D1683887

grandstand

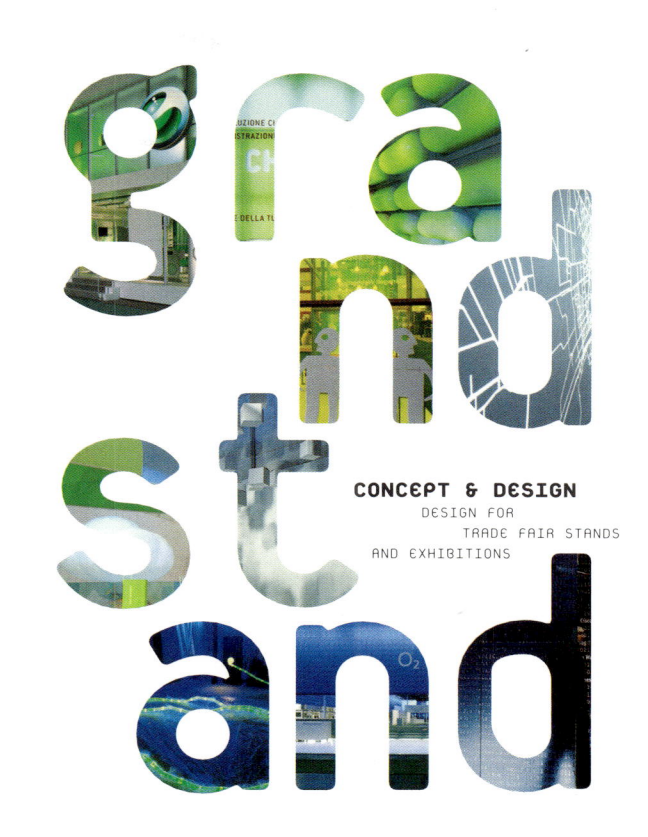

CONCEPT & DESIGN
DESIGN FOR
TRADE FAIR STANDS
AND EXHIBITIONS

CONTENTS

The Temporary Virtual	5
Arno Design	9
Atelier Markgraph	25
Cibic & Partners	41
Creneau International	57
D'art Design	73
Exhibits International	89
The GC Group	105
Kvorning Design	121
Land Design Studio	137
Lorenc + Yoo Design	153
Migliore & Sevetto	169
Oil for 3D	185
Promhouse	201
Raumschiff	217
Rotor Group	233
Schmidhuber + Partner	249
Totems Communication	265
Index	282
Colophon	286

page 9: ARNO DESIGN		page 25: ATELIER MARKGRAPH	page 41: CIBIC & PARTNERS

| page 57: CRENEAU INTERNATIONAL | page 73: D'ART DESIGN | page 89: EXHIBITS INTERNATIONAL | page 105: THE GC GROUP |

| page 121: KVORNING DESIGN | page 137: LAND DESIGN STUDIO | page 153: LORENC + YOO DESIGN |

| page 169: MIGLIORE + SEVETTO | page 185: OIL FOR 3D | page 201: PROMHOUSE | page 217: RAUMSCHIFF |

| page 233: ROTOR GROUP | page 249: SCHMIDHUBER + PARTNER | page 265: TOTEMS COMMUNICATION |

WELLCOME WING EXTENSION
SCIENCE MUSEUM, LONDON, UK

WHERE:
Science Museum, London, UK

WHEN:
2002

ARCHITECT:
Wilkinson Eyre, Johnson Banks

SIGNAGE SYSTEM:
Johnson Banks

Antenna is a latest news exhibition showing breakthroughs in modern day science, for example 'drugs in sport'.

THE TEMPORARY VIRTUAL

In the summer of 2000, two adjacent but very different exhibits opened at London's Science Museum. The first was the display entitled The Making of the Modern World, by architects Wilkinson Eyre and designers Farrow Design. It is a celebration of the best and most important works in the museum: over fifteen hundred objects, from a scalpel to a space missile, mainly displayed in formal cases, on white backgrounds and with simple, clear labels, set in Helvetica. Mark Farrow described it as 'designing a three-dimensional book.' The result is classical and cerebral, very cool, very balanced: an excellent frame for a world-class collection that includes Brunel's blockmaking equipment from the Royal Dockyards to an Apollo capsule, from a period beginning with the early industrial revolution and continuing up to the threshold of cyberspace.

WALKING THROUGH THE FORMAL GALLERY OF MAKING THE MODERN WORLD, THE VISITOR ENTERS THE VERY DIFFERENT SPACE OF THE WELLCOME WING. MacCormac Jamieson Pritchard were the architects for the wing, with design and signage by Johnson Banks. This was a new building of four storeys, which, as Michael Johnson explains, 'is targeted at the most difficult of audiences, children aged 9 to 15, in an attempt to engage them with science.' The space is named after the Wellcome Trust, which endowed and funded the project. It is a busy, bright space, with video and light-shows, hands-on displays, interactive commentaries. The emphasis is on contemporary technology and the contribution of science to the present and the future. Completely different from the Modern World gallery, the Wellcome Wing is aimed at an altogether different public, and it succeeds in its attractive and compelling way as much as the gallery does. Perhaps visitors leaving the Wing will be tempted to pause a little longer in the gallery after their experience!

THE LOGIC BEHIND THE TWO VERY DIFFERENT PRESENTATIONS OF SCIENCE IN THE MUSEUM IS SIMPLE: THEIR APPEAL IS TO VERY DIFFERENT AUDIENCES, scholars on the one hand, schoolkids on the other. Yet it is a dichotomy that also finds echoes in the contemporary world of trade fair stand design, where the public is more homogenous. Some stands invite the visitors to go at their own pace, absorbing information as they wish, other stands almost insist on the visitor becoming a participant, using both technology and human actors to involve them in what is being presented. Many of the best stands combine both approaches, with a more static area often surrounding a more dynamic presentation stage.

AS PHILIP URSPRUNG HAS POINTED OUT IN WRITING ABOUT THE ARCHITECTURAL EXHIBITIONS OF HERZOG AND DE MEURON, the *locus classicus* for the display of consumer goods is the Great

"THE CONCEIT WAS THAT EVERYTHING VISITORS COULD SEE WAS IN PRINCIPLE AVAILABLE TO EVERYONE"

WELLCOME WING, ANTENNA EXHIBITION
SCIENCE MUSEUM, LONDON, UK

WELLCOME WING EXTENSION
SCIENCE MUSEUM, LONDON, UK

Pattern pod is a gallery designed for 2 - 8 year old childeren which allowed them to discover patterns which were always around them in everyday life, for example from there pet's footprints to their own heartbeat.

Exhibition of 1851, the great spectacle that marks the beginning of the 'phenomenology of consumption,' in Baudrillard's phrase. 'The conceit was that everything visitors could see was in principle,' Ursprung observes, 'available to everyone.' He goes on to suggest that 'the economic shift from production to distribution and information that took place during the twentieth century has not fundamentally changed the power of the spectacle, only its mechanisms.'

THIS IS CERTAINLY TRUE OF THE TRADE FAIR. IN RECENT YEARS THE 'MECHANISMS' AVAILABLE TO EXHIBITORS HAVE INCREASED EXPONENTIALLY, whether in terms of display, from banners and large scale printing to video walls, or of communications, using on-screen units or large format projections. And the transformation in technologies which has benefited the armoury of techniques available to the stand designer, has also created a demand for more events and fairs to present the innovations of the technologies themselves to a wider and wider audience. Competition and complexity have increased the sophistication of the trade fair market and its penetration into new areas.

ONE POTENTIAL CONCLUSION FROM THE DEVELOPMENT OF NEW TECHNOLOGIES MIGHT HAVE BEEN THE DISAPPEARANCE OF THE TRADE FAIR CONCEPT, AND ITS REPLACEMENT BY AN ONLINE VIRTUAL REALITY SYSTEM, in which, like a super-animated version of the World Wide Web, everything could be on show all the time. There was indeed a move to create just such a virtual fair, using Superscape as the motor, some years ago, but it came to nothing. The web has indeed moved up the running

WELLCOME WING, PATTERN POD
SCIENCE MUSEUM, LONDON, UK

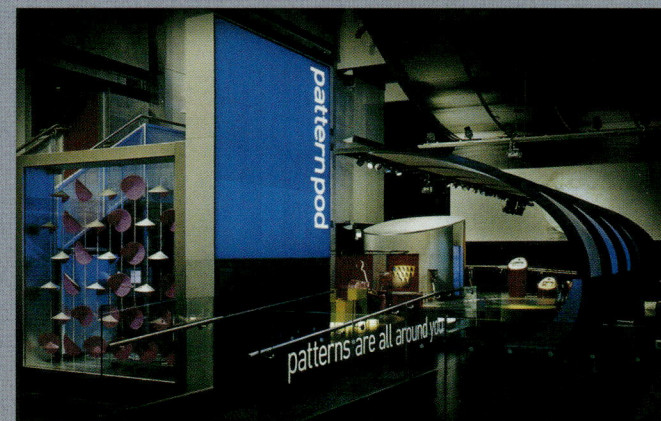

dramatically as a means of attracting clients and customers, sharing information with them, and selling products and services, but this has been in parallel with the development of larger trade fairs and more complex trade fair stands, not at their expense.

IF ONE ACCEPTS THAT THERE ARE TWO BROAD MODELS FOR STANDS, THE SHOWCASE AND THE FAIRGROUND, into which category should a virtual show go? One might assume the showcase, in that the visitor can move around at will. Or maybe the fairground, because of the interactivity that is implicit in the system. But the virtual model fails because it also lacks, in a sense, the patience and the performance of the actual event. And by always being available, it destroys the temporary nature of the fair. For the concluding irony seems to be that it is the fact that a fair is only on for a limited time; that the stands, however complex and seemingly permanent, are taken down a week later, that gives the fair its special character. Any visitor to a fair is inevitably a participant in the whole event, yet the event is in a sense unrea; part, to quote Ursprung again, 'of a game of concealing and revealing, illusion and dis-illusion, transparency and opacity.' Unlike the museum, where the actuality of the objects displayed is essential to the understanding of them, the very artificiality of the trade fair engages the attention of the visitor, as designers in both contexts use strategies of display performance and seduction to make the encounter real. And it is the opportunity for reflection and for involvement, for presence and distance, for levels of engagement, that the Science Museum exhibits so eloquently deploy.

arno design

ARNO DESIGN
MUNICH, GERMANY

ABOUT
arno design

Situated in a large house in the heart of Munich, with high ceilings, spacious rooms, and profiled doors, the offices of Arno Design don't give the impression of a firm devoted to trade fair presentations. In fact, these rooms contain nothing one would associate with trade fairs. The Advent wreath on the discussion table evokes a much more personal world than the thoroughly consistent, cool and sober trade fair presentations one is typically used to. One thing is immediately clear to the visitor before a word has been spoken: the right atmosphere is very important to Arno Design.

ARNO DESIGN'S PERMANENT STAFF INCLUDES 13 ARCHITECTS as well as project managers, CAD specialists and a management team of three (two men, one woman). Mirka Nassiri, Peter Haberlander and Claus Neuleib describe their projects in great detail and with a great deal of passion. Theirs is a firm characterised by much energy – that which enables them to enter heated debates between opposite opinions. At this discussion table one will never find executive officers who, as a result of the processes of rationalisation and institutionalisation, are no longer able to discuss controversial opinions and positions. Claus Neuleib explains: 'We initially approach a task as though we were consumers approaching a product. If, for example, wireless internet is involved, we keep asking the client questions until we really understand how the product can benefit us as potential "consumers." Then, we break down this message until it is understandable to the target group.' A very productive method, especially when it involves one or more merciless discussions.

'IT IS ALWAYS OUR ULTIMATE GOAL TO CREATE THE RIGHT ATMOSPHERE,' emphasises Mirka Nassiri. 'Trade fair visitors want to be entertained; they want to experience something. That's why it's important for the product itself never to be in the foreground as a sort of advertisement.' Arno Design concentrates on unconscious stimuli – atmosphere, or in other words, how one relates to one's surroundings. The result: a high-quality trade fair presentation. Their installation for Sto is a perfect illustration of this process. Sto restores façades, produces and sells paint, lacquers and plaster, materials that all require considerable space, and, if possible, natural surroundings, to be appreciated properly, and are consequently difficult to display adequately using a trade fair installation. In and of themselves, they can be technical and unexciting. Arno came up with 'a quite radical concept'. They produced an installation for Sto that accurately demonstrated their products' advantages as they are used, i.e. in the context in which consumers experience them. Their paints, for example: neither a plaster bucket nor sample cards

PROJECTS:
ARNO DESIGN

PROJECT PAGE 12:
SPEEDO
ISPO, MUNICH, GERMANY

PROJECT PAGE 13:
ELLESSE
ISPO, MUNICH, GERMANY

PROJECT PAGE 14:
GRUNDIG
IFA AUTUMN 2001, BERLIN, GERMANY

were to be seen anywhere. Instead the presentation consisted of a series of rooms in different colours. The room colours enabled visitors to experience the effects and atmospheres attainable by means of colour. In this sense, Arno Design delivers a clear message without primarily directing itself toward the individual product itself. Such an approach offers great advantages when it comes to the three-dimensional picture by which a company wants to be remembered in the mind of the consumer. The visitor to this installation won't remember a dripping paint bucket, but rather the spatial possibilities of paint in the hands of a professional.

IT SHOULD COME AS NO SURPRISE, then, that Arno Design's ultimate dream would be to communicate just principles and concepts; not *products*, but *ideas*. From a look at the projects thus far realised, it is readily apparent how perfectly Arno Design would be suited for such *dream commissions*. The eyes of the three executives begin to sparkle at the mention of the word 'vision'. For example, the kind of vision that is always latent at the back of their minds and is typically activated when they are confronted with the constrained, bleak world of standard trade fair practice. Their reality is, of course, more pragmatic: 'The companies – our clients – need to attain their targeted numbers of visitors. The facts are often clear and hard. We carry a great responsibility, one we cannot afford to ignore.' And it is clear to Peter Haberlander that the trade fair installation is an important image carrier, the flagship with which a company sails to a trade fair.

THE COMBINATION OF PRAGMATISM AND IMAGINATION YIELDS AN INTRIGUING MIXTURE. On the one hand, Arno Design pays careful attention to the *facts* and their client's (economic) requirements, considerations far removed from these designers' impulse to excel. On the other hand, their playful, fantasising and visionary side, ultimately gives their installations the stamp of creative vision. These are optimal conditions for a future-oriented firm of designers.

COMPANY STATEMENT ARNO DESIGN
"ANYTHING BUT BORING"

PROJECT PAGE 18:
STO
FARBE SPRING 2002, MUNICH, GERMANY

PROJECT PAGE 22:
KICKERS
VARIOUS LOCATIONS

PROJECT PAGE 23:
MONTANA
HMW, COLOGNE, GERMANY

PROJECT:
SPEEDO
ISPO, MUNICH, GERMANY

WHERE:
ISPO, Munich, Germany
WHEN:
July 2001 and July 2002
CLIENT:
Speedo International
MARKET SECTOR:
sport
DESIGNER OF STAND:
Claus Neuleib, Peter Haberlander, Mirka Nassiri
PROJECT TEAM:
Karsten Reinhold, Detlef Biermann
GENERAL CONSTRUCTOR:
Arno Design
CONSULTANTS:
Müllermusic, Ute Dissmann
MANUFACTURERS:
Arno Design
MATERIALS:
floor: Minipearl slightly structured white coated chipwood
walls: alu frame elements covered on both sides with shiny white Plexiglas covered with MDF
garment racks: refind steel
curtain: projection folio
AREA:
234 m²
OPENING:
2001

SPEEDO, a division of Pentland Group in London, presented itself in an eye-catching and dynamic way at ISPO Summer 2001. SPEEDO is the leading manufacturer of technical and fashion swimwear and beach clothing worldwide.
The dramatically folded translucent curtains of reflective foil suspended from the ceiling were sensational stylistic elements. At the same time, Arno Design used the whole permitted height of 6 metres. Shining like watercolours and floating above both the rounded wall elements, they attracted attention to the stand and were visible from a distance. A gently pulsating colour-changing light animation transformed them into light sculptures symbolising rhythm and movement.
The walls in the interior of the stand stood out in round shapes, running into rostrums as curved floor elements similar to tubs. Rounded corners also added character to the rhomboid-shaped, asymmetric side window giving a view into the interior of the stand, where swimsuits were displayed according to colour and pattern or on glass busts.
Speedo attached great importance to a quiet working atmosphere on the stand. Every kind of campaign was consciously avoided for this reason. The usual fashion shows associated with the trade fair were organized separately before the trade fair dates.

PROJECT:
ELLESSE
ISPO, MUNICH, GERMANY

WHERE:
ISPO, Munich, Germany
WHEN:
August 2002
CLIENT:
Ellesse International
MARKET SECTOR:
sport
DESIGNER OF STAND:
Claus Neuleib, Peter Haberlander, Mirka Nassiri
PROJECT TEAM:
Detlef Biermann
GENERAL CONSTRUCTOR:
Arno Design
CONSULTANTS:
lighting, a/v: Müllermusic
MATERIALS:
floor: Minipearl slightly structure white coated chipwood
walls: alu frame elements covered on both sides with shiny white Plexiglas covered with painted MDF
bar: metal construction covered with orange frosted illuminated Plexiglas
decoration balls: steel structure covered with painted forex
decoration platforms: painted wood
AREA:
324 m²
OPENING:
2002

For Arno Design, the shape of the cut-open tennis ball was the ultimate solution for the design of these four product islands. Although the four round bodies were identical in size, they appeared to be different because of their individually rotated positions. Each individual display was allocated to one of the four Ellesse ranges – Tennis, Ski, Sport Shoes and Leisurewear – and decorated strikingly on arranged busts and tableaux locked into the base of the rostrum. Selected pieces of clothing and shoes were played against a background with motifs from the relevant sport, which were projected onto the inner wall of the shell as a stationary image by means of an overhead projector.

Theatrical lighting projected images of water and snow on the outer surfaces of the balls. Their diffuse play of light and shadow was reflected in a stand floor of white-coated synthetic plates. The colourful company logo was emblazoned onto the outer sides of the four tennis balls, which framed round, smooth white wooden rostrums.

The design began with the concept 'The Game with Shape', which created a sense of coherence through all elements of the exhibit.

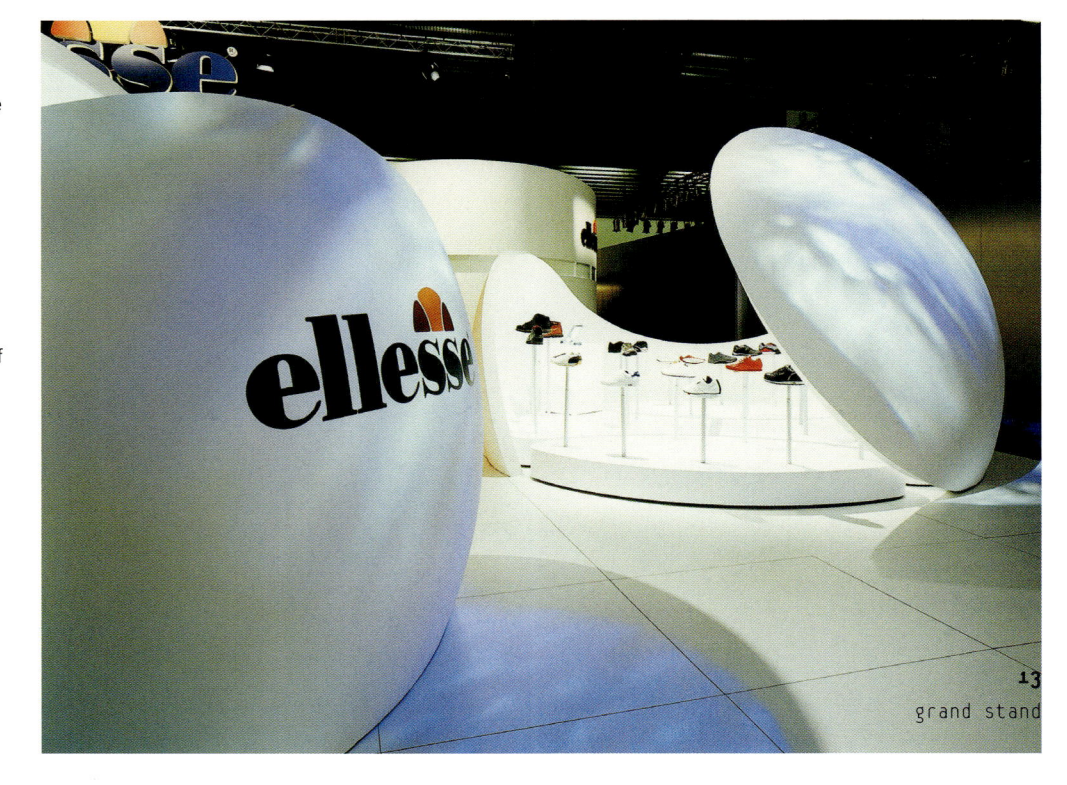

grand stand **AANO DESIGN**

PROJECT:
GRUNDIG
IFA AUTUMN 2001, BERLIN,
GERMANY

The IFA, International Radio and Television Exhibition, in Berlin, is the pinnacle for the Electronic and Home Entertainment Industry, not least because it is an audience magnet without comparison in Germany.

The challenge facing Arno Design can be described in a few short words: Aside from the technological competence of Grundig, the design strengths of Grundig should be dramatised and made into an experience. Product designs from the pen of Neumeister are to serve as an example.

The goals could be summarised as follows: first communicate the design of Grundig as a central theme. Second, add structure to the multitude of Grundig products. Third, create a large, self-confident appearance. Finally, create an experience from the visions of Grundig.

The starting point for the production was the concept of the 'Home Cinema' – the cinema experience in your own four walls. Human-sized letters from the logo float across the multifaceted scenery. The main axis is formed by a transverse aisle. An ambling mile with reflecting glass floors runs through the stand, with 12 mighty portals that guide the visitor through the entire product world of Grundig. Each of the portals is 4.5 metres high, 8 metres wide and has a side width of 2.2 metres. Additional mirrors at both ends continue the impression of infinity.

This creates a unit that focuses on the product. In its course, this develops into a stimulating, entertaining walk through the entire Grundig product spectrum. Aside from the important point of the product presentation, the hall includes also 'Home Infotainment' area developed for a second accommodation situation.

A show-arena with a lounge-like character, the 'Information Lounge' gives impressions and visions of the latest technologies and access to the Traders Centre. These areas are aligned to the cross axis and cross over the main aisle. >>

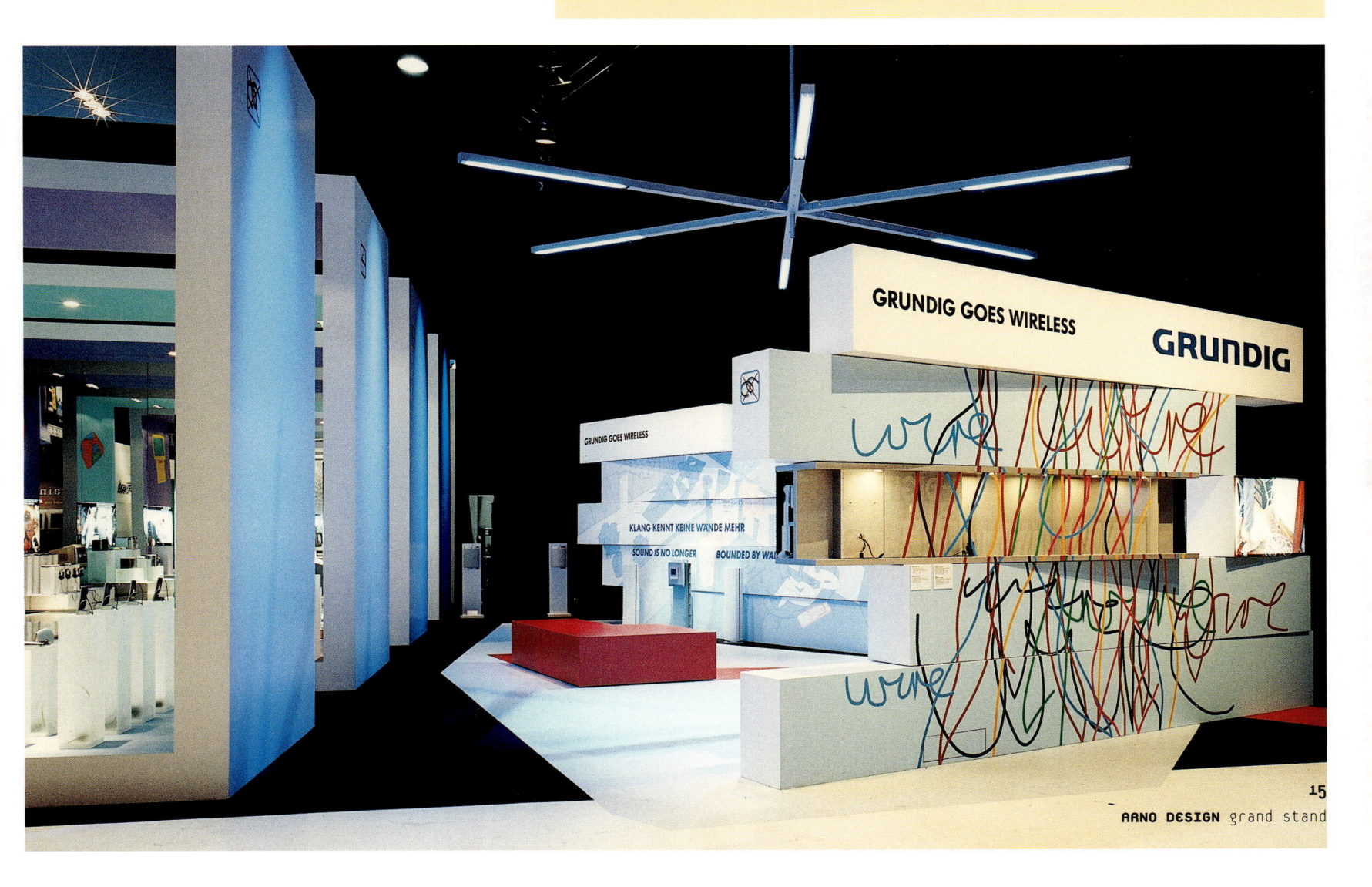

16

grand stand **ARNO DESIGN**

PROJECT:
GRUNDIG
IFA AUTUMN 2001, BERLIN, GERMANY

WHERE:
IFA, Berlin, Germany
WHEN:
August - September 2001
CLIENT:
Grundig
MARKET SECTOR:
media
DESIGNER OF STAND:
Mirka Nassiri, Peter Haberlander, Claus Neuleib
PROJECT TEAM:
Robert Gamohn, Uli Bauler, Martin Ritschel
GENERAL CONSTRUCTOR:
Arno Design
CONSULTANTS:
Müllermusic/Ute Dissmann
MATERIALS:
floor: recycled floor black rubber, structured glass grey security floor-stone
gates: wood, exterior paint concrete silver plait, metal translucent frosted Plexiglas
AREA:
2,200 m²
OPENING:
2001

This creates a close connection between the product, entertainment, information and experience.
The show-arena is the pulsating symbol of the hall: a 10 metres high, round tower, 14 metres in diameter, composed of 3 layers of transparent material. It is a construction which opens up a multitude of design possibilities. From outside it draws attention with projections and changing play of colours and inside it offers a cinema atmosphere. Next to competitions and presentations, the premiere showing of the DVD of Terminator 2 will take place in the show-arena and the first clip showing of the documentary epic 'Nomads of the air – The secret of the migratory bird'. A frontal presentation has been consciously avoided, to the strengthen emotional components. Therefore, the visitor finds a relaxing atmosphere on the inside. Self-designed 'bedding tablets' invite a relaxed viewing and experience. Due to this concept, the show-arena also provides the ideal location for the music-video mixes from VJ John de Kron and a group of DJ's.
The 'Information Lounge' forms the fourth focal point in the hall. 'Grundig goes Digital', 'Grundig goes Internet', 'Grundig goes Wireless' are the themes with which Grundig proves its strength in. The contents and the products requiring explanation are communicated in a relaxed and playful manner. Six-metre-long square columns lay on top of oneanother and bear messages as well as benefits. A coded design, such as the '0' and '1' signifying digital, striking statements and gimmicks with the individual themes invite one to discover additional depths in the presentation.
The interaction of the various perceptive possibilities neither excludes any of the visitors nor favours a specific target group. It allows the observation of Grundig from a very personal point of view, while imparting the experience of a brand name.

17
ARNO DESIGN grand stand

grand stand **ARNO DESIGN**

PROJECT:
STO
FARBE SPRING 2002, MUNICH, GERMANY

At the 'Farbe 2002' fair in Munich, the international trade fair for painting, decoration, and building protection, the current innovations and latest trends can be seen. It is also an occasion for the international professional brand Sto to show new products, too.

Arno Design, who have planned and realised fair appearances for Sto for more than 10 years, was entrusted by Sto with a fair appearance presenting the new revolutionary Sto Colour Fan.

The central briefing items were as follows: First to create an experience of the new Sto Colour Fan. Second, to intensify communication with the visitors, and third, to put forward a self-confident appearance, and fourth, to represent Sto's vision.

The architecture of the 700 m² fair stand portrays a town structure, i.e. an environment that exactly corresponds to the field of application of the Sto products. It includes 'building cubes' as rooms for informing and hosting, a 'main square' with a pool that is both a meeting and information point, as well projected 'advertising areas' for colour on transparent walls.

The architecture creates a stand that is very open and at the same time intimate, a feature that was appreciated by many visitors to the fair. The stand is consistently designed for communication. The actual pool in the centre is a quiet place for conversation and an attractive meeting place. It also gives a view of the entire stand. Within easy reach, there is a large model integrating Sto's entire world of colours and structures into one object. Around the centre are four catering areas, including a beer garden and a VIP lounge. One cube is dedicated to the 'New Colour Fan'. Two other cubes present Sto's range of products in display cases.

On the outside, the stand is grey. Except for the yellow house colour, there is nothing that points to the colourful inside. The 'grey giant' reveals its other face only to the interested visitor.

The idea of primary colours forms the basis of the colour design of the entire stand. With only four colours out of the Sto Colour Fan – orange, wine-red, pink, mustard-yellow – each of the places conveys new impressions and moods.   >>

PROJECT
STO AG
FARBE SPRING 2002, MUNICH, GERMANY

WHERE:	**GENERAL CONSTRUCTOR:**
Farbe Spring 2002, Munich, Germany	Arno Design
	CONSULTANTS:
WHEN:	Arno Design
April 2002	**MANUFACTURERS:**
CLIENT:	Arno Design
Sto	**MATERIALS:**
MARKET SECTOR:	*floor:* Minipearl, slightly structure grey coated chipwood
construction	*façade:* alu frame elements, MDF
DESIGNER OF STAND:	*cubes:* metal construction, translucent fabrics
Claus Neuleib, Peter Haberlander, Mirka Nassiri	**AREA:**
PROJECT TEAM:	704 m²
Karsten Reinhold	**OPENING:**
	2002

The sensuous aspect is supported by large coloured transparent areas on and between the cubes and by a series of movable projections.
The Colour Fan cube gives a dynamic multimedia dimension. Monochrome bases with monitors are located on a colour circle inside the cube. Here, associative clips, collages and images fill the colours with life. The drawers of the individual bases contain items that represent the respective colour. As an example, for yellow, the interested visitor finds bananas.
The colour fan idea has been consistently applied down to the last detail. Pink designer beer benches stand next to the orange walls of the VIP lounge. The multicoloured bar is composed of individual lacquered layers.
The colours separate and at the same time create a great unity, forming a close connection between product and emotion, information and experience.

ARNO DESIGN grand stand

PROJECT:
KICKERS
VARIOUS LOCATIONS

WHERE:
GDS, Düsseldorf, Germany
Moda Calzado, Madrid, Spain
Midec, Barcelona, Spain
Whos's next, Paris, France

WHEN:
March 2003

CLIENT:
Kickers International
contact: Hugh Sweeney, Bickers

MARKET SECTOR:
shoe/footwear

DESIGNER OF STAND:
Claus Neuleib, Peter Haberlander, Mirka Nassiri

PROJECT TEAM:
Susanna Kacer, Robert Gamohn, Klaus Hoffmann

GENERAL CONSTRUCTOR:
Arno Design

MATERIALS:
floor: Minipearl slightly structured white coated chipwood
façade: painted alu frame elements, illuminated infodesk
bar: illuminated frosted Plexiglas

DIMENSIONS:
12 x 8 m, 18 x 8 m, 14 x 8 m, flexible, modular system

DESIGN PERIOD:
November - December 2002

BUDGET:
£ 350 per m² incl. build up and down and transportation

The conception for the convention stand was formally coordinated with the advertising campaign and additionally developed architecturally. The campaign concept 'The Atmosphere of the Shooting Room' was adapted to the convention stand.
A view into the lounge area provides the opportunity to experience the 'white room' in a three-dimensional fashion.
The dramaturgy of the lighting, the shadowing effect and the accent-setting red furniture in the lounge support the fundamental ideas. This minimalist approach continues in the design of the closed areas.
An apparently material-less shoe presentation (transparent Plexiglas bent into various formats) focuses the attention exclusively onto the product with no distractions.
The outer façade surrounds the gleaming white entrance area with the illuminated Info-Counter. The view into the lounge is made possible by a glass front directly adjacent to the entrance area.
An apparently 'material-less' room is defined only by light and shadow, in which the modern seating furniture in red and an illuminated bar of frosted Plexiglas invite one to relax and stay a while. The only view from outside is made possible via a glass pane; a red glass pearl curtain may be deployed here. Opposite the seating corner, there is a changeable lighting box with current motifs. Alternatively, there would be enough space here to present the Shop Window Concepts. From here, the working areas are easily accessible.

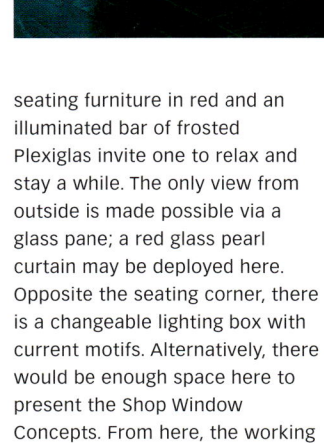

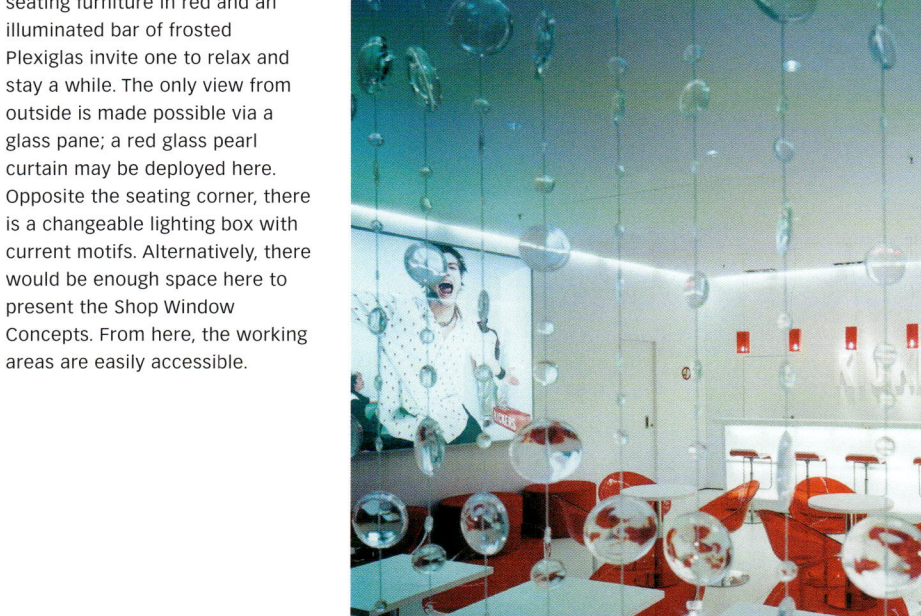

PROJECT:

MONTANA

HMW, COLOGNE, GERMANY

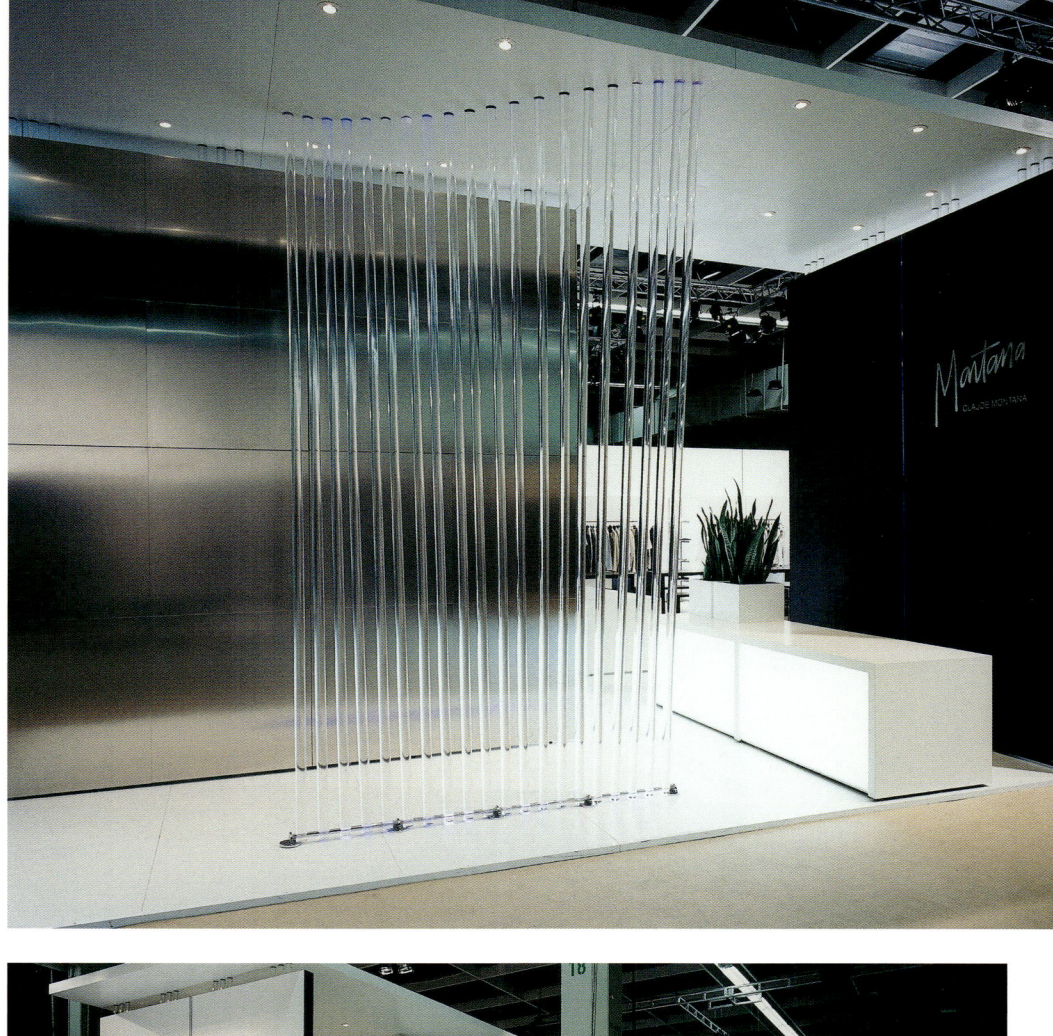

WHERE:
HMW, Cologne, Germany
WHEN:
1999
CLIENT:
Montana
MARKET SECTOR:
fashion
DESIGNER OF STAND:
Claus Neuleib, Peter Haberlander, Mirka Nassiri
PROJECT TEAM:
Robert Gamohn
GENERAL CONSTRUCTOR:
Arno Design
CONSULTANTS:
Müllermusic, Arno Design
MATERIALS:
floor: Minipearl, slightly structure white coated chipwood
façade: alu frame elements, Plexiglas on both sides
furnishing: Wenge, wood, dark
entrance element: Plexiglas tubes
AREA:
130 m²
OPENING:
1999

The relaunch of the Montana fashion brand started with a new exhibition stand at Men's Fashion Week in Cologne. The appearance was more than just a presentation platform for the new collections, it was a tribute to a fashion brand with cult status, a bow to its heyday in the eighties, and an indication of the future.
Design and materials are inspired by the eighties: clear, white-lacquered surfaces, severe shapes for chairs and benches, Plexiglas, stainless steel. Everything is cool and tidied-up. The stand cites central elements of the world of the Montana brand. Right at the entry, the cobalt blue typical of Montana is indicated in the Plexiglas harp that marks the great reception. The shop-like presentation area is designed in the form of a pavilion.
The fashion presentation is the focus of attention. Together with the accents of the dark wood of the chairs and tables, a straight and graphical shopping situation is created.

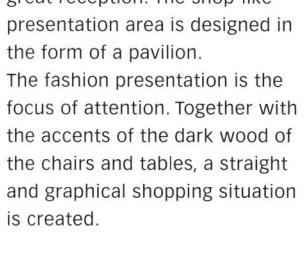

ARNO DESIGN grand stand

COMPANY NAME:
ARNO DESIGN

HEAD OFFICE:
Friedrichst. 9
80801 Munich
Germany

PHONE:
+49 (0)89 38 01 94 0

FAX:
+49 (0)89 33 71 08

E-MAIL:
office@arno-design.de

WEBSITE:
www.arno-design.de

OTHER LOCATIONS:
Stuttgart, Germany
Bad Homburg, Germany
Kempten, Germany
Athens, Greece
Bristol, UK
New York, USA

MANAGEMENT:
Mirka Nassiri
Claus Neuleib
Peter Haberlander

CONTACTS:
Mirka Nassiri
Claus Neuleib
Peter Haberlander

STAFF:
12

KEY DESIGNERS:
Claus Neuleib
Peter Haberlander
Mirka Nassiri

FOUNDED:
1994

COMPANY PROFILE:
Concept, design and realisation of trade fair booths, showrooms, stores. Arno Design was established in 1994 in Munich with a successful start. This success can be seen when browsing through important trade fair magazines and books, where you can almost always find the work of Arno Design. Even the list of well-known customers from every sector proves that the philosophy of the three creative heads Mirka Nassiri, Peter Haberlander and Claus Neuleib is convincing.

Success with individual concepts
Arno Design concentrates primarily on the construction of individual booths. That requires intense creativity, concentration on a clear concept and personal contact to find the best possible solution. At the same time the company values of efficiency and ecology are applied to every concept. That means that a trade fair booth built by Arno Design is not a 'disposable' product.
The art of attracting attention so comprehensively is mastered by no other means of communication than a trade fair booth. And in no other place are information and entertainment so close to one another than at a trade fair. Careful consideration of product presentation, the core of all trade fair participation, is at the centre of every project. Arno Design focuses on all senses in order to reach the hearts and minds of customers equally. Implementing diverse materials guarantees unexpected new impressions. Objects not only make products comprehensible, but conceivable at the same time, Multimedia techniques can convey a message over multiple communications channels. Installations shall be developed and realised specifically for the trade-show concept. The objective is to combine all of these facets in a unique, unmistakable and above all fascinating appearance.

Customers appreciate a clear stance
Only clear concepts and ideas produce results which are emotionally and rationally convincing. That is the reason why Arno Design safeguards the developed ideas starting with conceptual design up to implementation taking an unambiguous stance and pursuing it down to the last detail. Thus, customers also get results which distinguish themselves considerably from the others.

Arno Design is international
Arno Design undertakes projects ranging from conceptual design up to implementation all over the world. Successful trade fair participation on all continents offers customers the assurance that they can focus completely on the trade fair itself.

CLIENTS:
- ADAC
- Apple Autodesk
- Bäumler
- Berghaus
- Biodroga
- BMW AG
- Daimler-Benz Airport Systems
- Davidoff
- Dormeui
- Duravit
- Ellesse
- Escada
- Etienne Aigner
- Flow
- Gore
- Grundig
- Guy Laroche
- Hoechst
- La Chaussure Lacoste
- Loewe
- Louis Feraud
- Mercedes-Benz
- Mitre
- Montana
- Payot
- Pentland Group
- Pfleiderer
- Phenix
- Pierre Cardin
- Speedo
- STO
- Telefonica
- Windsor
- Yves Saint Laurent

SERVICES:
- Exhibition and stand design
- Exhibition and stand build
- Retail design
- Displays
- Graphic design
- Storage
- International transport

OPERATES:
Worldwide

ATELIER MARKGRAPH
FRANKFURT AM MAIN, GERMANY

ABOUT
atelier markgraph

Whether or not the exhibitions and trade fair installations of Frankfurt design studio Atelier Markgraph leave a lasting impression on their visitors is seldom questioned. The explanation for their memorability probably lies in their synergistic combination of architecture, communication design and art.

IT BEGAN TWENTY YEARS AGO: an interdisciplinary team of four comprised of a typesetter, a film architect, an educationalist and a graphic designer, entered uncharted territory in the field of event and exhibition design. Originally involving itself with individual room installations and exhibitions on a commission-by-commission basis, the group gradually developed a new, complex field of operations in three-dimensional communication in the interface between culture, industry, technology and society.

WITH ITS DARING AND SURPRISING PRESENTATIONS for such clients as DaimlerChrysler, Deutsche Telekom, Deutsche Bank and Heidelberger Druckmaschinen, as well as for internationally known cultural institutions and artists, the firm has established itself as a respected name all over the world. The small founding team grew in the course of years into a communication service with some 75 employees, specialising in brand communication and theme presentations. Offering services spanning the entire spectrum of three-dimensional communication, Markgraph supplies project concepts and designs for company and product presentations, trade fair appearances and showrooms, as well as for theme parks, cultural events and museum exhibitions.

AT MARKGRAPH, THE CONTINUOUSLY SHIFTING INTERFACE between classical communication disciplines gives rise to multifaceted designs, which transform architectonic space into substantial and durable experience-generating space. Gimmicks for their own sake are not used by Markgraph. Prior to each design, all minutiae of the specific themes and messages to be communicated are systematically analysed and, in turn, assembled around a core idea. This continuous process of focusing on the substance of a project, combined with a holistic approach to project realisation, characterises Markgraph's products. In place of an additive accretion of individual ideas or measures, organically connected complexes are developed. Even so, they always keep the essence at the forefront, ensuring that the visitor will experience the message to be communicated and be challenged to interact.

THE OFTEN COMPLEX TASKS INVOLVED IN THE FIRM'S PROJECTS CALL FOR A GENERALIST APPROACH, as well as the close cooperation of a variety of specialisms. For this reason,

PROJECTS:
ATELIER MARKGRAPH

PROJECT PAGE 28:
LAB.01 - DISCOVER THE NEXT EXPO 2000, HANNOVER, GERMANY

PROJECT PAGE 30:
SHAPING THE FUTURE OF PRINT MEDIA DRUPA 2000, DÜSSELDORF, GERMANY

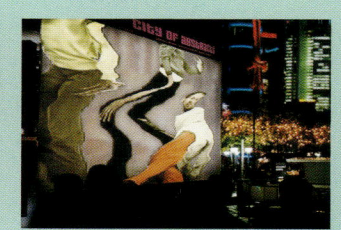

PROJECT PAGE 31:
CITY OF ABSTRACTS FRANKFURT AM MAIN, GERMANY

PROJECT PAGE 32:
UNDER ONE ROOF TRADE FAIRS WORLDWIDE 2000 - 2002

Markgraph is able to draw on a team from a wide range of fields: architects, designers, creative and art directors, editors, as well as its own media department. Where needed, the creative team can, in addition, draw on a large network of external specialists who regularly collaborate on the formulation and realisation of projects. Yet another of the firm's strengths is the close cooperation it enjoys with artists and artistic institutions. In addition to André Heller and Peter Gabriel, Markgraph's long-standing partners include Stephen Galloway, Laurie Anderson, Ron Arad, Peter Schwalm and Brian Eno. Another important aspect of the firm's unique approach is its openness toward cultural, scientific and societal developments, from which it gathers new ideas and impulses for its projects.

MARKGRAPH'S AIM IS TO DEVELOP INSTALLATION concepts which, going far beyond the purely commercial, succeed in sparking the visitor's imagination. A trade fair culture with a clear tendency toward excess and a time characterised by information overload pose a challenge to which Markgraph enjoys responding with cultural relevance and clearly defined communication experiences. Markgraph's team structures the visitor experience from beginning to end, a technique they sum up as 'time-shaping'. In addition to the 'classical' design methods, such as sketches, plans or 3D simulations, the design team also employs media such as theatre and film. Dramaturgy and storylines with special content are translated into cinematically arranged spatial sequences, yielding intense communication experiences.

MARKGRAPH'S TEAM WORKS WITH DEDICATION, purpose and courage toward the formulation of innovative concepts: 'Never leave well enough alone,' Raymond Loewy's motto, is their catchphrase. The professionalism of this experienced communication firm is apparent in its constant demand of quality from its own strategic and design concepts and planning to its realisation processes. The firm has frequently been the recipient of internationally recognised awards for the high creative level of its work. However, for Markgraph, the highest possible compliment lies in involving the visitor interactively, sparking his or her imagination and making a visit to an experience whose effect will long remain in the visitor's memory.

COMPANY STATEMENT ATELIER MARKGRAPH

"THE HIGHEST POSSIBLE COMPLIMENT LIES IN SPARKING THE VISITOR'S IMAGINATION"

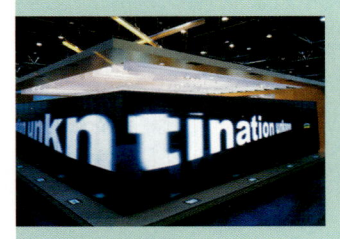

PROJECT PAGE 34:
LET'S GO MILES
GDS 2000, DÜSSELDORF, GERMANY

PROJECT PAGE 35:
VERKEHRSZENTRUM DEUTSCHES MUSEUM MÜNCHEN
MUNICH, GERMANY

PROJECT PAGE 36:
CONSTRUCTING ATMOSPHERES
LIGHT + BUILDING 2002, FRANKFURT AM MAIN, GERMANY

PROJECT PAGE 38:
THE STORY OF PASSION
IAA 2001, FRANKFURT AM MAIN, GERMANY

grand stand **ATELIER MARKGRAPH**

PROJECT:
LAB.01 - DISCOVER THE NEXT EXPO 2000, HANNOVER, GERMANY

WHERE:
EXPO 2000, Hannover, Germany and various locations

WHEN:
TOUR: 1 July 1999 - 7 November 1999
EXPO: 1 June - 31 Oktober 2000

CLIENT:
DaimlerChrysler

ARCHITECTURE:
Atelier Markgraph

COMMUNICATION CONCEPT AND DESIGN:
Atelier Markgraph

LIGHTING DESIGN:
Atelier Stromberg

VIDEO:
Atelier Markgraph with 3000.films

GENERAL CONSTRUCTOR:
Ernst F. Ambrosius & Sohn

PHOTOGRAPHY:
Sandra Mann, Marc Trautmann, Daniel Woeller

LAB.01, DaimlerChrysler's contribution to EXPO 2000 in Hanover, was conceived as a mobile exhibition project, merging future technologies with pop culture. Futuristic technological themes relevant to the world today were presented in the form of experiences – like interfaces between young people's daily lives and DaimlerChrysler's fields of research and development. The exhibits invited visitors to explore and experiment with futuristic technologies hands-on. To achieve maximum plausibility and thematic impact, all mention of DaimlerChrysler's products or technological achievements was omitted from the project.
After a year touring six European cities, LAB.01 docked onto Hall 2 at the EXPO 2000, becoming a landmark on the open space in front of the hall. The interior architecture adapted the style of a provisional research station and reflected the mobile character of the project.
While the LAB.01 tour introduced visitors to a wide range of themes, at EXPO 2000 the emphasis was placed on the aspects of 'Interfaces' and 'Interaction', especially the idea that all technological developments have been attempts to extend the functions of the human body. The theme areas were respectively arranged according to our physical senses. The exhibits allowed visitors to experiment with technologies which act as interfaces between humans and machines. The youth-oriented approach to communication implemented visual language and pictograms which were easily understandable in different countries.

<< Touch Ground: the technology responds to a visitor's touch and hand movements.

< Body Zone: body movements activate cascades of light and sound, allowing visitors to communicate with each other non-verbally.

PROJECT:
SHAPING THE FUTURE OF PRINT MEDIA DRUPA 2000, DÜSSELDORF, GERMANY

WHERE:
Drupa 2000, Düsseldorf, Germany
WHEN:
18 - 31 May 2000
CLIENT:
Heidelberger Druckmaschinen
ARCHITECTURE:
Atelier Markgraph
COMMUNICATION CONCEPT AND DESIGN:
Atelier Markgraph
LIGHTING DESIGN:
Media Spectrum
GENERAL CONSTRUCTOR:
Ernst F. Ambrosius & Sohn
PHOTOGRAPHY:
Vaclav Reischl

At drupa 2002, the world market leader for offset printing presses, Heidelberger Druckmaschinen, presented itself for the first time as a Solutions Provider for the entire printing process – from Prepress to Postpress. The challenge was to communicate the strategic realignment of this otherwise traditional manufacturer in response to market globalization and rapid technological changes. Within the framework of Heidelberg's new, global Brand Identity, Atelier Markgraph developed a trade fair communications strategy built around comprehensive, long-term corporate communication.

The defining design component of the stand – which took up two halls with a total area of 10,000 square metres, including a pavilion, VIP lounge and showroom – was inspired by the way paper moves through a printing press. The modular stand system was based on simple architectonic shapes, structuring the stand according to the various phases of printing, including spaces for products, live presentations and personal talks with clients.

In order to provide an approachable, easily-understandable scenario which actively encouraged visitors to get to know Heidelberg's new solutions, a finely-tuned overall concept of architecture, design and presentation materials was created. A unique new approach, in both style and content, was thereby established for the new Corporate Identity. An approach which could be immediately recognized worldwide and which delivered on the traditional Brand Values of Solidity, Trust, Strength and Customer Proximity but also represented new values: Heidelberg as a solution-oriented and future-shaping concern.

The communication concept let the printing industry speak for itself. The renowned photographer Jim Rakete took portraits of printers from all over the world, giving a face to the changes taking place on the market – and a voice. By applying feedback from a global customer survey, Atelier Markgraph composed authentic statements which accompanied the photos in an international, pre-fair print campaign.

PROJECT:
CITY OF ABSTRACTS
FRANKFURT AM MAIN, GERMANY

WHERE:
Three centrally located public spaces in Frankfurt am Main, Germany
WHEN:
14 November - 7 December 2000
CLIENT:
Frankfurt Ballett
COMMUNICATION CONCEPT AND DESIGN:
Atelier Markgraph with the Frankfurt Ballett
GENERAL CONSTRUCTOR:
Ernst F. Ambrosius & Sohn

In a highly unusual campaign in the inner city of Frankfurt, dance theater was temporarily brought to the streets – raising awareness for the Ballett Frankfurt's upcoming season, having just returned from a worldwide tour in the winter of 2000.

'City of Abstracts' was the name of this project conceived by choreograph William Forsythe and Atelier Markgraph. Large video walls installed on three central spaces in Frankfurt inspired passers-by to break into spontaneous dance. A camera captured their movements and projected them onto the video walls. The software IMAG/INE reproduced their movements in real-time, distorting the images depending on their dynamics. The effect: bodies became liquid or twisted into spirals. The public was enthusiastic, every passer-by became a performer. Managers, couples, teenagers began to hop, skip, jump – just to see how it would be distorted.

The video installations were at the opera house on Willy-Brandt-Platz, in the heart of the shopping district on Hauptwache and in front of the TAT on Bockenheimer Depot. All drew crowds like magnets, bringing a surprising moment of reflection in the pre-Christmas bustle. New performers emerged, spontaneous audiences formed, 'regulars' returned every day. The return of the renowned dance group was woven into the fabric of daily urban life in an 'overture of public space'.

PROJECT:
UNDER ONE ROOF
TRADE FAIRS WORLDWIDE
2000 – 2002

WHERE:
Internationale Luft- und Raumfahrtausstellung (ILA), Berlin 2000
International Airshow Farnborough 2000
Salon international de l'aéronautique et de l'espace, Paris-Le Bourget 2001
Internationale Luft- und Raumfahrtausstellung (ILA), Berlin 2002

WHEN:
6 - 12 June 2000 (Berlin)
24 - 30 July 2000 (Farnborough)
16 - 24 June 2001 (Paris-Le Bourget)
6 - 12 May 2002 (Berlin)

CLIENT:
European Aeronautic Defence and Space Company (EADS)

CONCEPT:
Atelier Markgraph in collaboration with Kauffmann Theilig & Partner Freie Architekten BDA

ARCHITECTURE:
Kauffmann Theilig & Partner Freie Architekten BDA

COMMUNICATION CONCEPT AND DESIGN:
Atelier Markgraph

LIGHTING DESIGN:
Four to One: scale design

VIDEO:
Atelier Markgraph with die manufaktur

GENERAL CONSTRUCTOR:
Ernst F. Ambrosius & Sohn

PHOTOGRAPHY:
Juraj Liptak, Andreas Keller

With the merging of the German company DaimlerChrysler Aerospace, the French Aerospatiale Matra and the Spanish CASA, in 2000 the largest aerospace company in Europe was formed, and one of the three leading aerospace companies worldwide: the European Aerospace Defence and Space Company (EADS)
In cooperation with the architects Kauffmann Theilig & Partner, Atelier Markgraph developed a trade fair concept for the new company based on the central design element of the circle. Serving as a symbol of unity and identification, the main stand component, the 'Space Tower', is a two-story construction formed by aluminum lamellar rings growing from its base and stretching over the entire exhibition area in the shape of a circle. The various business sectors, brands and products of the three founding members are thereby presented 'under one roof'.
The finely tuned interaction of the various design elements ensures corporate communication which is easily recognizable. Architecture, graphics, lighting, exhibits and media presentations support the personal dialogues at the fair, creating an atmospheric and consistent communication space. The design principle behind the EADS stand allows for easy adaptation, ensuring immediate recognition in different spatial contexts. Aside from implementation at the major trade fairs in Berlin, Farnborough and Paris-Le Bourget, the concept has also been applied at smaller fairs and company presentations around the world.
For the first time in Paris-Le Bourget, a separate hall was constructed for the exhibition. The so-called 'Pavillon' further extended the geometric attributes of the Space Tower towards the outside and clearly identified the umbrella brand EADS from a distance.

grand stand **ATELIER MARKGRAPH**

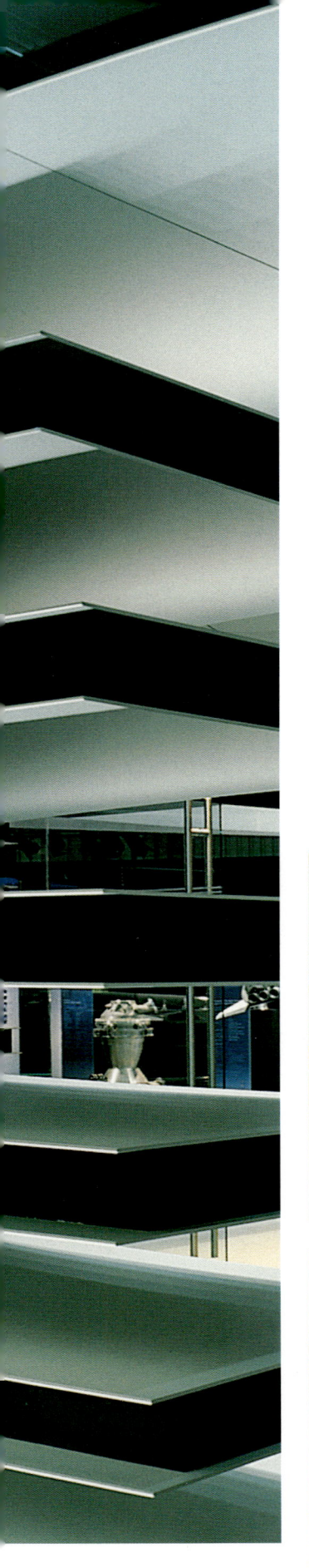

ATELIER MARKGRAPH GRAND STAND

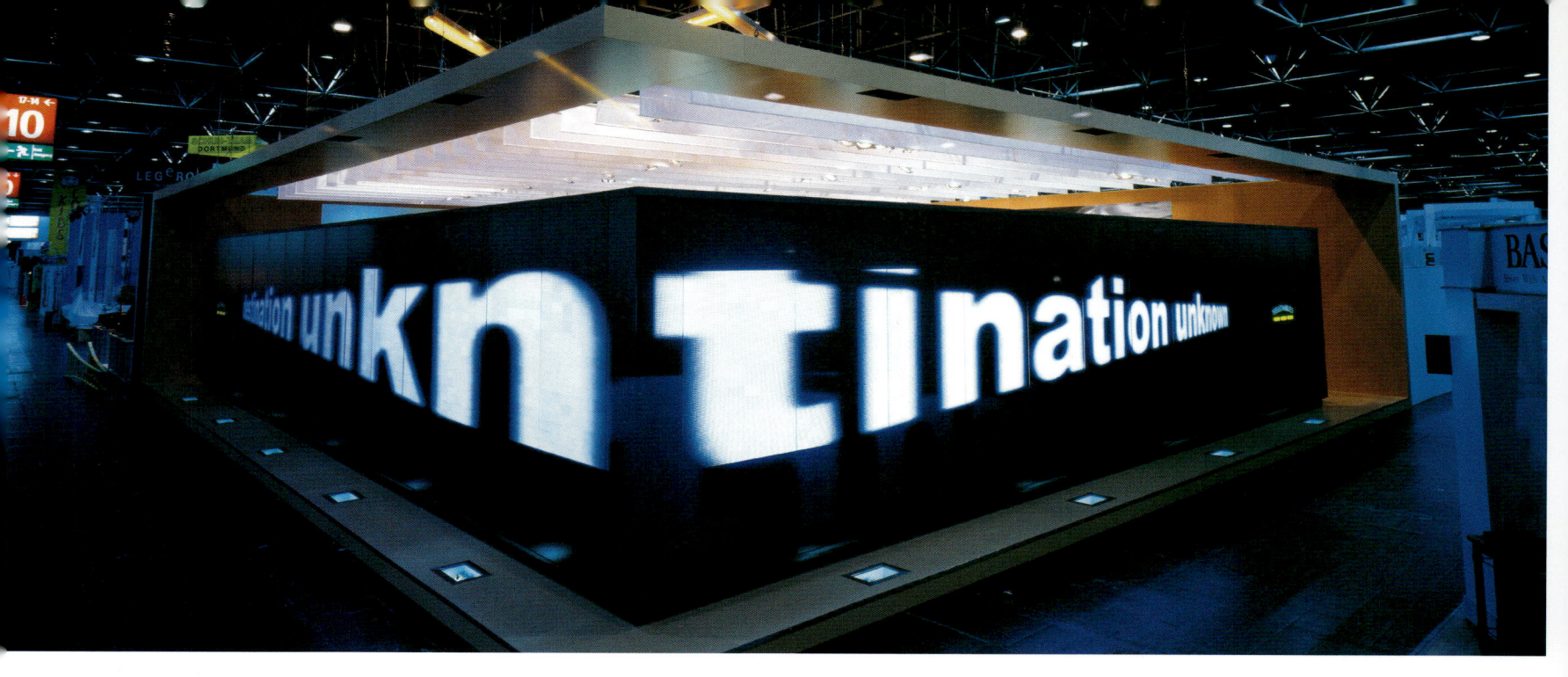

PROJECT:
LET'S GO MILES
GDS 2000, DÜSSELDORF, GERMANY

WHERE:
GDS 2000, Düsseldorf, Germany
WHEN:
14 - 17 September 2000
CLIENT:
YelloMiles
ARCHITECTURE:
Atelier Markgraph
COMMUNICATION CONCEPT AND DESIGN:
Atelier Markgraph
LIGHTING:
Showtec
GENERAL CONSTRUCTOR:
Display International
PHOTOGRAPHY:
Vaclav Reischl

As a new brand, YelloMiles was intent on grabbing the attention of the GDS audience with a remarkable and surprising debut. An atmospheric, brand-consistent space for communication and experience was conceived, with the primary function of facilitating dialogue with potential customers. A sense of mystery was achieved through the slightly inset black glass running around the outside of the stand. The light-emitting facade featured films running in LED windows, arousing curiosity for the world of YelloMiles. The spacious inner room was distinguished by a sense of suspense, accented by the object-like arrangement of the exhibition furniture. Once an hour, the display window for product exhibition was lowered and revealed a show window of unusual format: 11 metre wide by 50 centimetre high. In cooperation with theater, music and dance professionals, a dynamic show of footwork was performed featuring YelloMiles shoes and the yellow lines on their soles.
As a whole, the architecture, live-performances, media, graphics and music created an unmistakable and clearly characterized context for the YelloMiles image to be experienced and communicated. YelloMiles – shoes for urban adventure.

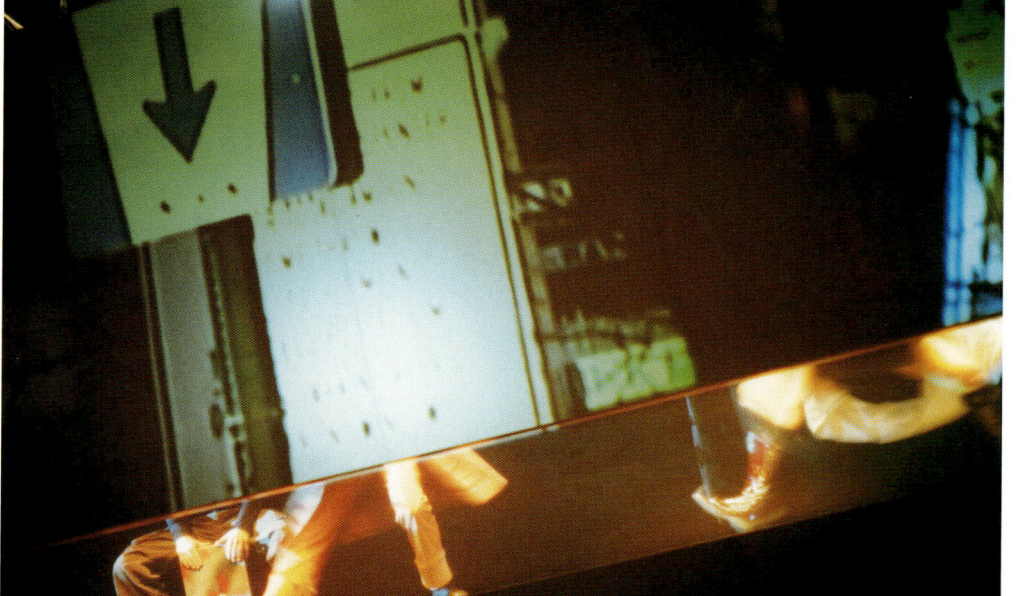

grand stand ATELIER MARKGRAPH

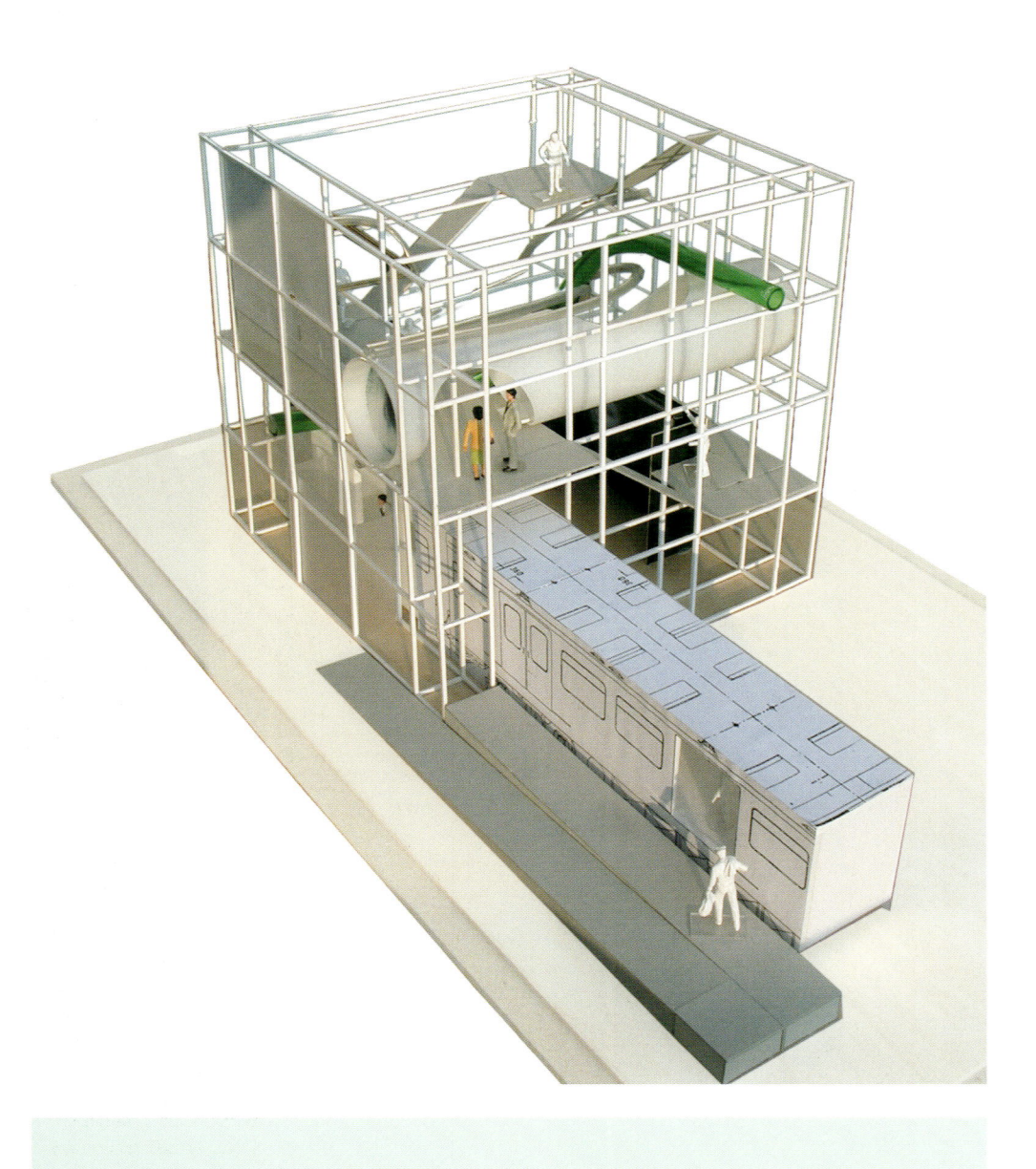

PROJECT:
**VERKEHRSZENTRUM
DEUTSCHES MUSEUM MÜNCHEN**
MUNICH, GERMANY

WHERE:
Messehallen Theresienhöhe,
Hall 1 and 2, München, Germany

CLIENT:
Deutsches Museum München

HALL RESTORATION:
RPM-Architekten

EXHIBITION CONCEPT AND DESIGN:
Atelier Markgraph

LIGHTING DESIGN:
Fischer Licht & Design

GENERAL CONSTRUCTOR:
Ernst F. Ambrosius & Sohn

OPENING:
Hall 3: 2003
Hall 1 and 2: 2005

PHOTOGRAPHY:
Atelier Markgraph

The 'Transport Center' on the Theresienhöhe in Munich is one of the most important future projects pursued by the Deutsches Museum. With this new branch, Europe's largest technology museum aims to reposition itself: as a worldwide first, the theme of transportation will be portrayed as a wide-reaching system, in all its dimensions, and designed to appeal to a wide audience. The experimental exhibition concept focuses on rooms for hands-on experience, offering visitors new access to the subject of transportation and a glimpse into the future. A careful blend of cultural science with an entertaining approach make the Transport Center an appealing public forum for interaction with the subjects of mobility and transportation.

The Transport Center is housed in three historical exhibition halls of the former Munich fair 'Theresienhöhe', where transportation exhibitions took place in 1925 and 1953. Each of the halls has its own theme: Hall 1 'City Traffic', Hall 2 'Travel' and Hall 3 'Mobility and Future'. Unique architecture characterizes each hall – identity and atmosphere reflect the respective themes.

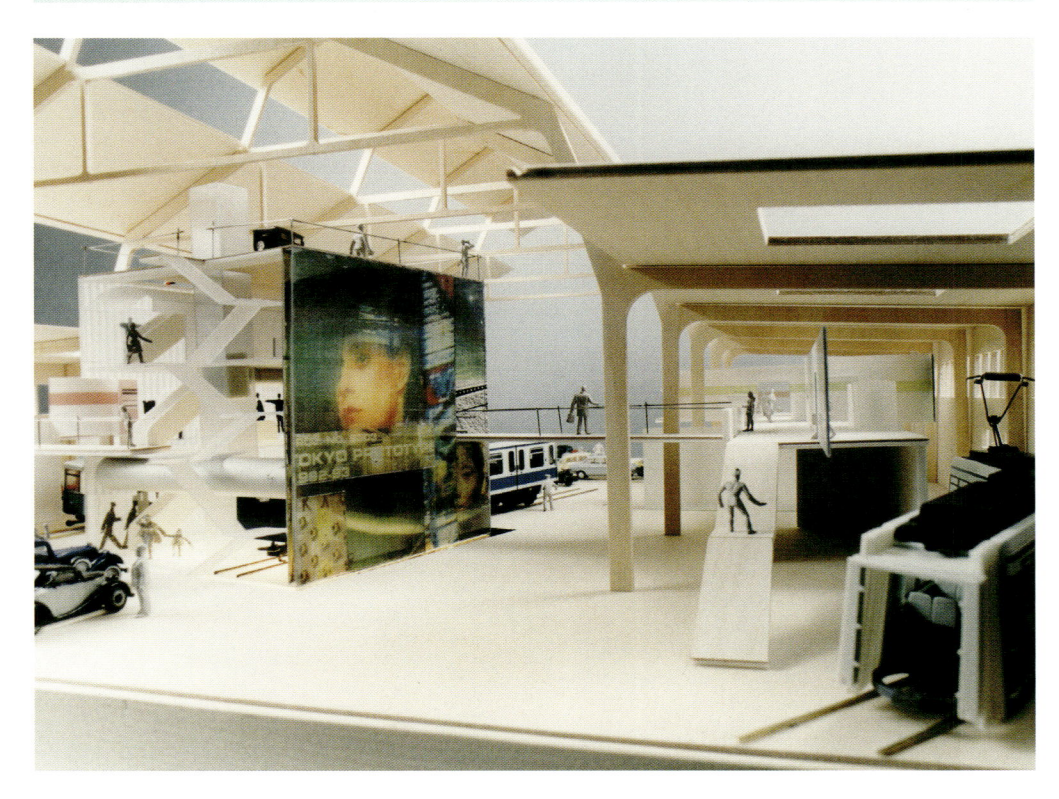

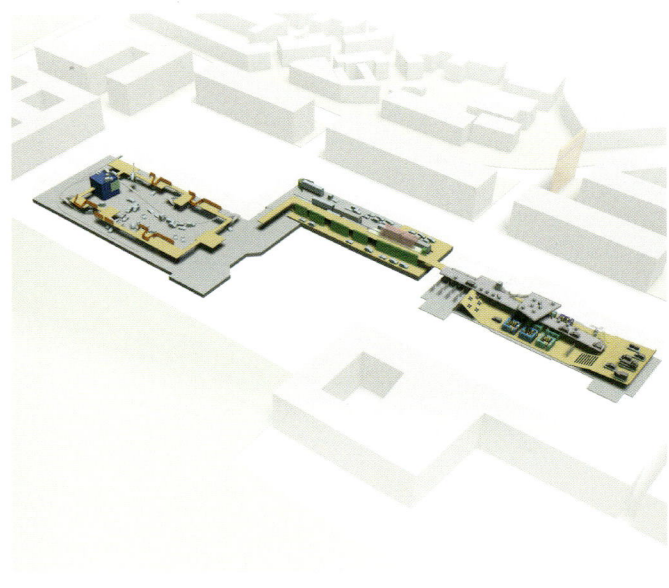

35
ATELIER MARKGRAPH GRAND STAND

```
PROJECT:
CONSTRUCTING ATMOSPHERES
LIGHT + BUILDING 2002,
FRANKFURT AM MAIN, GERMANY
```

WHERE:
Light + Building/Aircontec, Frankfurt am Main and Luminale, Frankfurt am Main, Germany

WHEN:
14 - 18 April 2002

CLIENT:
Messe Frankfurt

ARCHITECTURE:
Atelier Markgraph

COMMUNICATION CONCEPT AND DESIGN:
Atelier Markgraph

LIGHTING DESIGN EXPERIMENTAL CLOUD:
Atelier Markgraph with the Lighting Design Dept. at the Fachhochschule Hildesheim

ENERGY CONCEPT EXPERIMENTAL CLOUD:
Transsolar Energietechnik

GENERAL CONSTRUCTOR:
CL Veranstaltungsservice Freisteel

PHOTOGRAPHY:
Andreas Keller, Jürgen Zeller, Damir Tomas

In 2002, Messe Frankfurt featured a special attraction during the architecture and technology fair 'Light + Building': an exhibition entitled CONSTRUCTING ATMOSPHERES focusing on people and their perception of space and climate. The highlight of the show, which marked the integration of the 'Aircontec' climate fair, was undoubtedly the EXPERIMENTAL CLOUD – a genuine meteorological cloud which floated above visitors' heads in the spacious Galleria. The formation was several hundred cubic metres in size and generated twice a day – moderated by an engineer who explained how air layers of varying humidity and temperature were implemented. As a controlled reproduction of a natural phenomenon, EXPERIMENTAL CLOUD demonstrated the highly complex interaction between architecture, humidity, air and warmth, enabling visitors to experience the exhibition's theme at first hand. Some visitors even had the privilege of taking a ride up into the cloud.

Besides this firsthand experience of indoor climate regulation, in an innovative way CONSTRUCTING ATMOSPHERES also gave visitors insight into eight layers which serve to protect us from changes in weather and climate: from the human skin cell as the smallest climate sensor to a space station. Floating gauze walls demarcated the various thematic areas, 'grounded' by monochromatic bodies, acting as signposts as well as pillars for graphics and exhibits. Eye-catching key visuals led visitors down an intriguing informative path from interactive stations to spectacular exhibits. In July 2002, the exhibition was repeated as the Messe Frankfurt contribution to the XXI World Architecture Congress in Berlin. By night EXPERIMENTAL CLOUD turned into a striking light sculpture As a part of the city's first light culture festival 'Luminale', Messe Frankfurt established the cloud as a central icon, drawing hundreds of visitors every evening to relax in the CLOUD CLUB lounge or dance to ethereal vibes by selected DJs – the abstract cloud architecture crowning off the atmosphere as truly 'chill'.

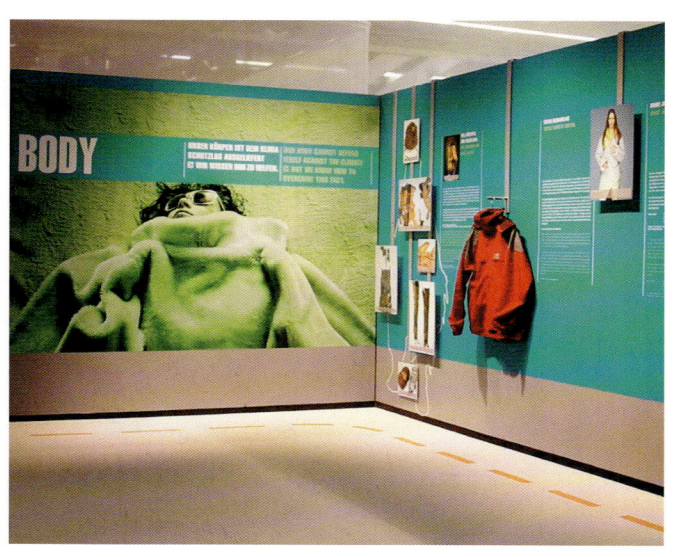

ATELIER MARKGRAPH GRAND STAND

grand stand ATELIER MARKGRAPH

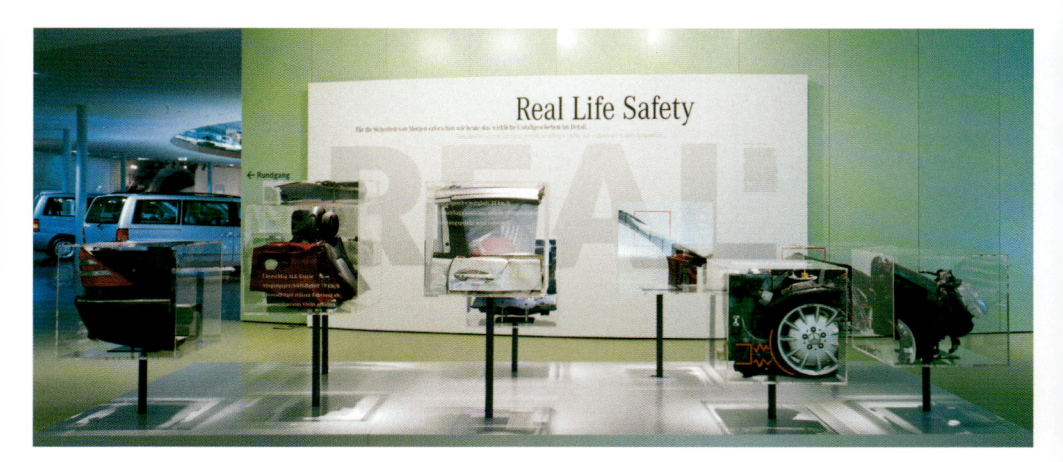

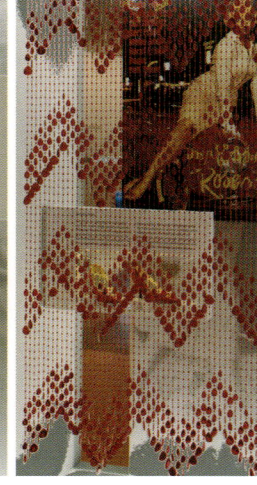

PROJECT:
THE STORY OF PASSION
IAA 2001, FRANKFURT AM
MAIN, GERMANY

WHERE:
Internationale Automobil-
Ausstellung (IAA) 2001,
Frankfurt am Main, Germany

WHEN:
11 - 23 September 2001

CLIENT:
DaimlerChrysler

ARCHITECTURE:
Kauffmann Theilig & Partner Freie
Architekten BDA

COMMUNICATION CONCEPT AND
DESIGN, LIVE PERFORMANCE:
Atelier Markgraph

GRAPHIC DESIGN:
design hoch drei

LIGHTING DESIGN:
Flaashaar Ingenieure,
TLD Lichttechnik

VIDEO:
Atelier Markgraph with
@ cineteam filmproduktion

GENERAL CONSTRUCTOR:
Ernst F. Ambrosius & Sohn

PHOTOGRAPHY:
Andreas Keller, Atelier Markgraph

The 100-year anniversary of the Mercedes brand was celebrated in the campaign 'The Story of Passion', running in all communication channels for the first 10 months of 2001 and finding its climax at the 59th International Motor Show in Frankfurt. The Mercedes-Benz IAA stand is traditionally in the Frankfurter Festhalle, a century-old concert hall. For the first time in 2001, the architectural character of the hall itself was implemented, especially the spacious inner room under the glass dome and its two circumscribing galleries. Visitors were led from the foyer to the upper gallery for a breathtaking overall view of the hall. The world premiere of the new SL class was in the center, above which a large LED screen featured 'The Story of Passion' film. The personality of the brand was celebrated and the basic message established – 'The Story of Passion' is a story about people.

The themes evolving from this story were Heritage, Customer Relations, Motor Sports, Design, Technological Innovation and Research – themes which could be discovered again in the exhibit and graphic design on all three levels of the exhibition. Together with the presentation of the latest models, a powerful, homogenic image of the brand Mercedes-Benz was communicated. 'The Story of Passion' gained new angles as employees and customers were shown talking about their passion for Mercedes-Benz, breathing life and emotionality into the brand. Visitors experienced in a dynamic way what the brand promises to be: 'The future of the automobile'. The representation of the themes on the four gallery halves was quiet and consistent in tone. The side rooms with the themes of Motor Sports, the world premiere of the Vaneo and Research were each characterized by a distinct architectural, media and graphic style.

COMPANY NAME:
ATELIER MARKGRAPH

HEAD OFFICE:
Hamburger Allee 45
60486 Frankfurt am Main
Germany

PHONE:
+49 (0)69 97993 1102

FAX:
+49 (0)69 97993 1183

E-MAIL:
contact@markgraph.de

WEBSITE:
www.markgraph.de

MANAGEMENT:
Rolf M. Engel
Meinhard Hutschenreuther
Roland Lambrette
Christoph M. Meyer

CONTACTS:
Angela Kratz, Public Relations

STAFF:
75

FOUNDED:
1986

COMPANY PROFILE:
Atelier Markgraph is an agency for brand communication and theme presentations. The agency conceives, plans and executes events and exhibitions from a communication standpoint for various brands and companies. Its range of services comprises:
Brand Communication
- Corporate Presentations
- Product Presentations
- Trade Fair Presentations
- Showrooms
- Customer Centers
- Shareholders' Meetings
- Press Conferences

Theme Presentations
- Museums
- Theme Parks
- Cultural Projects
- Events

CLIENTS:
- DaimlerChrysler
- Mercedes-Benz
- Dasa/EADS
- Heidelberger Druckmaschinen
- YelloMiles
- Deutsche Bank
- Messe Frankfurt
- Frankfurt Ballett
- Deutsches Museum
- Deutsche Sporthilfe
- Deutsche Telekom
- Europoint
- Deutsche Börse
- Peter Gabriel
- Brian Eno
- Roger Waters
- André Heller

SERVICES:
- Full Service
- Strategy
- Communication Concept
- Dramaturgy
- Research and Editing
- Text
- Architecture
- Graphic Design
- Exhibit Design
- Media Design
- Technical Equipment (Light, Sound, Media, Stage Technology)
- Software (Image and Sound, Mixing)
- Project Management
- Project Steering
- Project Controlling

AWARDS:
- **Merit Award,** D&AD 2003
- **Silver Medal,** 82nd Annual Award ADC New York 2003
- **Merit Award,** ADC Germany 2003
- **2 Awards,** iF design award 2003: Communication Design
- **2 Gold Medals,** EVA 2002
- **Silver Medal,** ADAM 2002
- **red dot award** 2002
- **3 Bronze Medals,** DDC Award 2001/2002
- **Finalist Award,** The New York Festivals 2001
- **2 Gold Medals, 1 Special Jury Prize,** EVA 2001
- **2 Silver Medals, 1 Bronze Medal, 1 Special Jury Prize,** ADAM 2001

OPERATES:
Worldwide

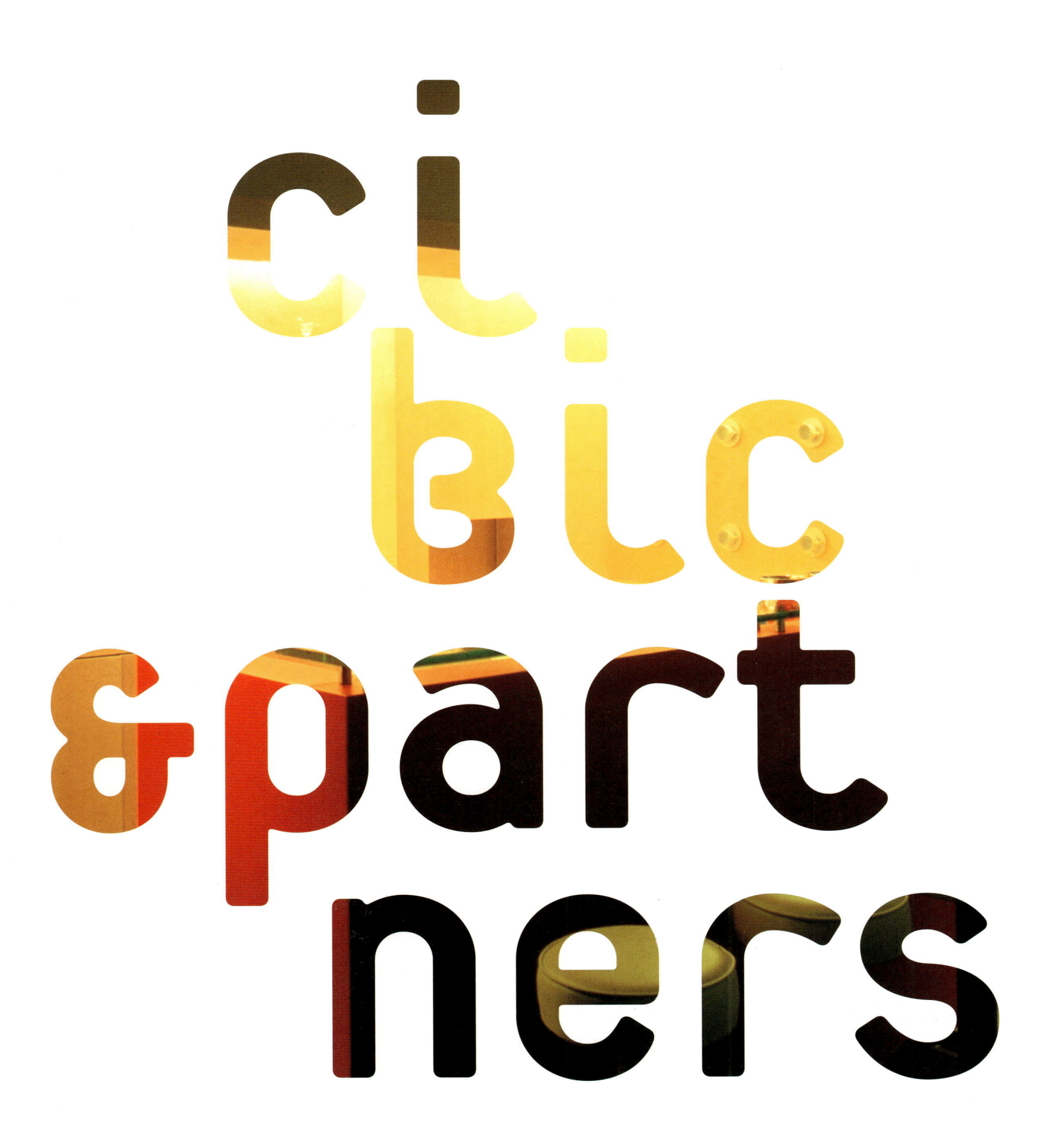

CIBIC & PARTNERS
MILAN, ITALY

cibic &partners

ABOUT

cibic &partners

Cibic & Partners, a well-known Italian design studio, was established in Milan at the end of the eighties. For over ten years it has operated in many parts of the world. The studio is a composite group that by choice and by calling has occupied itself with projects of diverse nature – ranging from architecture to interiors and from design to multimedia communications.

CIBIC AND PARTNERS IS GUIDED BY FOUR PARTNERS: Aldo Cibic is the design nucleus of the studio and along with Luigi Marchetti and Zoran Minic, is closely connected to the work groups that are dedicated to the various projects. Antonella Spiezio is the strategic core of the partnership and is responsible for the organisation and administration of financial and human resources. They are supported by a group of architects, interior designers, graphic artists, industrial designers, and a deep network of collaborating consultants of diverse professional and cultural backgrounds. The result is an environment where there is an intense exchange of stimulation and energy, and where the principal aim is the realisation of solid and innovative projects. The capacity for design and organisation are the two determining factors that make the studio a creative and reliable partner for major business groups world-wide.

ALDO CIBIC, BORN IN SCHIO IN 1955, moved to Milan in 1979 to work with Ettore Sottsass, becoming his partner the following year, together with Matteo Thun and Marco Zanini. That same year, 1980, marked the creation of Memphis, of which Cibic was one of the designers and founders, under the guidance of Sottsass. In 1989, he went out on his own, founding, together with Antonella Spiezio, Cibic & Partners, providing his personal design services for his own projects and for other companies, as well as expanding into the field of interior design and architecture projects in Italy and abroad. He also teaches at the Domus Academy, as part of the Industrial Design degree in the Faculty of Architecture at the Milan Polytechnic and as part of the Industrial Design degree in the Faculty of Design at the University of Architecture of Venice, as well as doing research on the relationship between design and society.

ANTONELLA SPIEZIO WAS BORN IN TORRE ORSAIA IN 1966. At the young age of 19 years, she embarked on two parallel roads that eventually met, transforming Antonella Spiezio into a versatile and well-rounded professional, as a result of her studies in Economics (she graduated in Milan in 1997) and her work at the Sottsass Associati Studio, where her organisational and managerial qualities immediately stood out. In 1989, she became founding partner and Managing Director of Cibic & Partners, a position she still holds today. She is the strategic core of the

PROJECTS:
CIBIC & PARTNERS

PROJECT PAGE 44:
TELECOM
GENEVA, SWITZERLAND

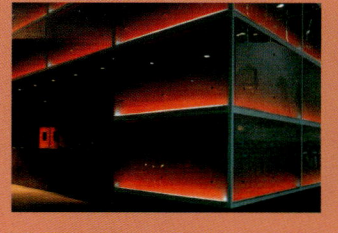

PROJECT PAGE 47:
X-NOVO
FIERA, MILAN, ITALY

Studio, handling the management of human resources and finances. Thanks to her unique brand of managing, having always grown within a highly creative environment, she guarantees the efficient organisation of work, following its development, management and day-by-day evolution.

LUIGI MARCHETTI, BORN IN LIVORNO IN 1967, obtained a degree in Architecture at the University of Florence in 1992 and, until the end of 1993, was assistant professor of Architectural Design at the University of Florence. He later went on to private practice, carrying out numerous refurbishment works of both flats and offices. From Tuscany, he moved to Milan, where he began collaborating with Aldo Cibic on various projects in New York (Pepe Jeans, offices and showrooms), Turkey (Beymen Department Store and refurbishment of the Executive area of the Istanbul Stock Exchange) and England (Habitat Shops). In 1995, he joined Cibic & Partners as Project Manager, signing off the main architecture projects realised by the Firm, consequently becoming partner in 2002. With the firm, he is currently responsible for the large Selfridges shopping centre project in England, the Medusa Multiplex Cinemas throughout Italy, the new Geox shops, and the Move In mixed-use entertainment complex in Legnano, as well as for the completion of the Una Hotel in Milan. He has also been in charge of the Pirelli Stand at the Bologna Motorshow (1996), the Marina Yachting (1997) and Esprit (1996) showrooms, and the creation and realisation of a new image for Henry Cotton's shops (1999).

ZORAN MINIC, BORN IN KRUSEVAC, YUGOSLAVIA, IN 1964, graduated in Architecture from the University of Belgrade in 1990; the following year, he moved to Germany, where he spent four years working for numerous architecture firms. He moved to Milan in 1994 and attended the Master's course in Industrial Design at the Domus Academy, participating in various seminars with Aldo Cibic, Andrea Branzi, Dante Donegani, and Stefano Giovannoni. In 1996, he began collaborating with Cibic & Partners, becoming partner in 2002. Since 1997, he has been Project Manager for important interior works and architecture, such as the Hometech Pavilion in Berlin for Whirlpool (2002), the new headquarters of publishing house Abitare Segesta (in progress), Pitti (design of new offices in the Leopolda Station, in progress), the new headquarters for I.Net British Telecom, the development of architecture and interiors for the Autogrill Fast Food project (1999), the Telecom Pavilion for the World Telecommunications Expo in Geneva (1999), and the architecture, interior design and image of the Valerio Catullo Airport (1998). Since 1998, he has been working on a self-produced design brand, 'POP SOLID FABRICATION': a series of design pieces, including lamps, furniture and objects ('Lamps', 'Solid Living', 'Flat', 'Home Tools').

COMPANY STATEMENT CIBIC & PARTNERS

"EVERY PROJECT IS A CHALLENGE TO CREATE A FEELING, EVEN A SUBTLE ONE, THAT CONSEQUENTLY GENERATES IDENTITY, VITALITY AND A SENSE OF BELONGING"

PROJECT PAGE 48:
WHIRLPOOL
BERLIN, GERMANY

PROJECT PAGE 52:
RELAXENSE
PITTI UOMO, FLORENCE, ITALY

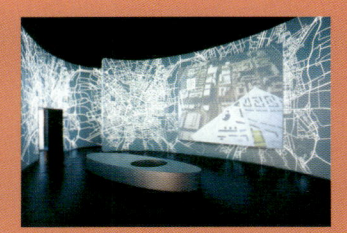

PROJECT PAGE 55:
RISANAMENTO
TERRITORIAL MARKETING EXHIBITION, MILAN, ITALY

PROJECT:
TELECOM
GENEVA, SWITZERLAND

WHERE:
World's Fair of Telecommunications, Geneva, Switzerland

WHEN:
October 1999

ARCHITECTURAL DESIGN:
Aldo Cibic, Zoran Minic and Carolina Suels, Cibic & Partners, Milan

LIGHTING CONSULTANT:
Studio Pollice, Milan

GRAPHIC DESIGN:
Michelangelo Petralito, Cibic & Partners

INSTALLATION:
Salvato Allestimenti, Pogliano Milanese, Milan

SPECIAL EFFECTS:
Creative Communications, Milan

AREA:
2,400 m²

BUDGET:
€ 1,500,000

PROJECT DURATION:
5 months

OPENING:
October 1999

The stand created for Telecom at the World's Fair of Telecommunications in Geneva is recognisable by the presence of an aluminium totem with a circular base. The stand is a large central open space bordered by two parallel oblong volumes of different lengths, connected by two raised passageways. The façades, made with rectangular panes of impact-proof glass, back-lit in red, conceal two levels. On the ground level of the longer wing, the reception, with three plasma video screens, occupies a protruding segment, leading to a portico punctuated by video screens on the walls or inserted in the columns in alucobond (aluminium panels). Behind this multimedia diaphragm are a screening room, a small theater and a storage area, all with blue wall-to-wall carpeting. The same carpet is also used for the upper level, which contains offices, a bar and a restaurant with a view of the central space through a glazing protected by a brise-soleil. An impressive videowall, faced in polyurethane foam and gray fabric, stands out at the center of the large central space, whose flooring is in maple panels. The space takes on the appearance of a piazza in a multimedia city, surrounded by glassy walls, which contain other, smaller videowall installations. The shorter wing is set aside for the TIM mobile phone affiliate, with other offices on the upper level.
All this technology is inserted in a warm atmosphere, thanks to the dominant use of red (at times alternated with segments of blue) in all the spaces, and the presence of maple and wall-to-wall carpet, in contrast with the coolness of the glass and the metals. The idea behind the design for Telecom combines the notions of encounter and communication in an architectural interpretation using imposing classical forms like the colonnade and the gallery, updated by the materials and the multimedia components of the installation.

CIBIC & PARTNERS grand stand

PROJECT:
TELECOM
GENEVAGENEVA, SWITZERLAND

PROJECT:
X-NOVO
FIERA, MILAN, ITALY

WHERE:
Fiera, Milan, Italy

WHEN:
March 2002

ARCHITECTURAL DESIGN:
Aldo Cibic, Zoran Minic, João Silva, Cibic & Partners

GRAPHIC DESIGN:
Michelangelo Petralito, Cibic & Partners

INSTALLATION:
D.S. Pubblicità with Francesco Migliaccio, Milan

AREA:
96 m²

BUDGET:
€ 25,000

PROJECT DURATION:
4 weeks

OPENING:
9 March 2002

Cibic & Partners was contracted to design a stand for 'X-NOVO', a new product line designed by Aldo Cibic, for Webert, a manufacturer of faucets. The small exposition space was to be contained within an 8 x 12 metres footprint and had to be produced in short time and on a 'shoestring' budget. The project layout and design echoed that of the products to be displayed, which add an ironic sense to their frank industrial declaration of function. The project is an almost graphic expression that presents the products in an honest, straightforward manner with a sense of serious fun.
An openly relaxed meeting point that flowed seamlessly into its surroundings, the stand allowed visitors passing by to effortlessly view the displayed objects.
An internally lit L-shaped volume was wrapped in diaphanous fabric printed with the product name 'X-NOVO', which provided a luminous canopy for the faucet displays below. A pale gray rectilinear enclosure bearing the new company logo contained a private meeting space and two offices.
Ultimately the stand proved to be a very simple and cost efficient means of announcing the firm's new direction in terms of art direction and extending the presence of its identity within the market.

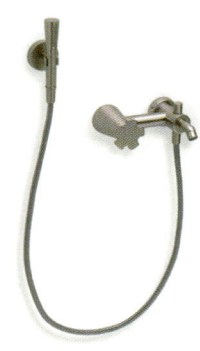

grand stand **CIBIC & PARTNERS**

PROJECT
WHIRLPOOL
BERLIN, GERMANY

The challenge Cibic & Partners chose to accept in building the Whirlpool pavilion for the prestigious electrical appliance show Hometech in Berlin, consists of responding to a particularly complex brief: 5,000 m² of floorspace occupying two distinct areas in which the group's two brands (Whirlpool and Bauknecht) must be united without ever neglecting their individual identities.

The first step towards the attainment of this goal was to create a structure that gave new life to the available space and that, at the same time, allowed the elimination of the subdivision of the areas so as to assure the visitor a sense of uniformity and homogeneity.

Cibic & Partners resolved this problem by building a wall of light around the perimeter of the space at their disposal; 270 metres long and 9 metres high, of an 'organic' form and thus in sharp contrast with the exhibition hall's rigid structure. Within this space the two main brands were positioned within two elements: Whirlpool in a 'Whirl' made of translucent inflatable material in which the products were displayed, and Bauknecht in the 'Bauknecht house', which consisted of a backlit box whose placement fulfilled the dual purpose of masking the space's subdivision in two parts and of creating a series of internal spaces for the display of the Bauknecht brand products. Between these two principal elements, Cibic & Partners positioned the bar, with its 'piazza' where informal encounters and the main events took place. The peripheral area contains the reception spaces near the entrances, the PROJECT F futuristic display, the Home Interactive pavilion, the Microwave area and the staff offices. The changing light, the use of video, the sound and colours, all form part of a complex production that eases the pavilion's conceptual transition from physical space to sensory setting distinguished by a sequence of emotions and experiences. The energy and the space thus take on their new dynamic forms based on modern technology seen, in this case, as a means of producing emotions.

PROJECT
WHIRLPOOL
BERLIN, GERMANY

WHERE:
Hometech, Berlin, Germany

CLIENT:
Whirlpool

ARCHITECTURAL DESIGN:
Aldo Cibic, Zoran Minic and Luis Almeida, Cibic & Partners

GRAPHIC DESIGNER:
Michelangelo Petralito, Cibic & Partners

INSTALLATION:
Mostrefiere, Turin

SPECIAL EFFECTS:
Creative Communications, Milan

MATERIALS:
floors: wood strip flooring
walls: backlit fabric screen, inflatable structure
furniture: plastic laminate

AREA:
5,000 m^2

BUDGET:
€ 4,000,000

PROJECT DURATION:
9 months

OPENING:
February 2002

51

CIBIC & PARTNERS grand stand

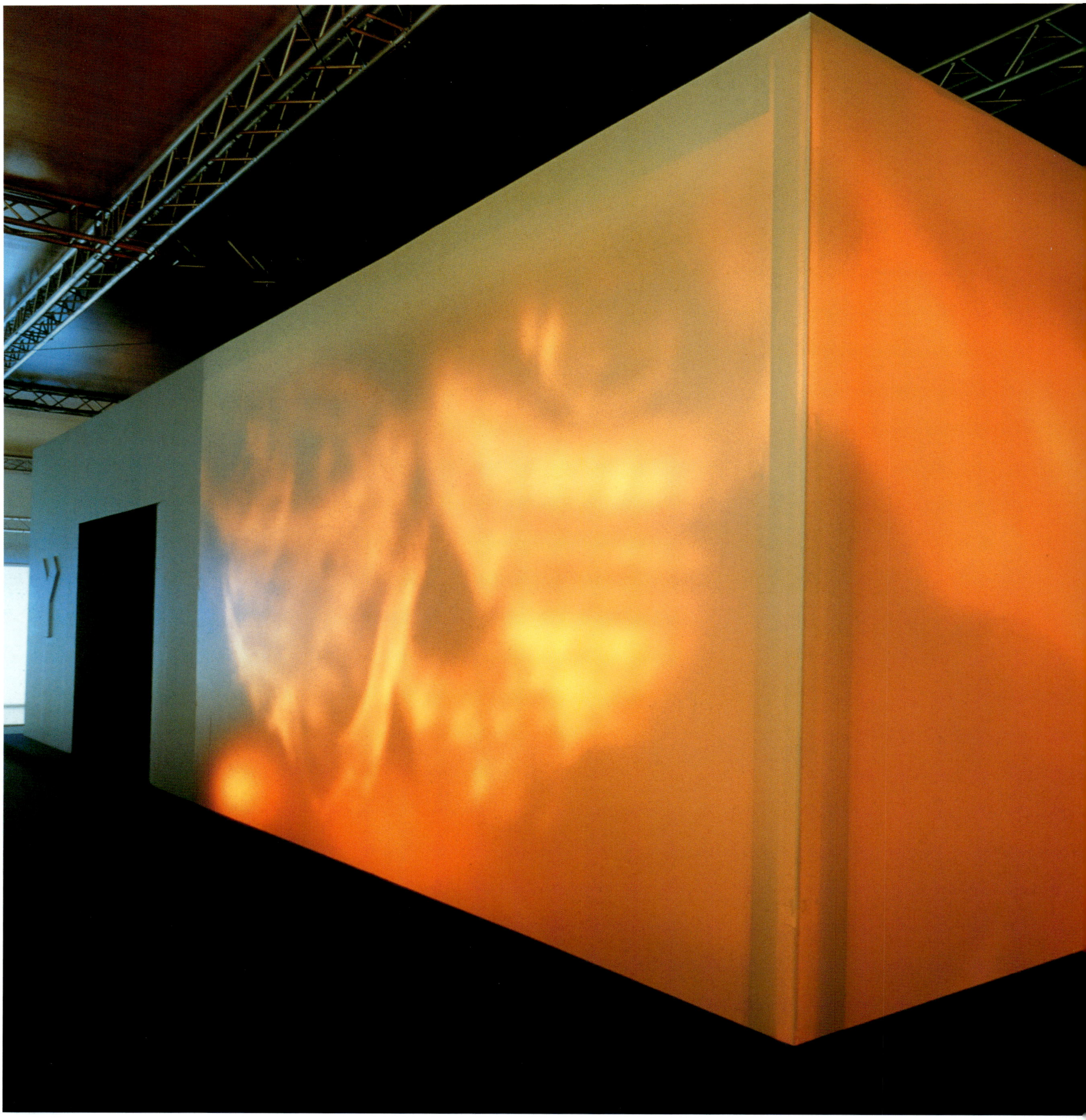

PROJECT:
RELAXENSE
PITTI UOMO, FLORENCE, ITALY

WHERE:
Pitti Uomo, Florence, Italy

WHEN:
June 1999

ARCHITECTURAL DESIGN:
Aldo Cibic and Francesco Messori, Cibic & Partners

INSTALLATION:
Salvato Allestimenti, Pogliano Milanese, Milan

SPECIAL EFFECTS:
Creative Communications, Milan

MUSIC:
Oscar Accorsi and Roberto Masotti (musiche ECM, München)

AREA:
400 m²

BUDGET:
€ 27,500

PROJECT DURATION:
1 week

OPENING:
June 1999

The Relaxsense stand, measuring 13 x 9 metres with a height of 3.5 metres, around which the entire itinerary of the Ynformal section of the Pitti Uomo event in Florence is arranged, takes on the look and the role of a sensorial box: a sort of womb with carpeted floors and walls made of fabric screens for back projection, creating a whirling collage of colors accompanied by sound effects and music.
The 'Stone' seat by Ron Arad, placed at the center of the stand, dominates the space which, like a vortex, offers the spectator two exit or entrance routes, opposite one another.
The colored projections, that gradually take on the warmer shades of oranges and yellows, then pass to greens and blues, transfigure a space that is intimate but also has a great visual impact, a sort of brief return to the prenatal state.

CIBIC & PARTNERS grand stand

PROJECT:
RELAXENSE
PITTI UOMO, FLORENCE, ITALY

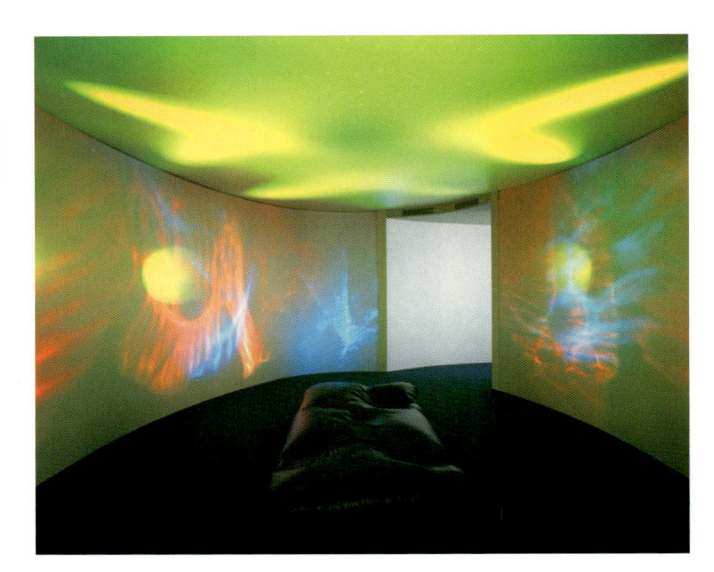

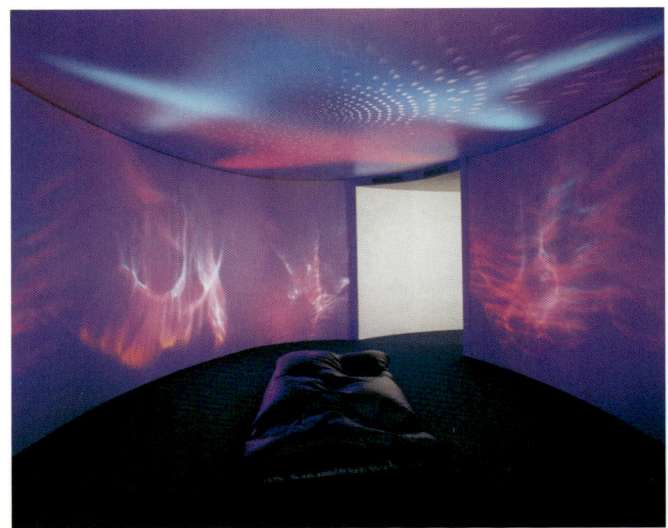

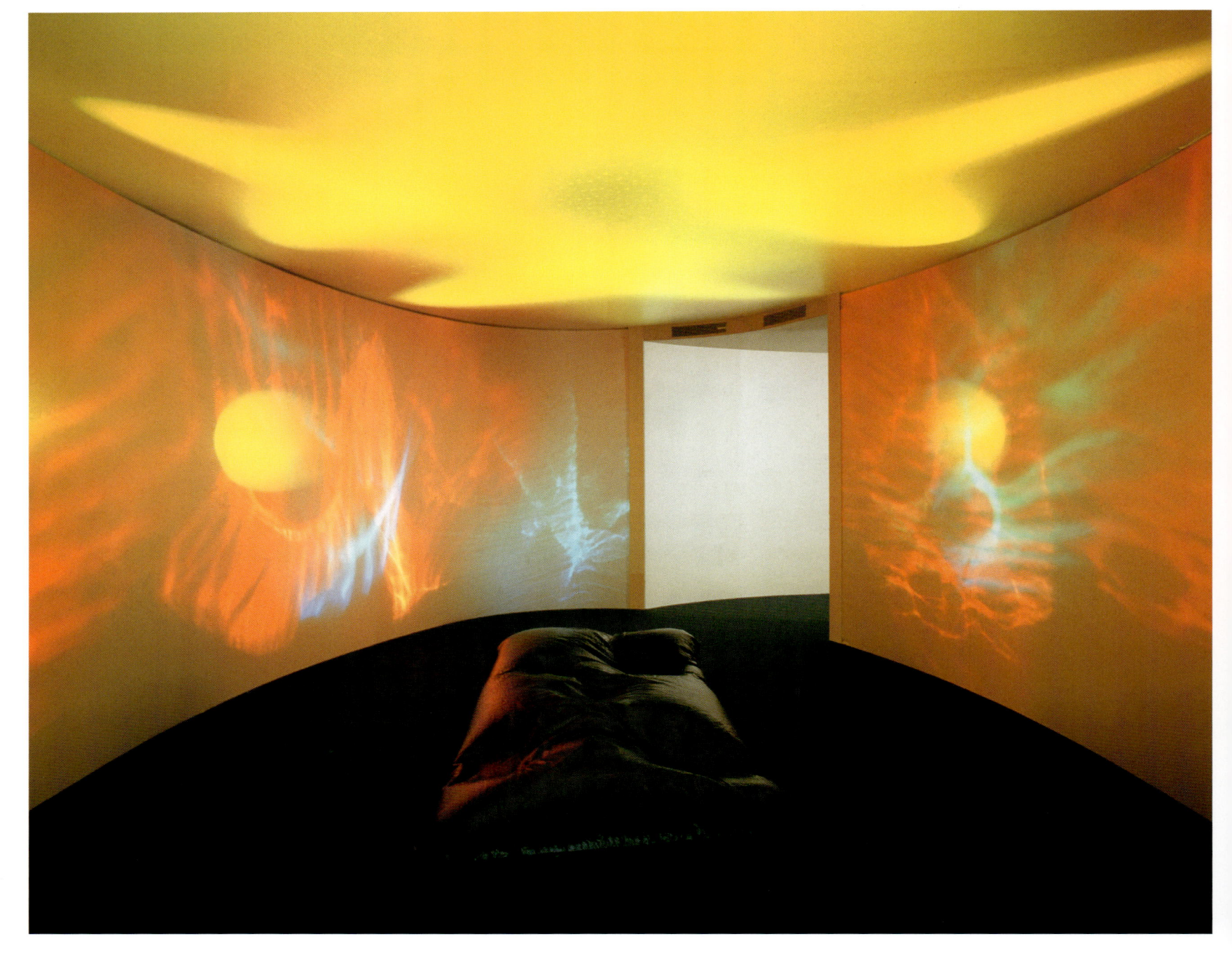

54
grand stand **CIBIC & PARTNERS**

PROJECT: RISANAMENTO
TERRITORIAL MARKETING EXHIBITION, MILAN, ITALY

WHERE:
Territorial Marketing Exhibition, Milan, Italy

WHEN:
February 2003

ARCHITECTURAL DESIGN:
Aldo Cibic, Luigi Marchetti, Marissa Morelli, Luigi Fumagalli, Cibic & Partners

LIGHTING CONSULTANT:
Creative Communications, Milan

GRAPHIC DESIGN:
Michelangelo Petralito, Cibic & Partners

INSTALLATION:
Mostrefiere, Torino

SPECIAL EFFECTS:
Creative Communications, Milan

AREA:
300 m²

BUDGET:
€ 115,000

PROJECT DURATION:
3 months

OPENING:
19 February 2003

Risanamento Spa, a leading firm in the Real Estate sector, contacted Cibic & Partners to design and build a stand for the 'Project City' exhibition in Milan.
The company requested that a space be created that appropriately represented the firm's identity – communicating solidity, commitment and institutional reliability – and at the same time be progressive and avant-garde. They asked that stand provide a place for meeting, that it be informative and communicative in order for visitors to the exhibition to become familiar with Risanamento's identity, its current projects and its plans for future development.
Cibic & Partners responded with a suitably particular and innovative form that adapted well to the programmatic functions: two architectonic volumes, each 3 metres high and painted blue, were intersected and united by a 5-metre-high luminous ellipse – all contained within a 300 m² floor area.
The reception area was located to the right of the entry and welcomed visitors along with a blue cube bearing the company's three dimensional logo, which was placed to the left of the entrance. At the center of the project, Cibic & Partners designed an elliptical helicoidal space that served as a multimedia piazza, with a video screen (14 x 5 metres) that presented the company's history and the interventions completed within the region.
Visitors entering the space were given the sensation of being totally immersed in the city by way of the enormous ground image of Milan printed on translucent PVC skin covering the wall structure – the walls were internally lit rendering the map luminously alive.

From main space, the curved walls led visitors into the two flanking exhibition areas contained within the blue rectilinear volumes intersecting the elliptical helix.
Located to the right was an interactive presentation with touch-screen terminals contained within niches. Visitors could research and discover the history of the Risanamento and current developments within the region. Three large-scale models of the firm's principal urban interventions in Milan (Montecity, Rogoredo, and Porta Vittoria) served as the central protagonists within the space.
The predominant thematic color of the space was dark blue (the company's corporate color) which was balanced by the gray mèlange carpeting and the luminous white PVC walls into which the computer monitors had been recessed.
Located to the left side of the elliptical helix, was an intimately scaled museum with an adjacent bar. On display were drawings of current projects as well as sketches of internationally recognized architects.
Various support spaces, including a wardrobe and spacious office, were located behind a dividing partition in order to be easily accessed by staff. These spaces were rendered in warm tones with ivory colored walls, gray mèlange carpeting, and soft upholstered chairs grouped around glass and stainless steel tables.

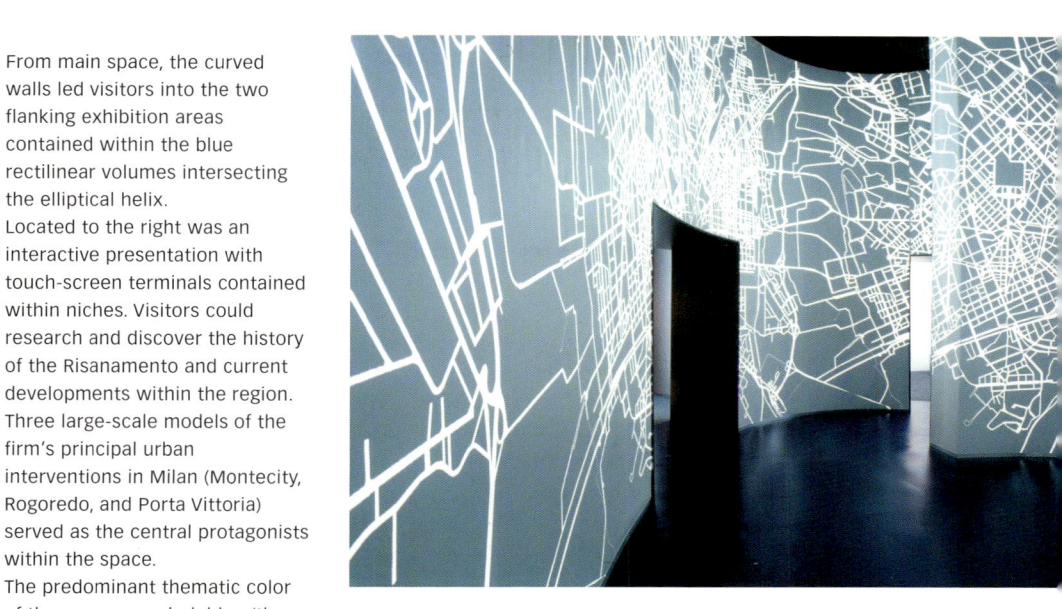

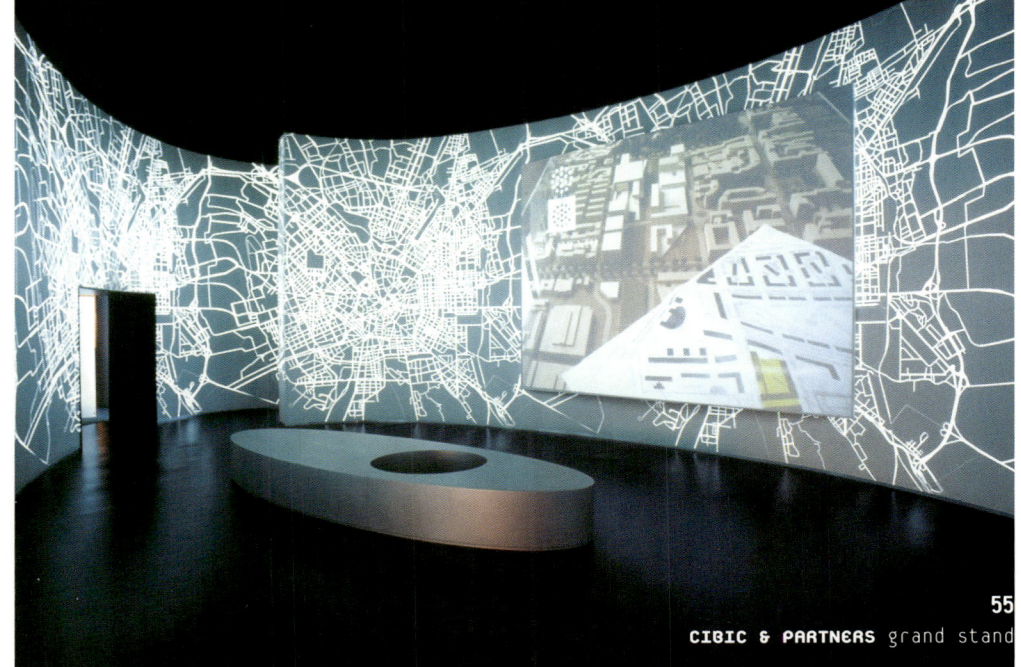

CIBIC & PARTNERS grand stand

COMPANY NAME:
CIBIC & PARTNERS

HEAD OFFICE:
Via Varese 18
20121 Milan
Italy

PHONE:
+39 02 657 11 22

FAX:
+39 02 290 60 141

E-MAIL:
info@cibicpartners.com

WEBSITE:
www.cibicpartners.com

MANAGEMENT:
Antonella Spiezio

CONTACTS:
Daniela Spiezio
danielaspiezio@cibicpartners.com

KEY DESIGNERS:
Aldo Cibic
Chuck Felton
Luigi Marchetti
Zoran Minic

FOUNDED:
1989

COMPANY PROFILE:
Cibic & Partners, one of the most well known Italian design studios, was established in Milan at the end of the eighties.
For over ten years it has operated in many parts of the world. The studio is a composite reality that by choice and by calling has occupied itself with projects of different nature – ranging from architecture to interiors and from design to multimedia communications.
Cibic and Partners is guided by four partners: Aldo Cibic is the design nucleus of the studio and along with Luigi Marchetti and Zoran Minic, is closely connected to the work groups that are dedicated to the various projects. Antonella Spiezio is the strategic core of the partnership and is responsible for the organisation, administration of financial and human resources. They are supported by a group of architects, interior designers, graphic artists, industrial designers, and a deep network of collaborating consultants of diverse professional and cultural backgrounds.
The result is an environment where there is an intense exchange of stimulation and energy, and where the principal aim is the realisation of solid and innovative projects. The capacity for design and organisation are the two determining factors that make the studio a creative and reliable partner for major business groups world-wide.

CLIENTS:
- **Autogrill Spizzico,** Typical architecture for Restaurants and Drive-thrus Bologna and Design of new Fast Food image
- **Abitare Segesta,** New Headquarters, Milan
- **Medusa,** Multiplex
- **Selfridges & Co,** Department Store, Manchester, Birmingham
- **I.Net British Telecom,** Headquarters, Milan
- **Geox,** Chain of shops
- **New England,** Showroom, Milan
- **Marina Yachting,** Showroom, Milan
- **Esprit,** Showroom, Milan
- **Habitat,** Shops, London
- **Cariverona Foundation,** Multi-use space, Verona
- **Verona Airport,** Departures area and VIP Lounge, Verona
- **Una Hotel,** Hotel, Milan
- **Risanamento,** Stand 'Progetto Città' Fair, Milan
- **Whirlpool,** Pavilion at Hometech 2002, Berlin
- **Telecom,** Pavilion, World Telecommunications Expo, Geneva
- **Pirelli,** Stand, Motorshow, Bologna
- **Pitti Ynformal,** Multimedia Lighting and Sound Stand, Pitti Immagine, Florence

SERVICES:
- Architecture
- Art Direction
- Interior Design
- Industrial Design
- Graphic Design
- Web Design

CRENEAU INTERNATIONAL
HASSELT, BELGIUM

ABOUT creneau

Conceived in Belgium in 1989, Creneau has since grown into an international design consultancy. Creneau specialises in building brand personality through the use of creative ideas and solutions for commercial environments. Creneau aims to be the most forward-thinking, European young design agency. Creneau brings brands to a new level of impact through cutting-edge design and concepts, breaking through the white noise of today's media-saturated world.

CRENEAU IS THE CREATIVE UMBRELLA FOR FOUR AREAS OF SPECIALISATION: ATMOSPHERE ARCHITECTURE For Creneau, retail is about breathing life into a brand and creating a physical brand presence that reflects its personality. Brand environments can be dynamic communication tools, building intense relationships with customers. Atmosphere architecture covers commercial interiors for shops, shop-in-shops, bars, restaurants, hotels, nightclubs, showrooms, offices, exhibitions, points-of-sale and visual styling.

GRAPHICS are a powerful, essential tool for creating immediate impact. Creneau gives a company's statement a unique profile, so nobody else says quite the same thing in quite the same way. Creneau produces graphics for print media, 2D corporate identities, house styles, packaging and catalogues.

PR AND EVENTS The tone and content of PR and events can often do more to dull a brand than to excite it. Creneau breaks the mould, creating events that people want to attend, events that are a demonstration of a brand's body and soul. Creneau PR and events' services range from product placements, media monitoring and analyses, press briefings and conferences to the organisation of fashion shows, meetings, workshops, parties, brainstorms and product launches.

MUTATIONSPOTTING Mutationspotting is a web-based intelligence network offering brands up-to-the-minute 'finger on the pulse' multimedia and global youth culture intelligence. In 2000 Creneau established a unique network, bringing together young style leaders and creative talent from all over the world to explore new ideas, underground trends and subcultural mutations. Mutationspotting (www.mutationspotting.com) is a unique concept in Europe, offering a network of youth reporters, or spotters, aged between 16 and 26 and based in 50 cities, among them Paris, Barcelona, Brooklyn, New York, Warsaw, Dublin, Madrid and Buenos Aires.

THE COMPANY'S PROJECTS ILLUSTRATE INNOVATION and an unconventional approach whilst remaining in touch with commercialism and practicality. The company is structured to maximise creativity, with a large 'creative core' in Belgium made up of forward-thinking individuals sourced

PROJECTS:
CRENEAU

PROJECT PAGE 60:
LEE JEANS 101
BREAD & BUTTER TRADE FAIR, COLOGNE, GERMANY

PROJECT PAGE 62:
LEE JEANS
INTERJEANS TRADE FAIR, COLOGNE, GERMANY

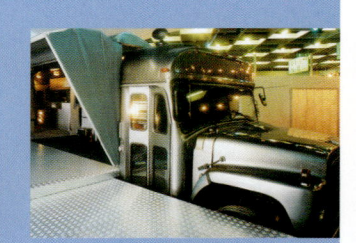

PROJECT PAGE 64:
LEVI STRAUSS EUROPE
INTERJEANS TRADE FAIR 2000, COLOGNE, GERMANY

from various nationalities. The 'creative core' initiates the concept creation and the project managers take over to develop the design for the specific client or home market, bringing in the practical knowledge and skills of manufacturing and project management required to build ground-breaking creative projects efficiently.

CRENEAU'S NOTORIOUS AND CLIENT PROJECTS INCLUDE the so-hip-it-hurts bar Markt in New York, a ground-breaking office environment for Exposure Promotions in London, Levi's brand promotion for Europe, Guess, Tommy Hilfiger, Dr Martens, Converse, Fila, XX brand launch for Mexx's European girls' range, Miss Selfridge, edc by Esprit, Pepe Jeans London, Lee Jeans, Wrangler, G-Star, San Miguel, Fosters, Interbrew, Coca-Cola, Douwe Egberts, L'Oréal, Watches Of Switzerland, Yo Japan, Chillypepper, Top Shop.

COMPANY STATEMENT CRENEAU
"EXPECT THE UNEXPECTED"

PROJECT PAGE 66:
LEVI STRAUSS EUROPE
INTERJEANS TRADE FAIR 1999,
COLOGNE, GERMANY

PROJECT PAGE 68:
XX BY MEXX
CPD FAIR, DÜSSELDORF,
GERMANY

PROJECT PAGE 70:
WRANGLER
INTERJEANS TRADE FAIR,
COLOGNE, GERMANY

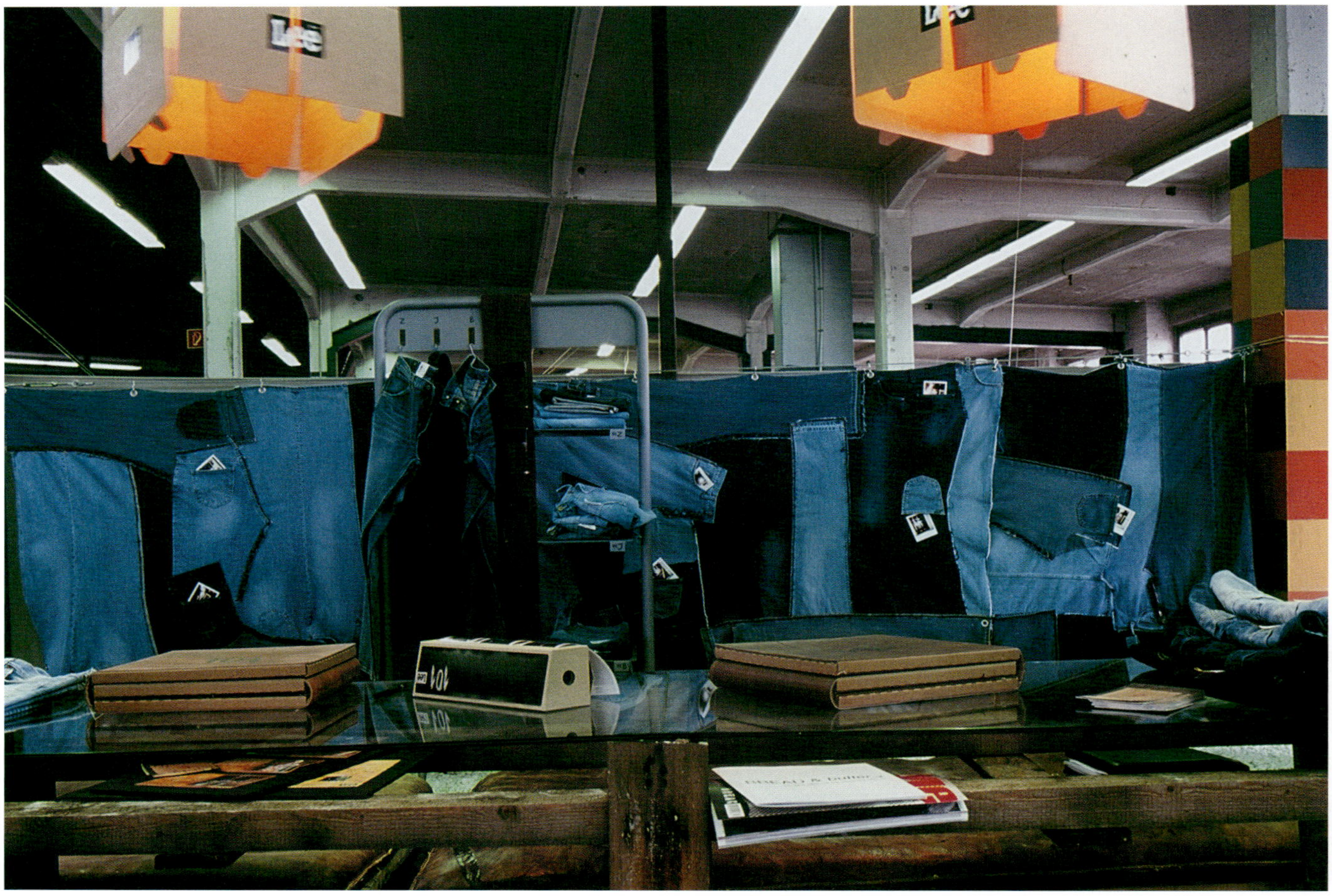
Lee
Lee
101

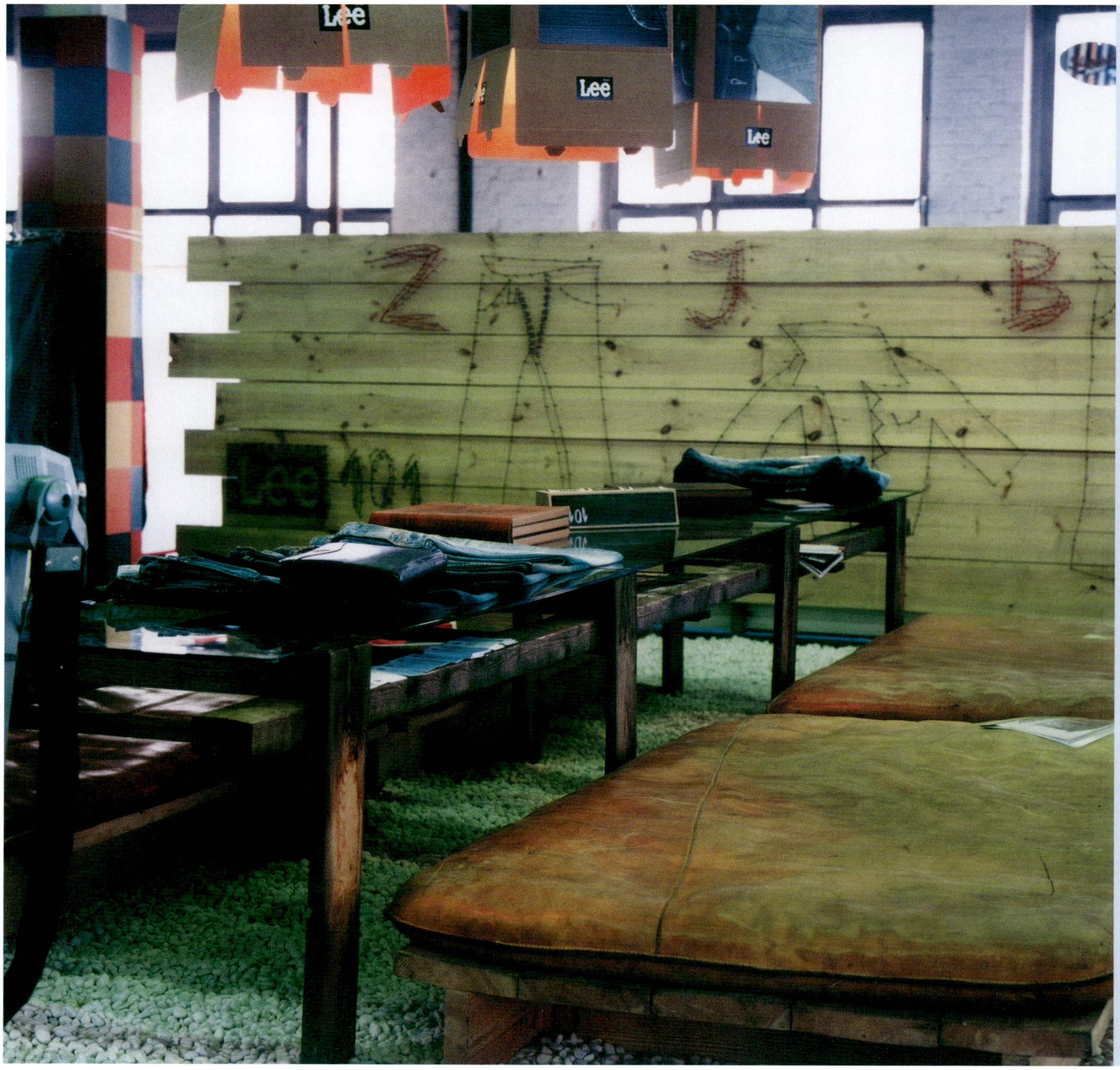
Lee
Lee
Lee
Z
J
B
Lee 101
101

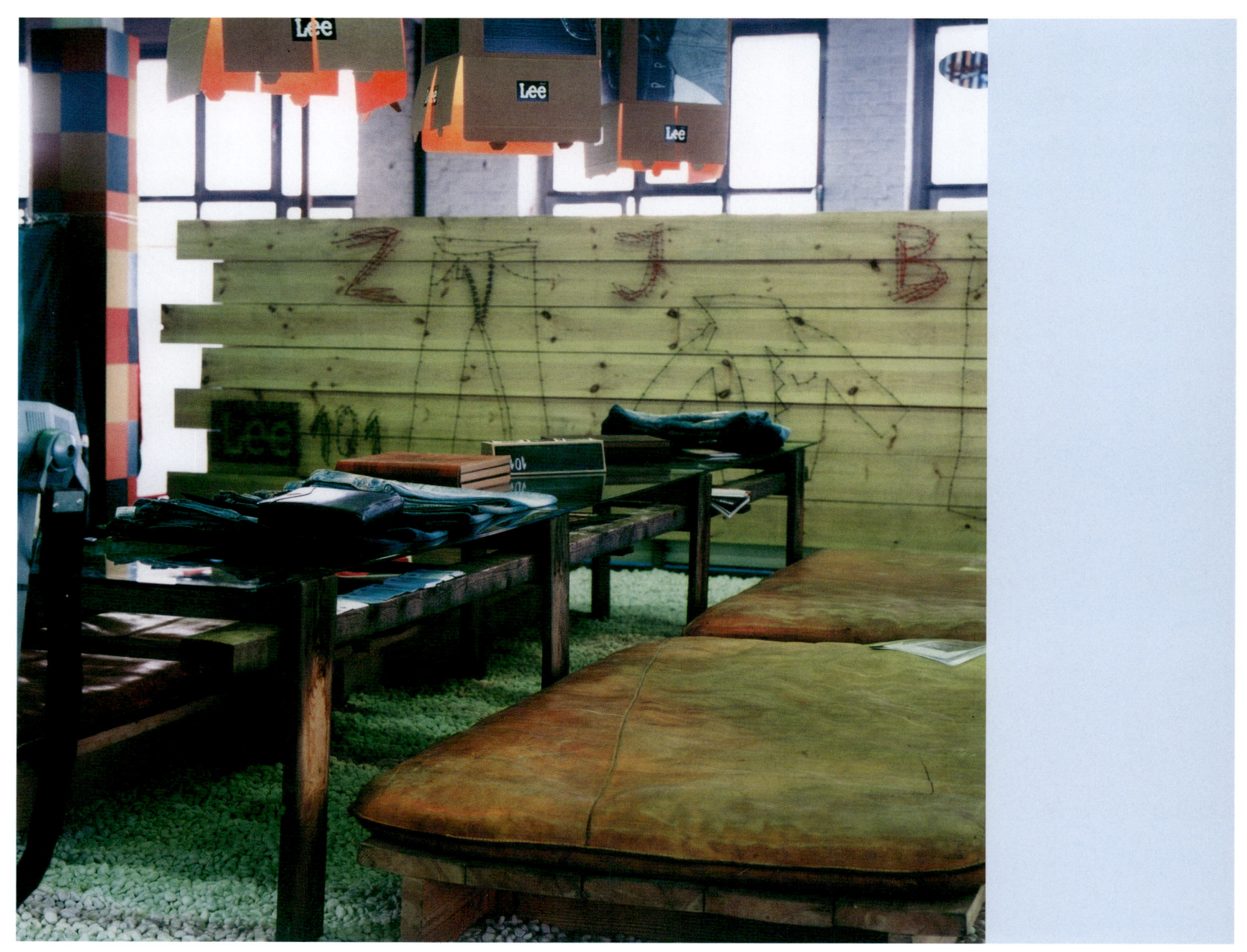

PROJECT:

LEE JEANS 101

BREAD & BUTTER TRADE FAIR, COLOGNE, GERMANY

THEME: LEE 101

Making a statement on a 33 m² surface is not easy! Creneau used materials such as a cobblestone floor combined with low wooden seats covered with vintage leather cushions to bring the values of the Lee 101 collection to the stand: heritage, quality, durability and authenticity.

The Lee logo was shown in a creative and innovative way on a wooden back wall: threads woven between nails created the graphic of the logo. The lights were covered with cardboard boxes showing the 101 logo and images. The exclusive Lee 101 collection was presented in metal cages.

In fact, all materials used – stone, wood, used leather, cardboard – were breathing the same authenticity and vintage feeling.

PROJECT:
LEE JEANS
INTERJEANS TRADE FAIR,
COLOGNE, GERMANY

THEME: FEEL THE BLUE
The concept for the stand 'feel the blue' was based on Lee's heritage as workwear. Creneau translated this concept into a modern factory environment.

The space was divided into two sections. The first section was a workshop giving the impression that the workers had just put down their tools and gone home. The second section was the canteen and management offices. In the canteen, Creneau communicated the Lee concept of 'feel the blue' by using light, sound and materials.

In the workshop, each product line had its own department where the clothes were displayed in their own unique way. For example, Originals were inside security transport cages because of their value, Icons were displayed in a self-contained area called the Spray Room, where the range of clothing was being customised. The stand was constructed of wire mesh outer walls, including triangular roofing. Painted panels in 'factory colours' lined the inner walls.

The furniture was actual workshop material such as benches, tool walls, lockers, cantilever systems, cheap and cheerful canteen furniture as well as a professional kitchen unit. Drinks were served from oil barrels (try our cocktails!). Posters of naked girls were replaced by 'Denim 42' images and information. Notice boards were used for displaying Lee promotional information.

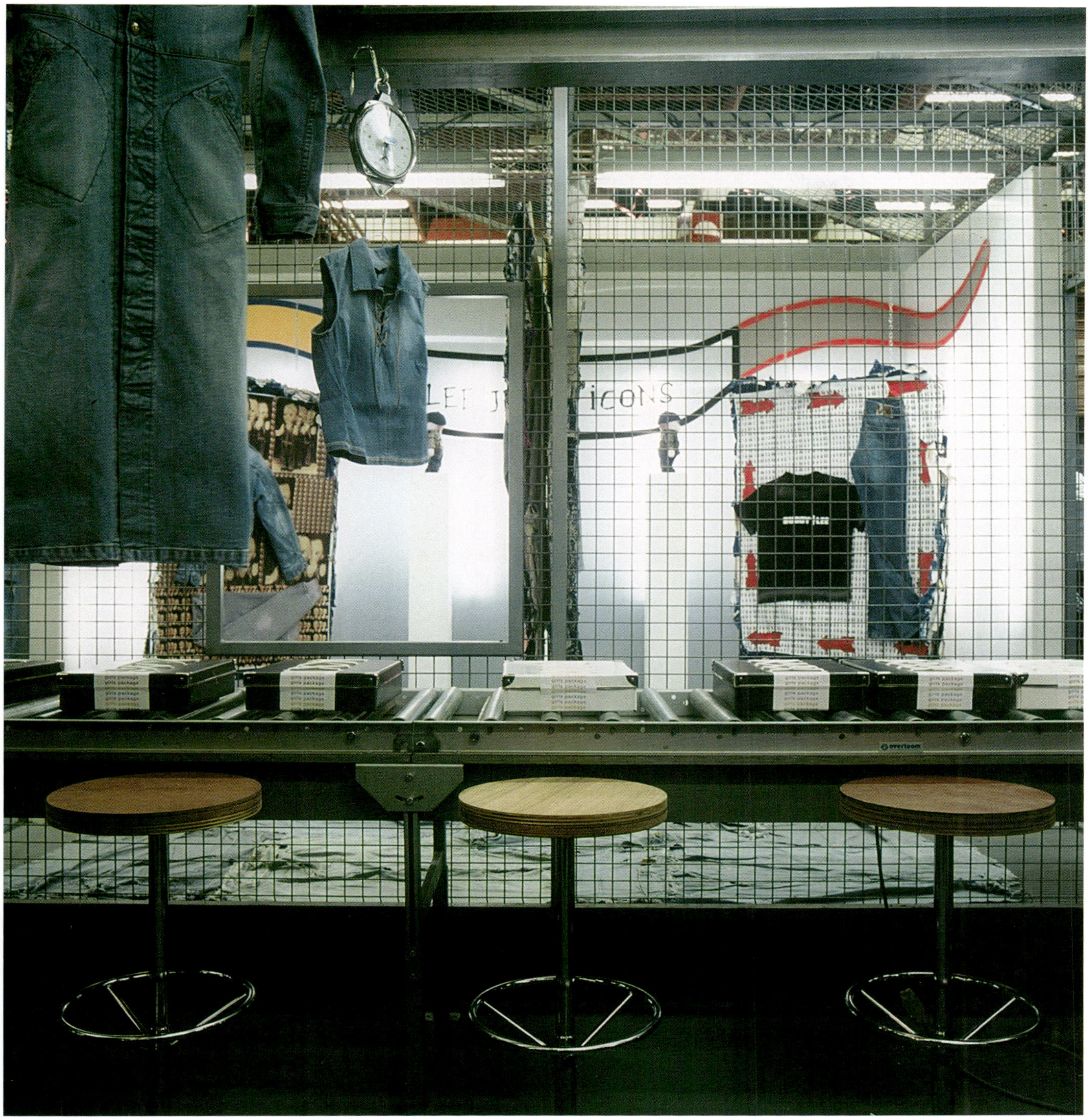
ICONS

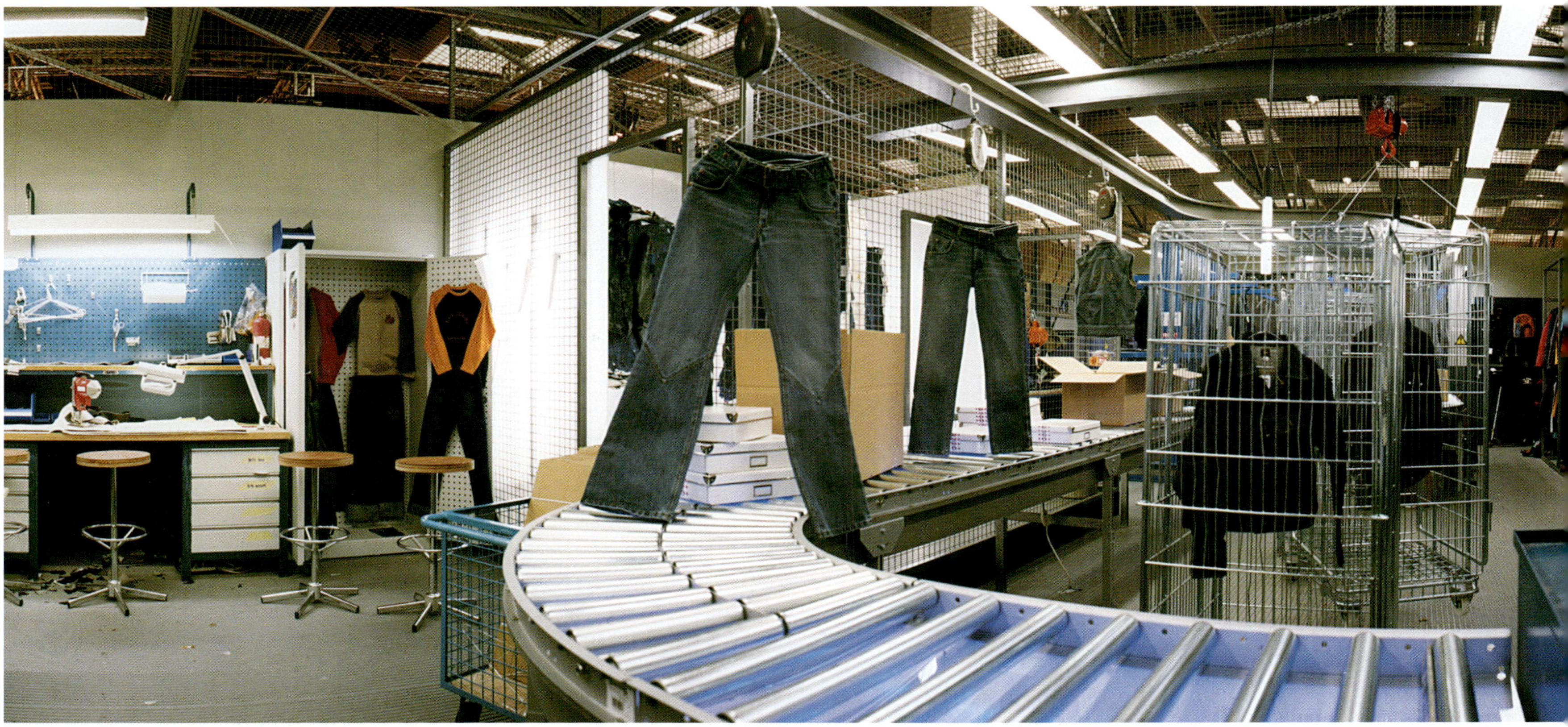

PROJECT:
LEVI STRAUSS EUROPE
INTERJEANS TRADE FAIR 2000, COLOGNE, GERMANY

THEME: YOUTH ON THE MOVE
Emphasis was put on the theme 'youth on the move', a contemporary nomadic environment for travelling people at the beginning of the 21st Century. Four converted American tour buses were positioned around a central chill-out arena, where young artistic talent was putting life into works of art. Moroccan lamps and oriental carpets, combined with contemporary art pieces, gave this central area the look of a modern kasbah or marketplace.
The whole area was covered with stretched fabric with a projected clear blue sky.
The different product lines of Levi's found their perfect home within the individual interiors of the buses. The buses excellently reflected the identity of the four segments and served as an innovative and creative background for the Levi's collection. The visitors were moved by the enthralling atmosphere.

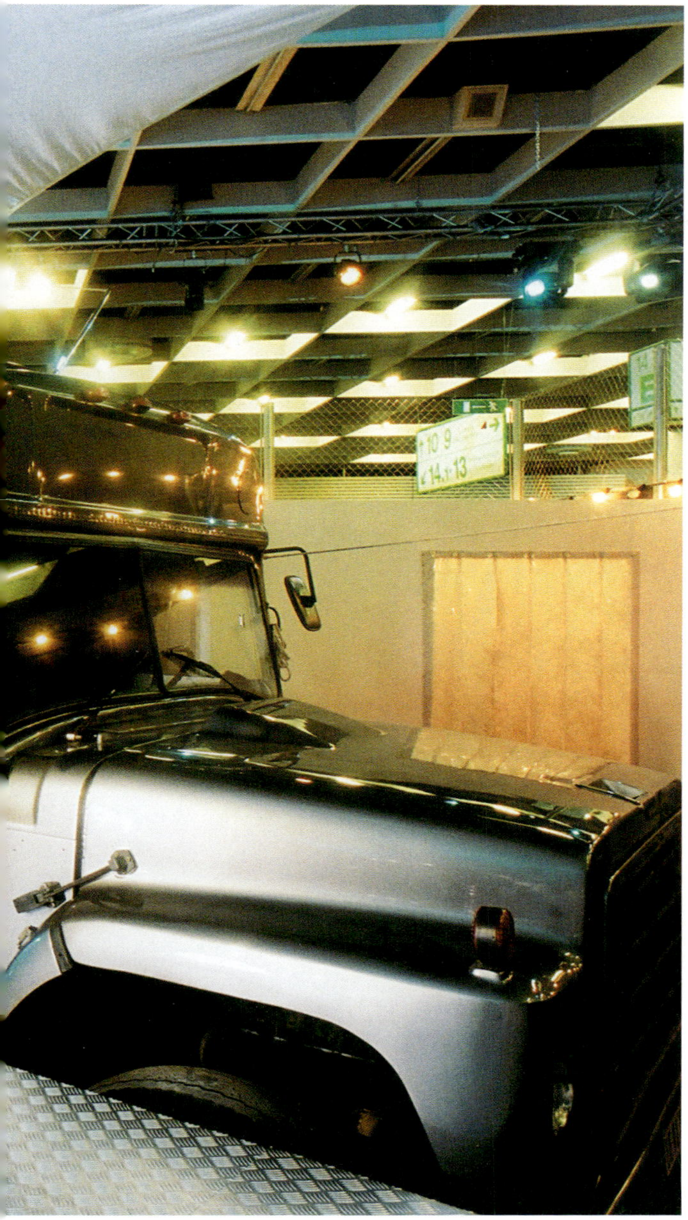

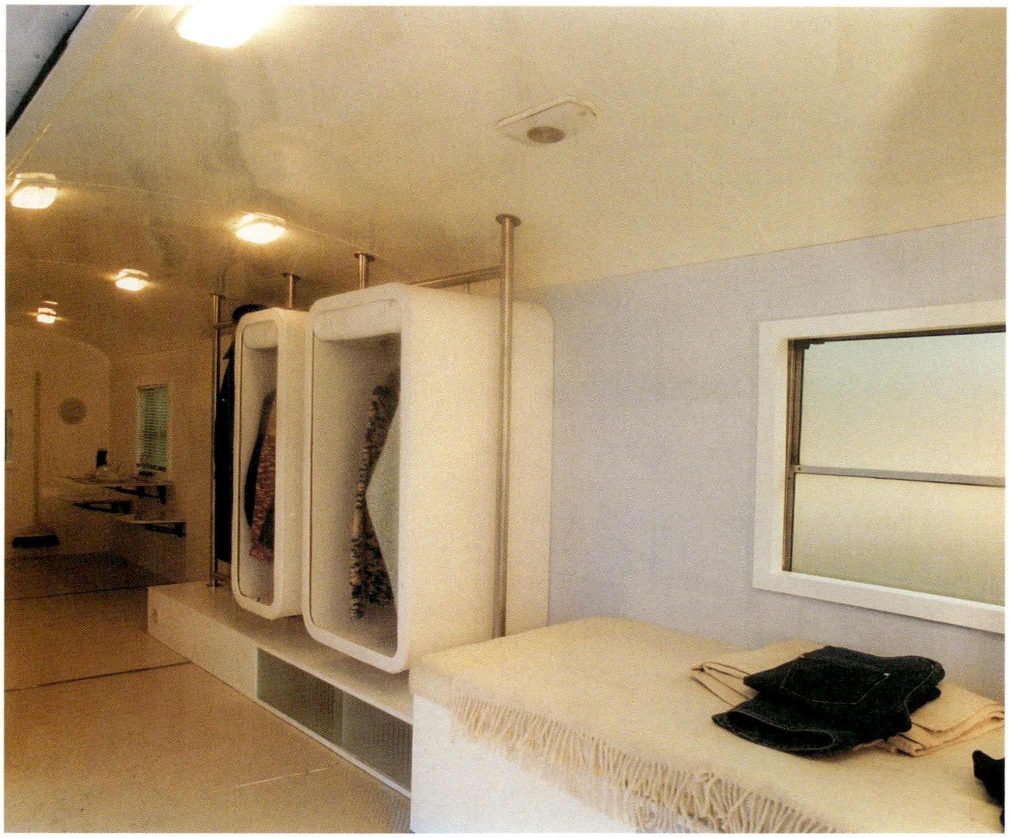

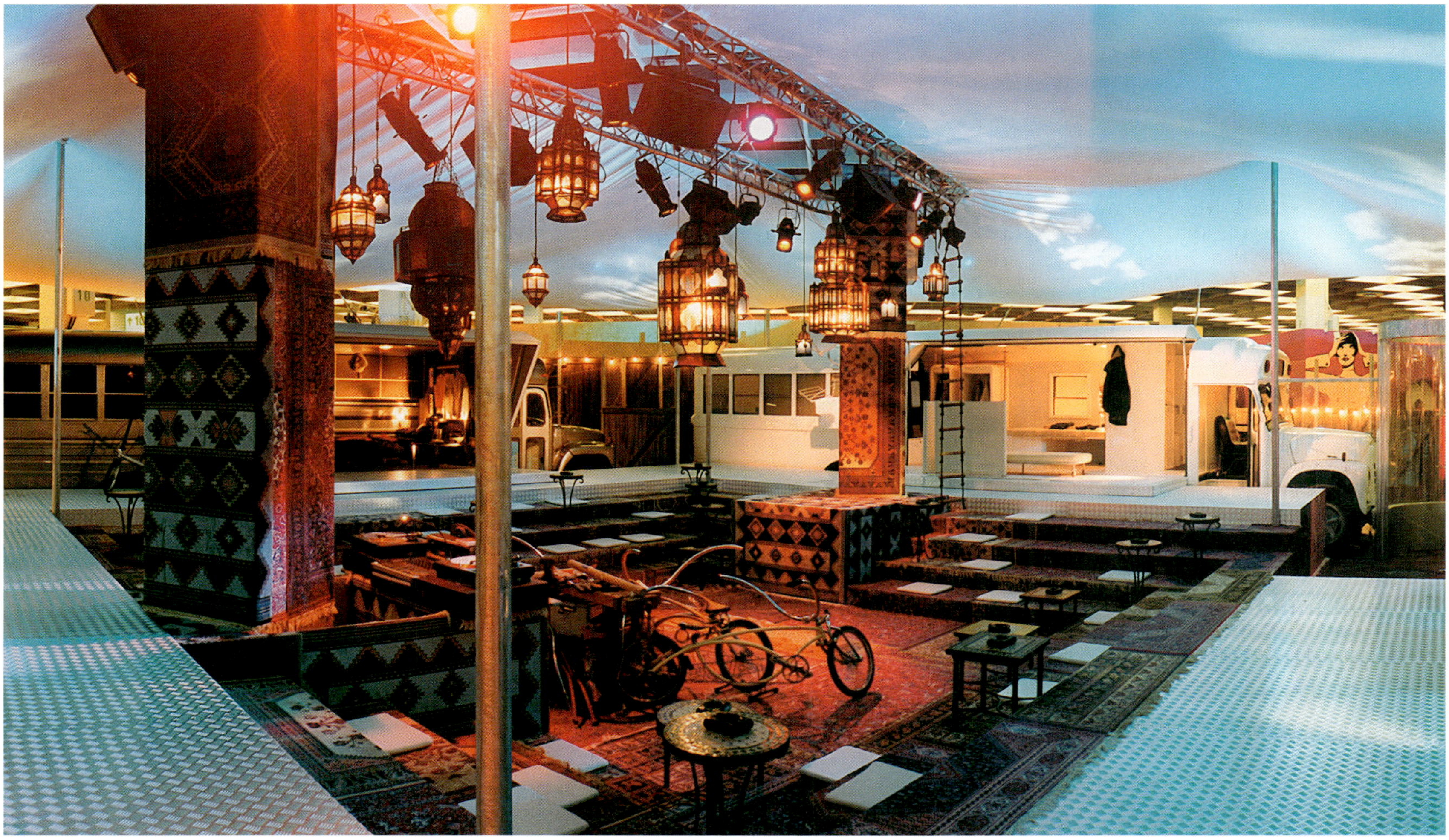

grand stand CRENEAU INTERNATIONAL

PROJECT:
LEVI STRAUSS EUROPE
INTERJEANS TRADE FAIR 1999, COLOGNE, GERMANY

THEME: NOSTALGIC FUTURISM
As a leading casual wear brand, Levi's is forced to constantly evolve its methods of communication. At the Interjeans trade fair in 1999 in Cologne, Creneau created a very special exhibition stand: an amazing reconstruction of a classic/contemporary house, based on the style and philosophy of the American architect Pierre Koenig. Responding to the theme 'nostalgic futurism', the house contained, among others, a garden, a garage, a kitchen, a living room, a study, a bedroom, and a guestroom. Those who visited the 462 m² stand had the impression that they entered a house where the owners had just popped out for a few minutes. Each product group shown was allocated to a specific part of the house that represented its character. Each room had an atmosphere incorporating details such as furniture, art and everyday objects that communicated the different philosophies behind each of the collections. The visitors could find the products put away within each room, giving them the feeling that they were peeking into someone else's cupboards. Certain components of the stand at Interjeans were used afterwards for the Levi's stand at the London trade fair, 40 Degrees.

68
grand stand

PROJECT:
XX BY MEXX
CPD FAIR
DÜSSELDORF, GERMANY

THEME: MIX AND MATCH
The concept of this stand was based on Creneau's philosophy of 'mix and match'. Creneau first took this basic theme as inspiration for a communication tool that they developed for XX by Mexx: a book where 50 girls from different European countries were photographed in their favourite environment, showing their own clothes mixed (and matched) with the XX by Mexx-collection. This marvelous book became a trend book which gave an accurate picture of the XX target group. The girls' environments were 'copied' within the stand to create the feeling of breathing and living the atmosphere in the book: a typical girls' bedroom, the bathroom, a student's kitchen. The XX by Mexx-collection was integrated into the different environments.
In front of the stand 50 little white tables brought the images of the book alive: XX's made with strawberries, spaghetti, candies, paint tubes, just like the book. The front was a mix and match of different materials attracting the visitors with its multi-coloured patchwork.

69

CRENEAU INTERNATIONAL grand stand

PROJECT:
WRANGLER
INTERJEANS TRADE FAIR
COLOGNE, GERMANY

THEME: WHATEVER YOU RIDE
The concept of the stand was based on the new Wrangler image 'whatever you ride', from which Creneau took the most powerful images and the expression of the feelings of movement, including train-box carriages and herds of running buffalo.

Creneau created an authentic space with key features and large graphics using tri-vision panels. These key features included buffalo swings, a humorous take on the image of the running herds. One room had a retro American bar for socialising and also relaxation and featured a disco dance floor. In both areas, large projections conveyed the sense of travel and the theme of 'whatever you ride'. The two spaces (authentic and retro) were linked by a tunnel which was a metaphor for a journey.

The whole stand was constructed of double-layered wood with indirect lighting between the walls to create a warm and dynamic space. On the exterior, the boxes were surrounded by a printed layer of mosquito net, reflecting the use of the material for fly doors in most southern US homes. Televisions were displayed to show the launch of their advert for the new brand image.

The furniture consisted of classic wooden tables and stools, felt seating based on horse blankets and a cheap and cheerful dark wood veneer bar. Clothing was displayed on meat hooks hanging from simple metal bars and the stock was displayed in hanging canvas containers.

CRENEAU INTERNATIONAL grand stand

COMPANY NAME:
CRENEAU
INTERNATIONAL

HEAD OFFICE:
I.Z. De Roode Berg
Hellebeemden 13
3500 Hasselt
Belgium

PHONE:
+32 (0)11 24 79 20

FAX:
+32 (0)11 24 79 59

E-MAIL:
info@creneau.com

WEBSITE:
www.creneau.com

OTHER LOCATIONS:
Brussels, Belgium

MANAGEMENT:
Werner Vanherle, General Manager

CONTACTS:
An Moors (an.moors@creneau.com)

STAFF:
Belgium: 30

KEY DESIGNERS:
Davy Grosemans
Pablo Hannon

FOUNDED:
1989

COMPANY PROFILE:
Creneau was conceived in Belgium in 1989. Creneau has grown to an international design consultancy. Creneau specializes in building *brand personality* through the use of creative ideas and solutions for commercial environments. Creneau aims to be the most forward-thinking, European young design agency.

CLIENTS:
- EDC by Esprit
- Pepe Jeans London
- Lee Jeans
- Interbrew
- L'Oréal
- Garnier
- Watches of Switzerland
- Dr. Martens
- Miss Selfridge
- Converse
- Coca-Cola
- Tommy Hilfiger

SERVICES:
- Atmosphere architecture: including commercial interiors such as shops, shop-in-shops, bars, restaurants, hotels, nightclubs, showrooms, offices, exhibitions, point-of-sale & display design, 3D corporate branding and visual styling.
- Graphics, brand development and hyper-graphics
- PR & events
- Mutationspotting

AWARDS:
- 1998: British Midland UK Export Award
- 2000: Cultural Prize Province Limburg
- 2001: Nomination Design Week Awards
- 2001: The Times Awards
- 2002: IFM Awards
- 2002: Best Global Self Promotional Agency festive mailings
- 2002: Best Bar & Presentation Award

OPERATES:
Worldwide

STRATEGIC PARTNERSHIPS:
Interbrew

D'ART DESIGN GRUPPE

NEUSS, GERMANY

d'art design gruppe

ABOUT

d'art design gruppe

Internal and external communication plays an important part in the success of a company at a trade fair, according to D'art Design Gruppe. But to be successful the message must be clear and the employees should be trained to communicate that message well. After all, the stand is an extension of the company and not a separate entity.

THE GERMAN DESIGN FIRM D'ART DESIGN GRUPPE develops and executes solutions for communicative presentations; its focus is on trade shows, exhibitions, showrooms, stores and fashion shows. The company started in 1990 and is based in a charming former train station in Neuss. The team currently consists of 25 employees, including product designers, interior designers, communication designers, art directors and project managers. The firm works for international clients such as Sony, Samsonite, Adidas, Gabor and Audi. Although the firm does not have a particular design style, there is a certain distinctive manner of working. Stands need to be clear and legible; the story should be clear at a single glance. Since a trade show typically suffers from imagery overkill, this is where the client should try to distinguish themselves. The trick is to compress the complexity of the corporate identity. Visitors only take two seconds to decide! By reducing the formal language and filtering the information to its essential components, the message comes across stronger and more clearly and is remembered longer. Communication is the most important starting point, while the design itself is the instrument to reach a solution.

REGRETTABLY, CLIENTS DO NOT ALWAYS SEE THE CHALLENGE and the opportunities that a trade show can offer. Companies get the opportunity to communicate directly with their business contacts only once or twice a year. No advertisement, brochure or website can compete with that. The stand is an extension of the company and not a separate entity. Moreover, for the corporate image it is important to develop continuity at trade shows. Especially now that the economy is failing, clients should present themselves continually, or they will lose the attention of their contacts. Doing a small stand every year is better than a big one every other year!

IN CONTRAST TO TWO-DIMENSIONAL MEDIA, AN EXHIBIT CAN STIMULATE the senses in every way: through optical tools, sound, touch, taste and smell. A good illustration of this is the firm's own presentation at on the EuroShop 2002. The design is an example of how to achieve optimal communication with minimal architecture – 'design without design' (page 78/79). The concept extended further than the stand itself, because before, during and after the trade show a stimulating publicity campaign was organised around a metaphorical character.

PROJECTS:
D'ART DESIGN GRUPPE

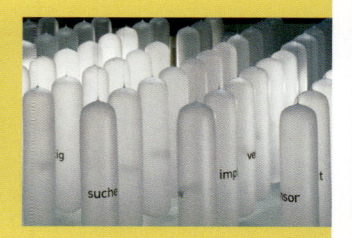

PROJECT PAGE 76:
SAMSONITE
TENDENCE, FRANKFURT, GERMANY

PROJECT PAGE 78:
D'ART DESIGN GRUPPE
EUROSHOP, DÜSSELDORF, GERMANY

grand stand D'ART DESIGN GRUPPE

BY APPROACHING THINGS FROM A DIFFERENT PERSPECTIVE it is possible to reach a specific audience in a better and more focused way. For D'art Design Gruppe the challenge lies in convincing the client of this. It is an interactive process, in which the client gets to discover his own core values. Many clients hide behind a mask or reflect on themselves through the competition. Their corporate identity is often unclear, and far too often their own image is blown out of proportion. Through a re-briefing the design firm redirects a number of essential questions back to the client, in the hope that they will develop an open attitude and begin to form a clear image of his own identity.

NOWADAYS THE DIFFERENCE BETWEEN PRODUCTS has very nearly disappeared, and to reach the right target group, different perspectives are necessary. An established shoe company such as Gabor can no longer present itself at trade shows as only about selling shoes. The company needs to win the sympathy of its audience by engaging with societal issues, such as in this case a goodwill shoe-shine project for UNICEF.

WRAPPING UP A PROJECT DURING AND AFTER THE TRADE SHOW is as important to D'art Design Gruppe as the conceptual and design stages. Through exhibit care – a sort of customer support that is fundamentally different from a full-service practice – employees are prepared and trained in handling visitors because that is often missing.

IN REALITY, EMPLOYEES ARE FREQUENTLY UNPREPARED, or have just come out from behind their desks. Often they head to a trade show at a moment's notice, and it often takes place in an unfamiliar environment. To prevent their feeling unsettled, the firm advises the client to bring them to the trade show a day early. Thus they can already adjust to the surroundings and the stand. In a 'kick-off' meeting they are then given instructions on how the stand was conceived. Without this preparation, the first results will not come in until the third day, which is naturally too late for a four-day trade show.

OFTEN D'ART DESIGN GRUPPE ALSO REMAINS PRESENT FOR THE FIRST DAY after the transferral to support the employees and to determine on the spot the succes of the concept. This is important for the debriefing, in which the lessons learned are studied together with the client: what can be done better, what does not work, etc. The client is typically focused on the number of new contacts the trade show has resulted in. But that can only be determined at a much later stage, because new relations do not present themselves within three days after the end of a trade show!

COMPANY STATEMENT D'ART DESIGN GRUPPE
"HANDLE WITH CARE!"

PROJECT PAGE 80:
PHILIPS AEG LICHT
EUROSHOP, DÜSSELDORF,
GERMANY

PROJECT PAGE 82:
VDP
INTERPACK, DÜSSELDORF,
GERMANY

PROJECT PAGE 84:
MONO
TENDENCE, FRANKFURT,
GERMANY

PROJECT PAGE 86:
ZANDERS
DRUPA, DÜSSELDORF, GERMANY

76
grand stand **D'ART DESIGN GRUPPE**

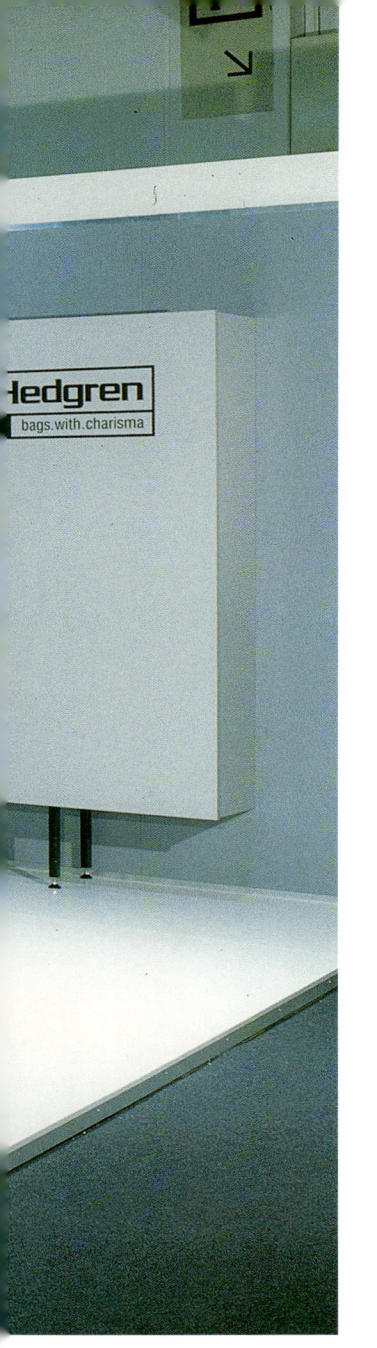

PROJECT:
SAMSONITE
TENDENCE, FRANKFURT,
GERMANY

WHERE:
Tendence, Frankfurt, Germany
WHEN:
2002
CLIENT:
Samsonite
MARKET SECTOR:
luggage
DESIGNER OF STAND:
Dominik Hof
DESIGN TEAM:
Jochen Höffler, Klaus Müller
GENERAL CONSTRUCTOR:
ACES Realisation, Neuss
AREA:
35 m²
PROJECT DURATION:
30 August - 3 September 2002

With its appearance at the 2002 Tendence trade fair, Samsonite demonstrated that it occupies a leading position in the fields of design and lifestyle. In both fields, it devotes a great amount of attention to effective product presentations and the aspect of communication. Correspondingly, in its installation, Samsonite's product range is grouped around a long counter decorated in silver and wenge. The counter contrasts beautifully with the blue-grey wall and high-gloss white floor of the open installation. Many of the bags presented on the 5 x 7 metres corner stand come from the Samsonite by Starck collection. Backpacks, accessories and briefcases are displayed in front of brightly coloured cut-outs in yellow, green and orange in front of the narrow rear wall. This in turn serves as a backdrop for the elegant, straight-lined anthracite bags in the foreground. The colour accent gives the installation a cheerful ambience and doubles as an effective eye-catcher. The larger objects, for example trolleys or travel bags, are exhibited on angular 'presenters' on the side facing the passage area. The long wall surface is dominated by a silver-coloured structure used to present the Hedgren Series, which appears suspended before the wall. These sport bags are exhibited to good effect in a rectangular cut-out with rounded corners.

D'ART DESIGN GRUPPE grand stand

PROJECT:
D'ART DESIGN GRUPPE
EUROSHOP, DÜSSELDORF,
GERMANY

WHERE:
EuroShop, Düsseldorf, Germany
WHEN:
2002
CLIENT:
D'art Design Gruppe
MARKET SECTOR:
(interior) design
DESIGNER OF STAND:
Jochen Höffler, Guido Mamczur
DESIGN TEAM:
Dominik Hof, Karin Blanke, Silke Eimanns, Jonas Reinsch, Conny Cavlek
GENERAL CONSTRUCTOR:
ACES Realisation, Neuss
PROJECT DURATION:
23 - 27 February 2002

For their self-presentation at 2002 EuroShop, D'art Design Gruppe opted for a direct approach in place of a retrospective of projects already realised. In a space measuring 200 m², they used hollow volumes and surfaces to create interaction.
154 different words on 154 balloons suspended from the ceiling produced a half-transparent volume made up of suggestions – suggestions without a coherent message. This challenged visitors to make their own associations. The balloons' freedom of motion, volume and position in space led to associations with landscaping (a park, a garden, a clearing), and they activated slowly changing soundscapes with the sounds of crickets, seagulls, etc. In this imaginary world of balloons there was yet more to discover: the same situation could be further explored virtually with the help of playstations and joysticks.
A table-like object which provided information about the designers and their projects was located between the hollow structures. The installation caused every visitor who entered it automatically to become involved with its underlying communication principle.

grand stand **D'ART DESIGN GRUPPE**

79
D'ART DESIGN GRUPPE grand stand

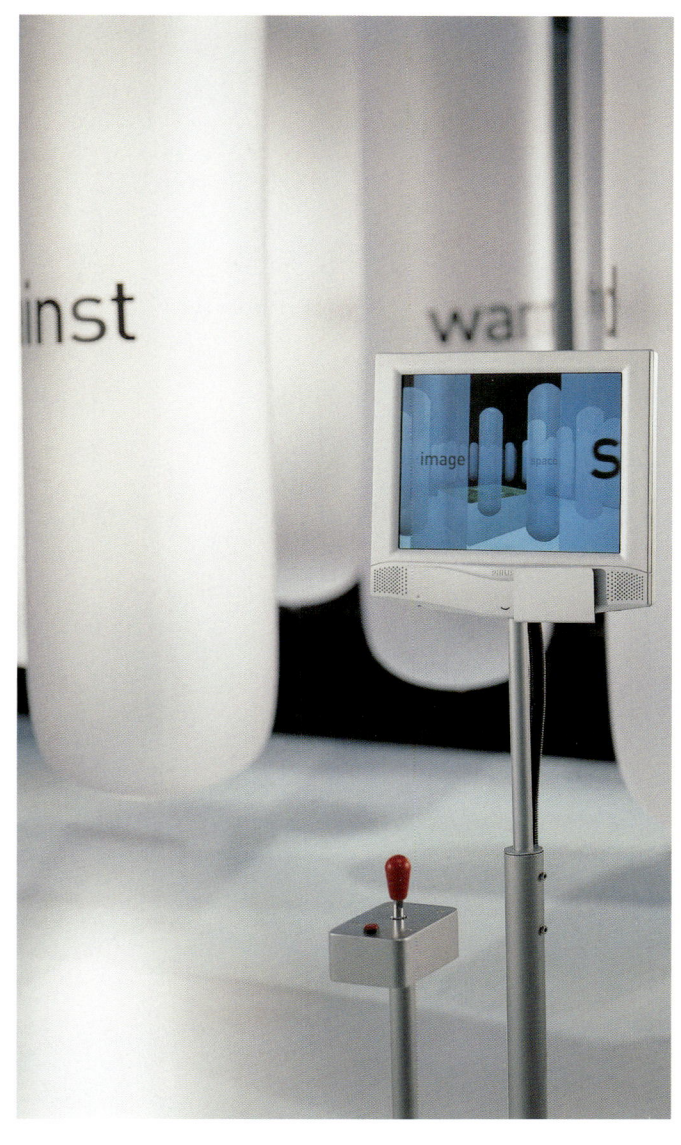

80

grand stand **D'ART DESIGN GRUPPE**

PROJECT:
PHILIPS AEG LICHT
EUROSHOP, DÜSSELDORF, GERMANY

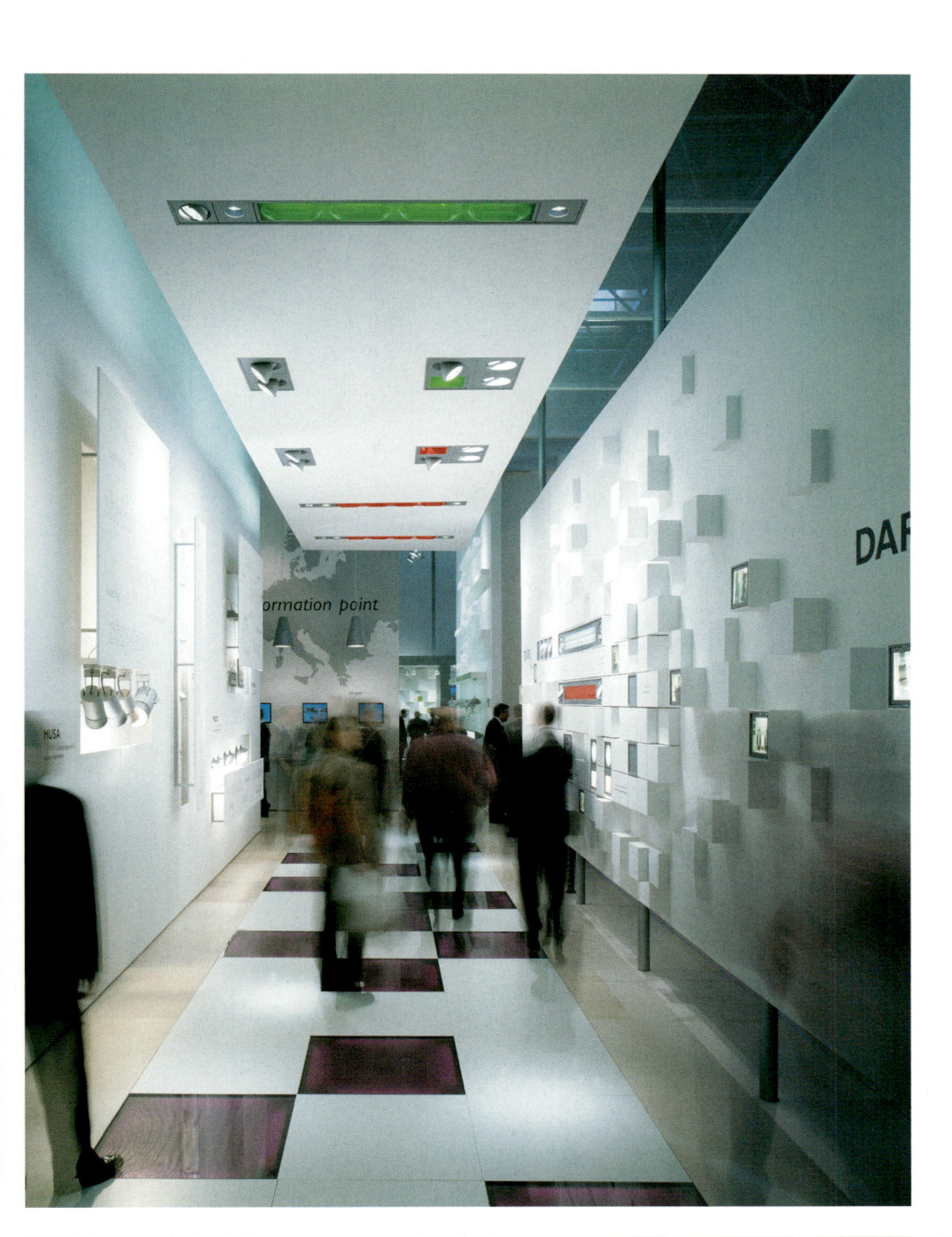

WHERE:
EuroShop, Düsseldorf, Germany
WHEN:
2002
CLIENT:
Philips AEG Licht
MARKET SECTOR:
lighting engineering
DESIGNER OF STAND:
Jochen Höffler
DESIGN TEAM:
Guido Mamczur, Klaus Müller
GENERAL CONSTRUCTOR:
Holz und Technic, Springe
AREA:
304 m²
PROJECT DURATION:
23 - 27 February 2002

With Goethe's last words 'more light', Philips AEG Licht sums up its presentation at the 2002 EuroShop, where products are displayed while integrated in natural lighting contexts. Visitors are treated to a sensual supermarket scenario, in which the apple is connoted as an instrument of desire.

The presentation concept focuses on three different lighting segments. In order to convert these into visual form, three different associative 'shopping worlds' were created. Together, they represent user-oriented purchase worlds, which, alternated with a range of function zones and information categories, create a spatial structure without demarcations. For the area 'Ambiance Lighting', the new product family DARUMA was introduced alongside a range of add-on and built-in systems. Their distinguishing feature – individual segmentable frames on a square-shaped floor plan – serves as the keynote for this sculpture-like presentation.

A bar overflowing with apples forms the centrepiece of the 'Lighting Solutions' area. Here, power spotlights are presented: these employ a range of light temperatures which make it possible to influence the effect of product colour intensity. Analogous to typical product images in self-service markets, strip-lighting systems illuminate giant jam jars.

A modular strip-lighting ceiling system is the highlight of the 'Lighting Experience' area. The individual modules can be controlled by means of a light manager, with which colour and intensity can be varied to obtain a range of atmospheric effects.

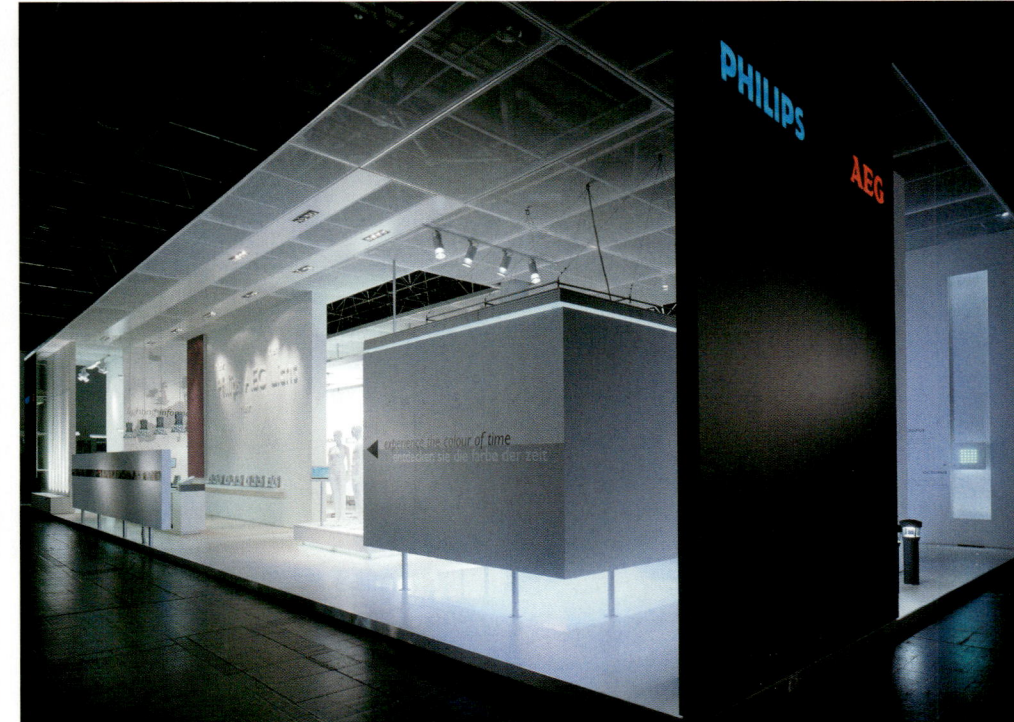

papier, karton, pappe –

PROJECT:
VDP
INTERPACK, DÜSSELDORF,
GERMANY

WHERE:
Interpack, Düsseldorf, Germany
WHEN:
2002
CLIENT:
Verband Deutscher Papierfabriken
MARKET SECTOR:
paper
DESIGNER OF STAND:
Jochen Höffler
DESIGN TEAM:
Karin Blanke, Dominik Hof
GENERAL CONSTRUCTOR:
ACES Realisation
AREA:
100 m²
PROJECT DURATION:
24 - 30 April 2002

The Verband Deutscher Papierfabriken (VDP) represents the German paper industry. Typically, its role is to make the industries further down the production chain aware of the product advantages of paper, cardboard and pasteboard as packaging materials. However, at the Interpack trade fair, its aim was to underscore its role in the service-provision area. Consequently, the primary function of its installation was communication with the visitor. Its task was to stimulate interest and curiosity about the many uses of paper.
An unusual approach to the material, and the reduction of the communication task down to its essential functions were the starting points for the design concept. A large sculpture composed of pasteboard boxes gave the installation its keynote whilst also serving as an excellent eye-catcher. All structural components were white, making it possible to achieve interesting silhouette effects, these being projected on the rear wall by the sculpture. Visitors in the discussion area typically had the impression that they were sitting under a treetop blowing in the wind.

D'ART DESIGN GRUPPE grand stand

PROJECT:
MONO
TENDENCE, FRANKFURT, GERMANY

WHERE:
Tendence, Frankfurt, Germany
WHEN:
2001
CLIENT:
Mono Seibel GmbH
MARKET SECTOR:
home furnishings
DESIGNER OF STAND:
Jochen Höffler, Klaus Müller
GENERAL CONSTRUCTOR:
ACES Realisation, Neuss
CONSULTANTS:
Buttgereit und Heidenreich
AREA:
90 m²
PROJECT DURATION:
24 - 28 August 2001

The family business Mono is known for its sense of lifestyle and special approach to design. The concept for their presentation at the Tendence trade fair is based on a triangular floor plan. A central structure housing a small office and a portion of the product presentation area divides the exhibition area into three zones, each with a different function. Free-standing black wall panels, which separate the central space from the passage areas, present a range of product groups. Cutlery designs, such as the classic monoa, are integrated in graphically stylised table arrangements. Tea and coffee pots and porcelain series are displayed in back-lit wall niches. Separate presentations for accessories, bowls and glass objects are arranged on free-standing elements in the central space, complementing the presentations in the passage areas. strong contrast is created between large, brightly coloured graphics and black wall panels, and between untreated fibre cement boards on the floor and matted glass. The installation concept communicates high quality, elegance and timelessness, mirroring in an effective manner the company's culture and products.

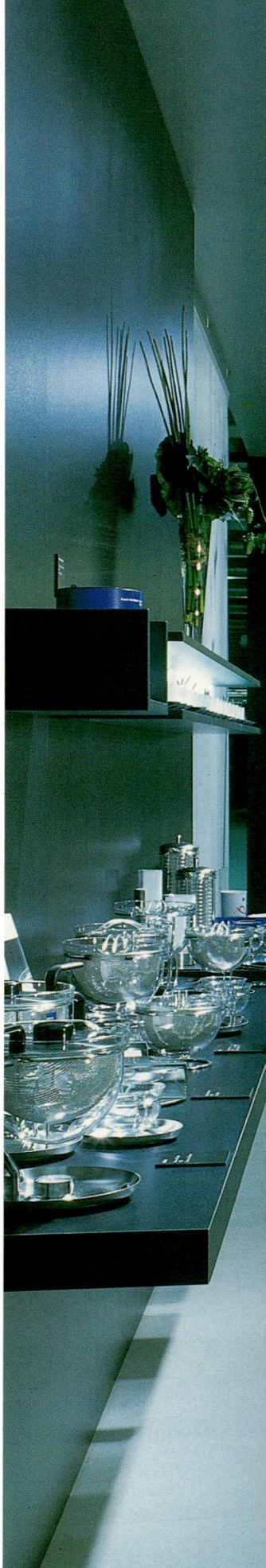

D'ART DESIGN GRUPPE grand stand

COMPANY NAME:
D'ART DESIGN GRUPPE

HEAD OFFICE:
Kulturbahnhof Norf
Bahnstrasse 33
41469 Neuss
Germany

PHONE:
+49 (0)2137 910730

FAX:
+49 (0)2137 910744

E-MAIL:
info@d-art-design.de

WEBSITE:
www.d-art-design.de

MANAGEMENT:
Dieter Wolff
Jochen Höffler
Freddy Justen

CONTACTS:
Gülcin Durmus

STAFF:
25

KEY DESIGNERS:
Dieter Wolff
Jochen Höffler
Freddy Justen
Guido Mamczur

FOUNDED:
1990

COMPANY PROFILE:
Intelligent design and optimal project realisation are the D'art Design Gruppe's objectives. Our work is characterised by the interaction of surface and content. We devise and realise communication. We see ourselves first as suppliers of ideas and impulses, and only secondarily as interior architects, graphic designers and product designers. We regard the classical modes of realisation, such as architecture or graphic design, only as instruments to be used for the realisation of fantasies.

CLIENTS:
- Adidas-Salomon AG
- Allianz
- ASYS
- Audi AG
- Curiavant
- EDG
- Fresenius
- Gabor Shoes AG
- Karstadt AG
- LLOYD Shoes GmbH
- Mercedes-Benz
- MFI
- Mitsui
- Mono
- Philips AEG Lichttechnik GmbH
- Richter Junge Schuhe
- Rimage
- RWE AG
- Samsonite GmbH
- SONY
- Verband Deutscher Papierfabriken
- Zanders

SERVICES:
- Communication design
- Exhibition/stand design
- Shop/retail design
- Product design
- Graphic design

AWARDS:
- IF Product Design Award 1997: Graphic-Holder
- IF Product Design Award 2000: Graphic-Wall
- ADAM Award 2002: Trade Fair Design
- IF Communication Award 2003: Trade Fair Design

OPERATES:
Worldwide

EXHIBITS INTERNATIONAL
AMSTERDAM, THE NETHERLANDS

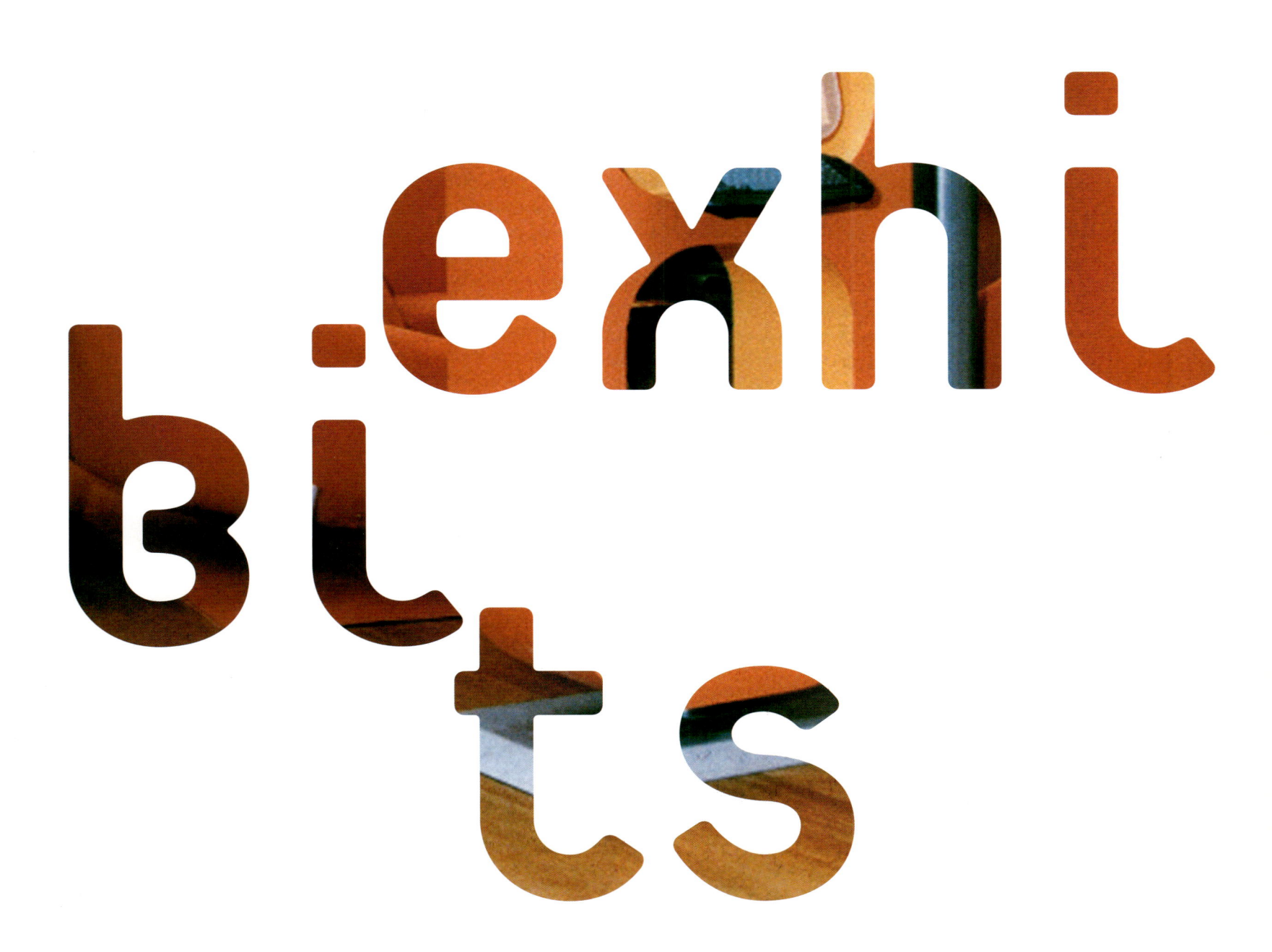

PROJECT:
'JA, IK WIL'/'YES, I DO'
DE NIEUWE KERK, AMSTERDAM,
THE NETHERLANDS

This exhibition was to commemorate the marriage of the Dutch crown prince Willem Alexander to Máxima Zorreguieta in the New Church in Amsterdam.
Royal weddings are a celebration for the public too, often attracting worldwide attention. The 'Ja, ik wil' exhibit attracted 125,000 visitors in the first two months of opening alone. In order to further involve the people, both young and old, it was considered appropriate to share in the excitement and history of royal weddings since 1791, all leading to this event. Whilst revelling in history, all graphics and 3D elements created had a fresh, modern feel and tone of voice to engage the younger audiences. >>

ja
ik wil
yes, I do

PROJECT
'JA, IK WIL'/'YES, I DO'
DE NIEUWE KERK, AMSTERDAM,
THE NETHERLANDS

The design concept was applied to all elements of the exhibition, from catalogues, flyers, invitations, billboards, and souvenirs, to a window in the Bijenkorf department store and even a miniature version of the Church in Madurodam amusement park! The entire project concept to execution was all managed by Exhibits International.

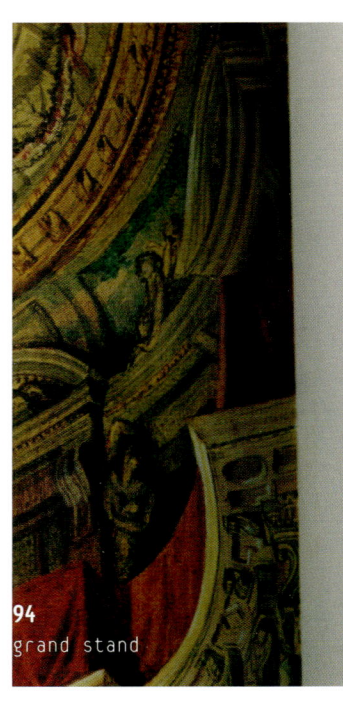

DE HUWELIJKEN VAN
KONING WILLEM III (1817-1890)
1839 & 1879

Sophia Frederika Mathilda, prinses van Wurtemberg (1818-1877)
Toen de koning van Wurtemberg in de zomer van 1837 met zijn beide huwbare dochters Marie en Sophie Nederland aandeed, vatte erfprins Willem, de latere koning Willem III, serieuze gevoelens voor Sophie op. Zelf vond ze de prinsen 'grote sterke jongens zonder goede manieren en matig onderlegd'. Sophie was de dochter van koning Willem I van Wurtemberg en Catharina Paulowna, grootvorstin van Rusland, een zuster van erfprins Willems moeder, Anna Paulowna. Deze verzette zich heftig tegen

EXHIBITS INTERNATIONAL grand stand

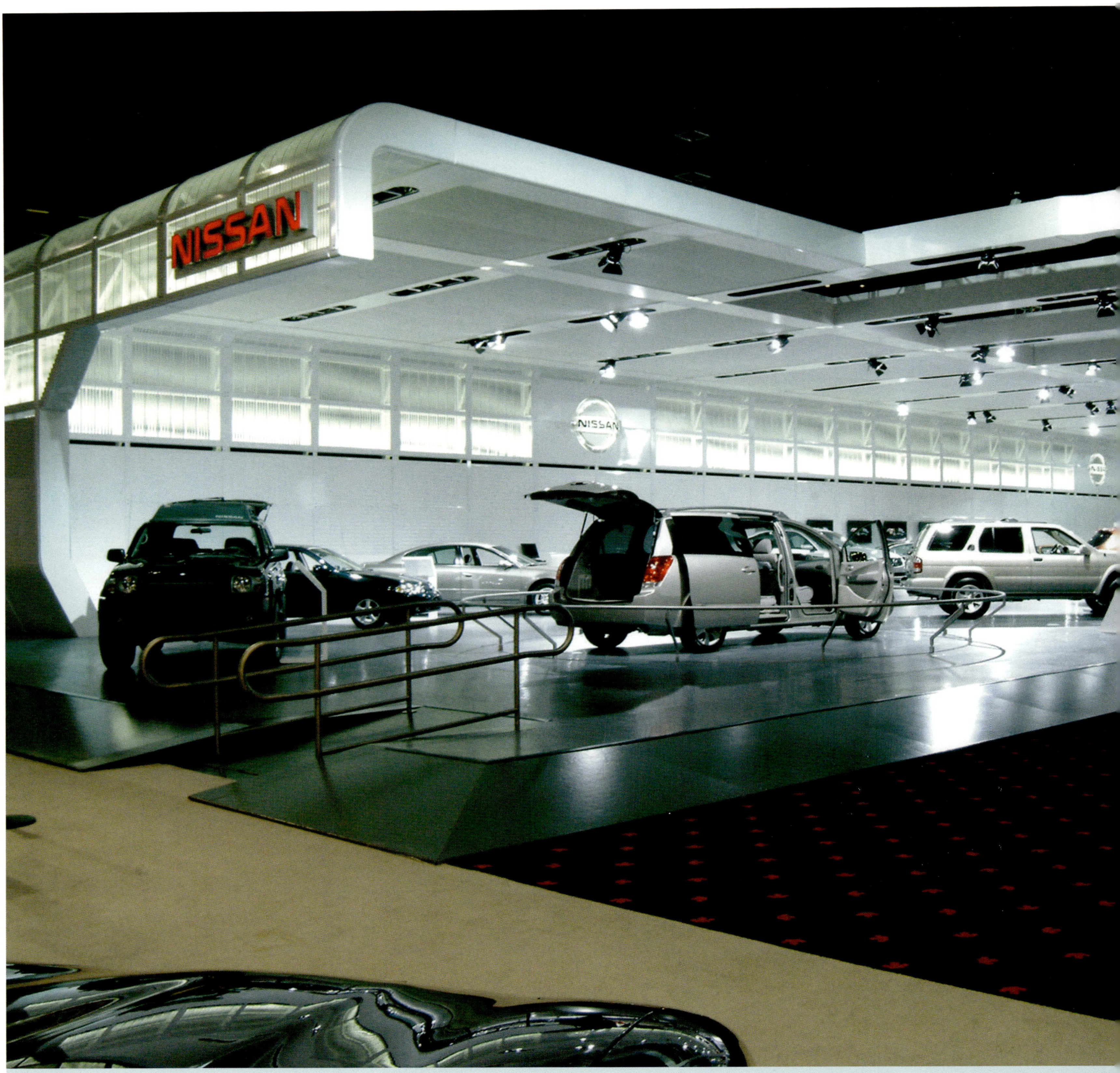
NISSAN
NISSAN

PROJECT:
NISSAN
GLOBAL EXHIBITION PACKAGE,
NORTH AMERICA

This project was designed for Nissan to reflect the dealer program developed for Tokyo. The essence was to provide a clean and simply-defined space where the cars would be the heroes. The entire exhibit was white with materials, finishes and lighting providing added definition and variation.

Lifestyle aspirations are key in selling cars and the exhibit design needed to exceed these aspirations. The individual personalities of Nissan vehicles came to life here so it was imperative to set the scene with an impressive visual statement that can drive Nissan into the future.

PROJECT:
UNILEVER
AMSTERDAM, THE NETHERLANDS

Exhibits International faced the challenge of defining the Unilever Internet marketing strategy in a visitor centre. The goal of this visitor centre was to train product managers and marketing managers in using new media in the marketing mix.
The modern, crisp interior was designed to create greater awareness and definition of Unilever's brands by incorporating all elements of the individual brands right into the wall graphics and furniture programs.

EXHIBITS INTERNATIONAL grand stand

PROJECT:
MICROSOFT: WAAR IS HANS?
AMSTERDAM

Partnering with Microsoft's advertising agency, Blueberry Frog, Exhibits International created a guerilla marketing campaign based on a treasure hunt concept to raise awareness of the MSN website in the Netherlands. Traditional and new media ideas were integrated to direct people to the website for clues to find the missing 'Hans'. Blueberry Frog chose Exhibits International to help in this challenge based on its intimate experience and knowledge of the integrated use of media and the youth consumer market through its work with major sportswear manufacturers and retailers.

PROJECT:
TOYS R US
TIMES SQUARE,
NEW YORK CITY, USA

Competing with a ferris wheel and a life-sized Barbie house for attention meant that Exhibits International's designs for the 'World's Fair' area in the Toys R Us flagship store not only had to differentiate but blend into the fantasy world created here. New products and media launches were to take place in this area so the firm wanted to add to this excitement without stealing the thunder.

The circus big top was the inspiration for this backdrop, employing light and audio visual aids to create the necessary 'big bang' required in product launches in 'the world's largest toy store'. This unique location on Times Square remains a launching pad for many of the leading toys going to the market.

PROJECT:
NASDAQ MARKETSITE
TIMES SQUARE,
NEW YORK CITY, USA

What is NASDAQ? It is the first electronic stock market for global financial transactions and worldwide investments, or the power and intensity created when global leading companies come head to head with bullish, savvy investors. NASDAQ embodies all this excitement and more. Exhibits International was asked to capture these qualities in a visitor presentation centre. Highly engaging, fast-paced, hands-on and exciting were just a few of the requirements in explaining NASDAQ's technological advancements. A ringside view of the NASDAQ trading floor combined with interactive and hands-on displays bring NASDAQ to life and illustrate its position at the forefront of innovation.

Visitors are guaranteed to leave this impressive Time Square location in awe of the immense capabilities of NASDAQ, and with a first hand experience of living life in the fast, dynamic world of global trading.

PROJECT:
CHELLO
EUROPEAN EXHIBITION PACKAGE

Chello is Europe's leading broadband cable Internet provider, with an extensive marketing communication program in which product presentations and events are key. Exhibits International designs, produces and manages the event program, including this travelling modular exhibit and a variety of 'surf stations' used to present the product.

EXHIBITS INTERNATIONAL grand stand

COMPANY NAME:
EXHIBITS INTERNATIONAL

HEAD OFFICE:
431 Horner Avenue
Toronto, Ontario
Canada, M8W 4W3

Plotterstraat 1
1033 RX Amsterdam
The Netherlands

PHONE:
+(416) 252 2818 (Canada)
+31 (0)20 581 30 30 (NL)

FAX:
+(416) 252 3708 (Canada)
+31 (0)20 581 30 31 (NL)

E-MAIL:
info@exhibits-intl.com

WEBSITE:
www.exhibitsinternational.com

MANAGEMENT:
Louk de Sévaux, Managing Director (Europe)
Sam Kohn, President

CONTACTS:
info@exhibits-intl.com

STAFF:
125

KEY DESIGNERS:
Aram Leeuw
Volker Licht
Adriano Almeida
Walter Rhoddy

FOUNDED:
1983

MEMBER OF:
- Design Management Institute, Boston
- GVR
- BNO, Association of Dutch Designers

COMPANY PROFILE:
Exhibits International brings brands to life by adding a third dimension. With more than 125 skilled professionals in Canada and Europe, we work with many global companies to put the face and personality of their brands on the street.
Having begun 20 years ago designing and producing highly acclaimed exhibit stands, we have subsequently been called upon by our clients to create live events, theme parks, retail interiors and brand experiences of many kinds.

CLIENTS:
- Nike
- Levi Strauss Europe
- Lego
- Heineken
- Nissan
- Nasdaq
- Unilever
- Ahold
- Microsoft
- AOL Time Warner
- Camel
- Infinity
- Callaway
- Douwe Egberts
- Kia
- Chello
- Toys R Us

SERVICES:
Our business is divided primarily into four divisions: exhibitions and stands, retail, events and museum/visitor centres. We offer services from strategic brand concepting, graphic design, 3D design, production, implementation, transport and storage. We also have an online inventory management system.

AWARDS:
- Eddi awards - various
- Exhibitor Magazine - Edge award 2002

OPERATES:
Worldwide

THE GCGROUP
ZURICH, SWITZERLAND

grand stand

PROJECT:
ORANGE CUBE
ROADSHOW, VARIOUS LOCATIONS, SWITZERLAND

WHERE: roadshows, various locations, Switzerland
CLIENT: Orange Communications, Zurich
MARKET SECTOR: telecommunications
DESIGN/AGENCY: The GCGroup
MANUFACTURERS: The GCGroup
DIMENSIONS: 7 x 7 x 7 metres
AREA: 49 m²
WEIGHT: 30 metric tons
SET-UP TIME: 6 hours
TAKE-DOWN TIME: 4 hours

The Orange Cube is boxed and ready to go. Anywhere. Set up within just six hours, it's living proof that a portable sales area does not necessarily have to be a tent in order to offer complete mobility and flexibility. And yet no functional compromises have been made. Automatic glass sliding doors, air conditioning and heating are all built in, and the Cube contains the complete infrastructure for a fully optimised information and sales pavilion. From displays, plasma screens, product presentations and cash desks, to computers with network and internet access, discussion areas and sales terminals, everything is provided. The structure is built on two storeys, which are internally connected by a staircase placed in the middle of the lower element. It's so easy to set up that the Cube is a perfect illustration of 'Plug and Play', the global mantra of the information technology business. When it's all over, the installation crew just removes a few screws and stores each component in its place on a customised truck ready to drive to the next event location. The next crew then conjures a magical Orange presence out of thin air and connects the fully-equipped module to power lines for more plug and play, the easy Orange way.

orange™

Orange speaks Business

110
grand stand THE GCGROUP

PROJECT:
ORANGE DOME
ORBIT COMDEX, BASEL, SWITZERLAND

WHERE:
Orbit COMDEX, Basel, Switzerland
WHEN:
2002
CLIENT:
Orange Communications, Zurich with Nokia (Switzerland)
DESIGN/AGENCY:
The GCGroup
MANUFACTURERS:
The GCGroup
MATERIALS:
floor: hub flooring with white, high-gloss HPL panels, laid without gaps
internal walls: covered with 54 m² oak panels, natural stain
Dome: double membrane filled with 340 m³ air, 1,800 Chesterfield back-stitches
furniture: Supérieur, Zurich, Wassily, Marcel Breuer, Barcelona, Mies van der Rohe (on loan from Knoll International, Zurich)
AREA:
640 m²

Unique. Tempting. Impressive. With its mixture of together male and female, hard and soft, simple and complex; this clear statement by Orange cannot be confused with any other competitor. The brief was to convey consistency, quality and a continuation of the existing brand values, taking into account every product in the range. The brand and its people should be clearly visible in an ultra-modern setting that somehow guarantees competence and reliability. The realisation of this vision will remain shining in the minds of the many visitors. A soft and light-flooded dome is sharply contrasted against a clearly structured, two-storey, fully air-conditioned internal building. Feminine and masculine in equal measure, the hardness of the white flooring is juxtaposed with the internal infrastructure. The appearance doesn't suggest a stand. It has a simple but complex appearance that guarantees both recognition and the promise of order. The straightness of the internal elements combines with the soft and fanciful air-filled dome to give the impression of quietness. It's a world in which man is the focus of attention, but products and presentations are in perfect perspective. With no prior advertising, this Orange presence became a memorable event, a unique experience of something that no one could have imagined. The future is indeed bright. The future is Orange.

grand stand THE GCGROUP

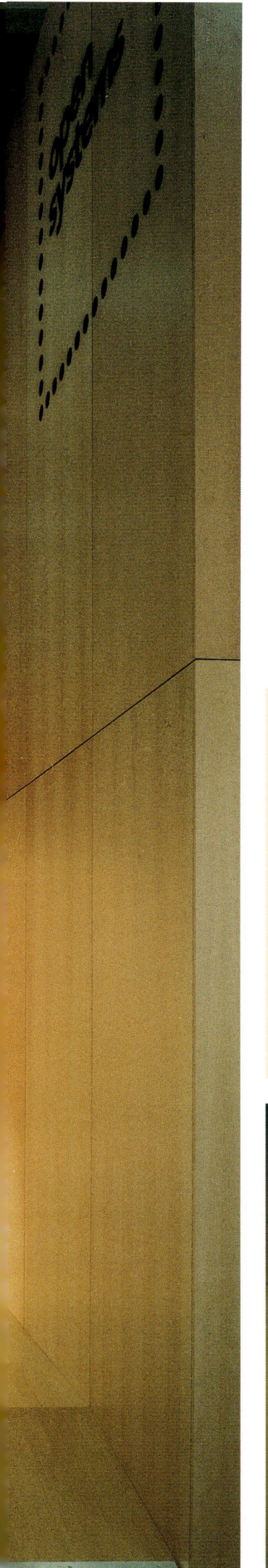

PROJECT:
OPEN SYSTEMS
I-EX 02, ZURICH, SWITZERLAND

WHERE:
I-EX, Zurich, Switzerland
WHEN:
2002
CLIENT:
Open Systems
DESIGN/AGENCY:
The GCGroup
MANUFACTURERS:
The GCGroup
KEY MATERIAL:
beech

This is an open-plan structure for Open Systems. Deceptively simple, it was designed to create an oasis of tranquility. The beautiful beech surfaces, on walls and floors, have a timeless quality which helps guests to relax and enjoy the experience. The structure is built on two levels, giving participants both openness and intimacy; two ways of being on the inside.

113
THE GCGROUP grand stand

114
grand stand **THE GCGROUP**

PROJECT:
ORANGE BOAT
EXPO 02, SWITZERLAND

WHERE:
Expo, various locations, Switzerland
WHEN:
2002
CLIENT:
Orange Communications, Zurich
DESIGN/AGENCY:
The GCGroup
MANUFACTURERS:
The GCGroup
PROJECT DURATION:
2002 - 2004
BOAT:
'Petersinsel'

Orange branding outside, Orange feeling inside: after a top-secret project, the Petersinsel was transformed in a specially built dock. Local craftsmen executed a total transformation inside and out, launching the boat in April 2002 to the surprise and concern of those competitors who had undertaken larger financial commitments as Expo sponsors. The result was an instant and remarkable Orange presence at all the various exhibition areas (Arteplages), and a long-lasting, unique experience for all visitors from youngsters to pensioners, whatever their gender, whatever their language. Habbo terminals, Internet stations and plasma screens guaranteed high-tech entertainment, while the Orange Sundeck, Orange Lounge and Orange Coffee provided the feel-good factor. All Orange customers had free access to the boat, with the Orange sign on their mobile phone display acting as the free ticket. Passengers were given full Expo information and updates, and VIP guests were invited by SMS to special events on the boat. Many will remember their participation in the Expo opening ceremony from one of the best vantage points on the waterfront, the warm summer nights on three different lakes, and the Orange rubber boats, innertubes, sun caps, air mattresses and many other giveaways. As well as achieving a complete Expo presence at a minimum cost, the experience can also be repeated. Orange became a sponsor of Bieler Schifffahrt-Gesellschaft and now has the opportunity to use the Petersinsel as an action boat for different communication markets and regional events.

THE GCGROUP grand stand

PROJECT:
ERICSSON
ORBIT COMDEX, BASEL,
SWITZERLAND

WHERE:
Orbit COMDEX, Basel, Switzerland
CLIENT:
Ericsson
DESIGN/AGENCY:
The GCGroup
MANUFACTURERS:
The GCGroup

Four product categories, one strong brand placing the heterogeneous within the homogeneous, this unique presentation of Ericsson products has all the self-confidence and competence that people expect from the brand. The appearance is right up-to-the-minute, a strong presence, and a practical presentation that was never meant to look like a 'stand'. The four different product categories, ranging from consumer to carrier solutions, are all clearly identified as one single, very modern brand. The low, complex appearance guarantees immediate recognition and reflects order, a calmness amidst the noise of the exhibition hall. And, yes, this platform is a solutions platform, the x-y-z of axis management, and the a-b-c of simply doing it right.

grand stand **THE GCGROUP**

THE GCGROUP grand stand

PROJECT:
ORANGE MODULARE
BUSINESS SHOWS, VARIOUS LOCATIONS, SWITZERLAND

WHERE:
various locations, Switzerland
CLIENT:
Orange Communications, Zurich
DESIGN/AGENCY:
The GCGroup
MANUFACTURERS:
The GCGroup

From human resources events to business meetings, from students to CEOs, from 5 m² to 150 m², the Orange Modulare system does business wherever it appears, whatever the event. A totally reliable tool for cost planning and control, it allows simple handling and a minimum set-up time, while presenting Orange as an innovative, honest and future-orientated company with the highest quality standards. The modular system lives and breathes transparency through transparent plastic furniture and open views. Barriers are torn down. Desks, displays and monitor walls allow a continuous change in perspective. The softly-lit, tissue-covered walls give warmth and welcome. It's not about products or services. It's all about people, good feeling and the positive memory of being wrapped in a unique atmosphere while sharing thoughts with an innovative partner or an honest employer.

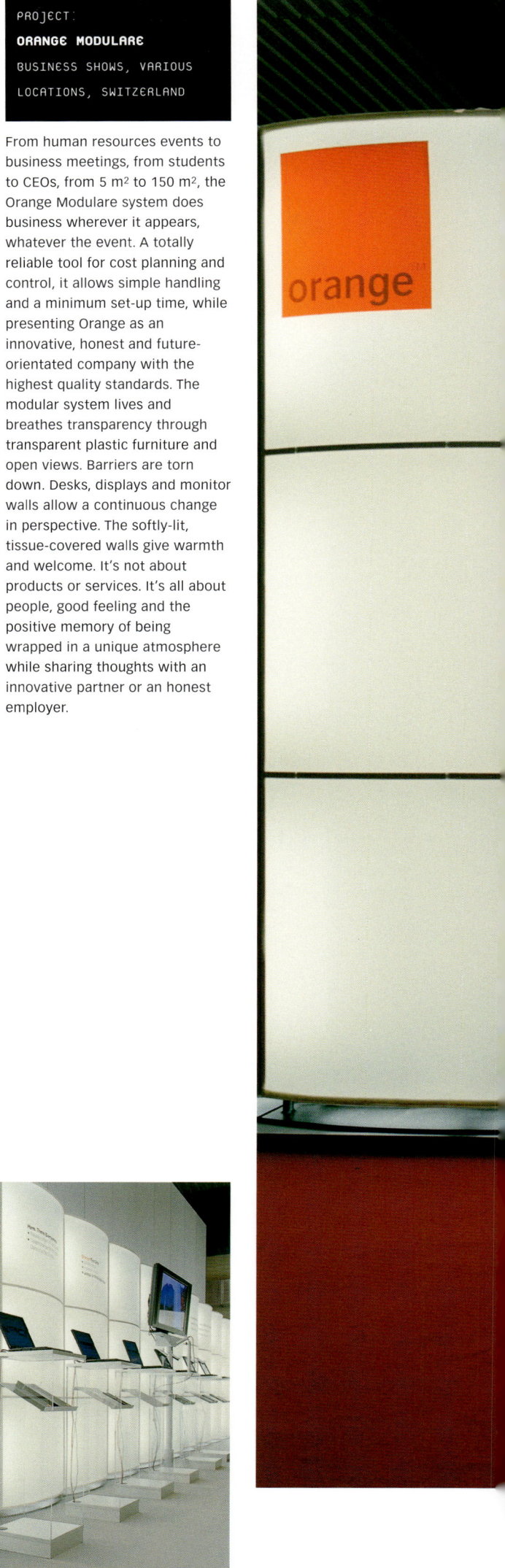

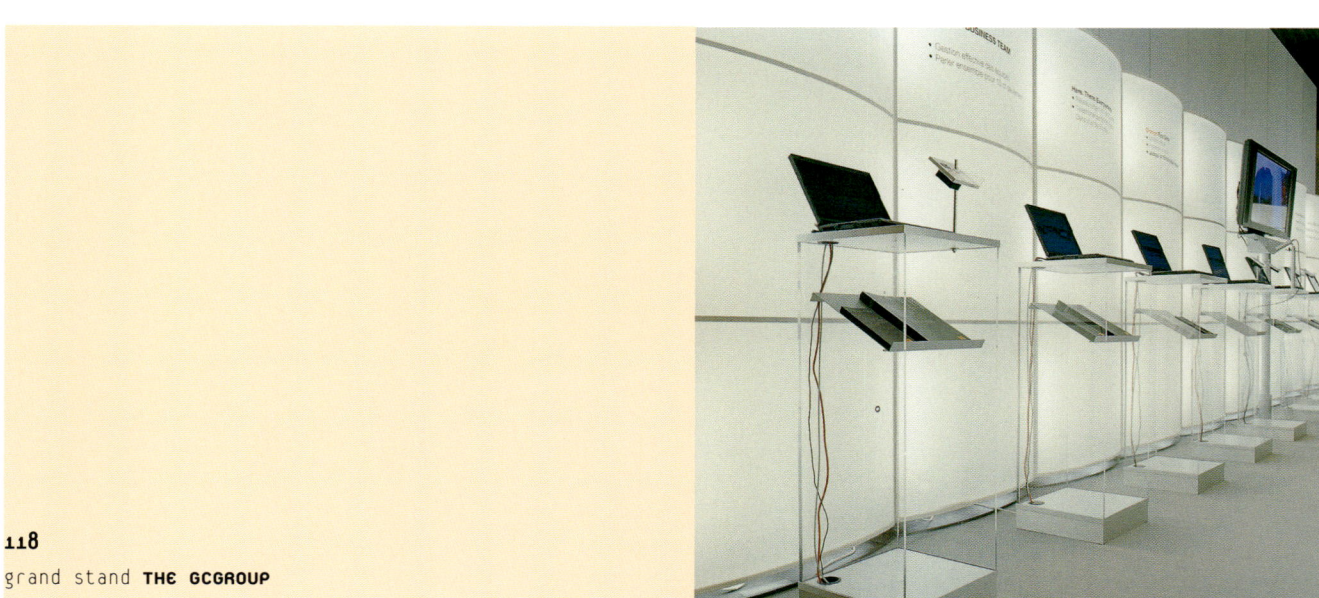

118
grand stand **THE GCGROUP**

THE GCGROUP grand stand

COMPANY NAME:
THE GCGROUP

HEAD OFFICE:
Weberstrasse 7
8004 Zurich
Switzerland

PHONE:
+41 43 322 13 13

FAX:
+41 43 322 13 14

E-MAIL:
info@gcgroup.ch

WEBSITE:
gcgroup.ch

MANAGEMENT:
Patrik Gubser

CONTACTS:
Patrik Gubser
Marianne Praxmarer
mp@gcgroup.ch

STAFF:
Design/Management 11
Production 137

FOUNDED:
1998

CLIENTS:
- Alcatel
- BEVAG Better Value
- Bluewin
- Cyberlink
- Dallia
- Deliciel
- Domotec
- Ericsson International
- GE Capital Bank
- Hostettler Autotechnik
- ID Interdiscount
- IP Mulitmedia
- Impact Music (Live at sunset)
- JHM Finanzmesse
- JVC / Spitzer Electronic
- Mitutoyo (Schweiz)
- OCÉ (Schweiz)
- Open Systems
- Orange Communications
- Procom Technology Switzerland
- Sager
- Steko
- Sunrise
- Swisscom
- WIFAG

SERVICES:
Retail design, trade fair architecture and installations. All the way from concepts and ideas to nuts and bolts.

AWARDS:
- Xaver Award, **silver 2002**
- Xaver Award, **silver 2002**
- Xaber Award, **bronze 2003**

OPERATES:
Switzerland and throughout the world

KVORNING DESIGN & COMMUNICATION

COPENHAGEN, DENMARK

ABOUT

kvorning

Kvorning Design & Communication is a Danish firm specialised and experienced in international stand and exhibition design. The company offers full-concept integrated solutions for a wide range of exhibition design areas varying from stands, projects to permanent exhibitions.

FULL-CONCEPT DESIGN IS A CORE ELEMENT in the creative work of Kvorning. An exhibition is a total experience where all elements from displays, furniture, graphic expression and signboards to corporate identity are used to create consistency and synergy in all the media and interfaces employed.

THE PERSONAL SIGNATURE PRESENT in many of Kvorning's exhibition works is the transformation of the exhibition area into conceptual scenery, where all perceived exhibition elements are present on the stage. Light is not only used as a functional device, but also serves as a delicate measure to provide a specific atmosphere or symbolic attachment to the context. For example, light animation and projections on the exhibition scene are often used as media for communicating statements.

PHYSICAL, CONSTRUCTED SOLUTIONS FOR OBJECT DISPLAY and division of space are not only created from the perspective of functionality and aesthetic. They also serve as additives to thrill and astonish the visitor. Kvorning's frequent use of sometimes very large but light construction elements for the purposes of display or the creation of atmosphere demonstrates a remarkable ability to create momentum behind the exhibition through its architecture. In this regard, many of Kvorning's works emphasise the idea of the exhibition as an extended space for experience. The use of non-traditional materials and media and a consistent focus on detail are other significant trademarks of Kvorning's works.

IN A BROADER CONTEXT, THE EXHIBITION WORKS of Kvorning reflect the democratic Scandinavian design tradition. Simplicity is not only valued on its own, as a signifier of style and glamour, but is also brought into use as a device to make things easy to handle and understand. Flexibility is a crucial part of usability and accessibility. For example, the design of flexible exhibition display systems such as Kvorning's 'BUG' system can be seen as a response to the need for travelling exhibition systems that are adaptable to different local conditions. Another striking aspect of Kvorning's work is the ability to create architecture that fits with its physical environment without loosing its individual identity.

PROJECTS:
**KVORNING
DESIGN & COMMUNICATION**

PROJECT PAGE 124:
THE DANISH WAVE
AUSTRALIA, BRAZIL, CHINA AND JAPAN

PROJECT PAGE 126:
INTERNATIONAL ARCHITECTURE BIENNALE THE DANISH PAVILION, VENICE, ITALY

PROJECT PAGE 128:
MINIMAL CONSTRUCTIONS
COPENHAGEN, DENMARK
CHINA

APART FROM THEIR INVOLVEMENT IN EXHIBITION DESIGN, Kvorning Design & Communication offers consulting services in visual design and identity programmes for private and public organisations, consultancy in print media marketing and public relations, product design, web design, architecture and interior design.

THE COMPANY HAS PLANNED AND IMPLEMENTED PROJECTS in more than 30 countries, including Denmark, Sweden, Norway, Finland, Iceland, the United Kingdom, Germany, Belgium, France, Switzerland, Italy, Spain, Poland, Ukraine, Hungary, Brazil, Estonia, Latvia, Lithuania, Romania, Slovakia, Russia, USA, China, Japan, South Korea and Australia.

COMPANY STATEMENT KVORNING DESIGN & COMMUNICATION

"NO PROJECT TOO BIG, NO DESIGN TOO COMPLEX, NO LOCATION TOO FAR FLUNG"

PROJECT PAGE 130:
IN PLACE OF DOMINIQUE PERRAULT COPENHAGEN, HELSINKI AND TALLINN

PROJECT PAGE 132:
MIDEM MUSIC FESTIVAL CANNES, FRANCE

PROJECT PAGE 134:
LIGHTWEIGHT SYSTEMS WORLDWIDE

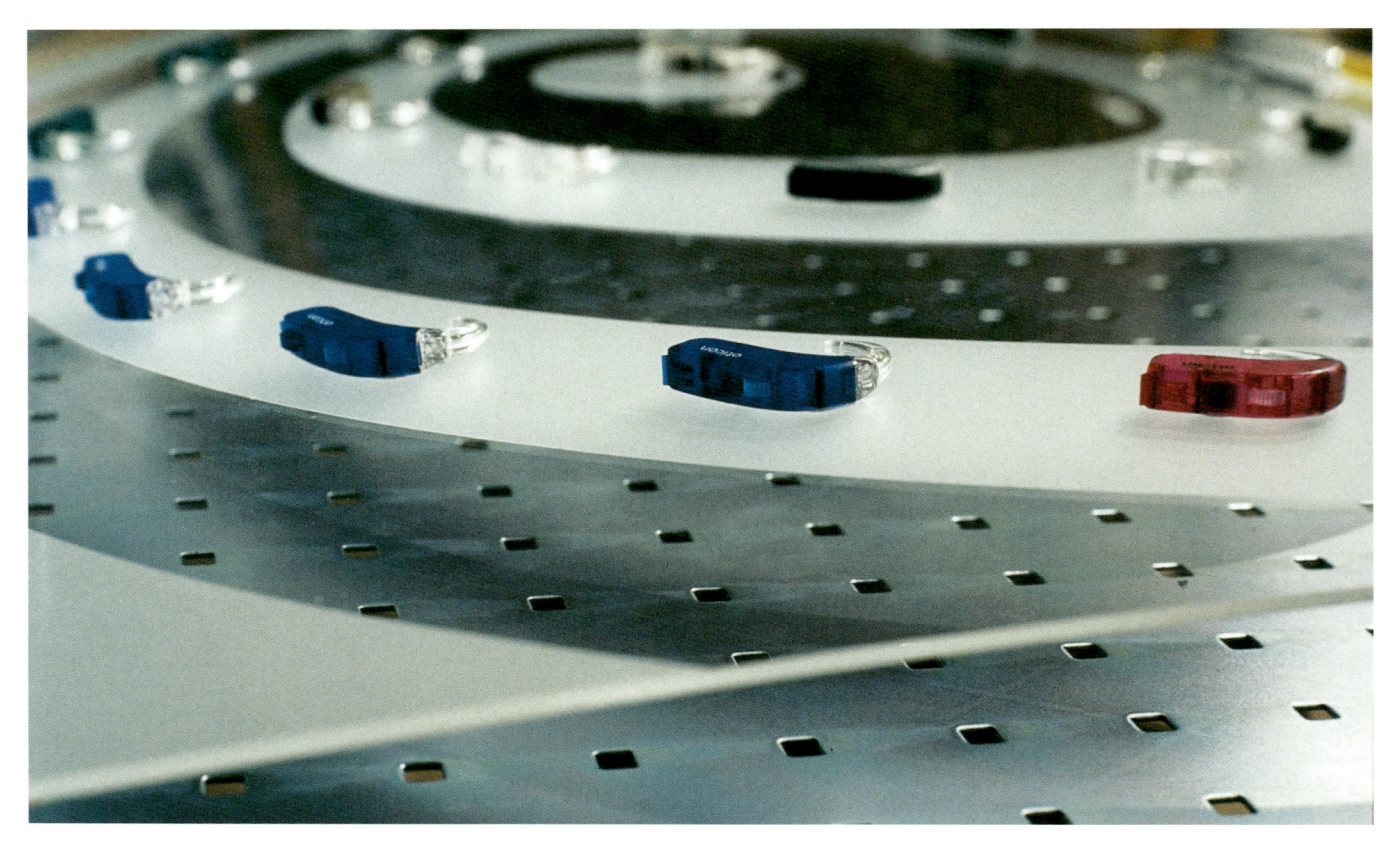

124
grand stand **KVORNING DESIGN & COMMUNICATION**

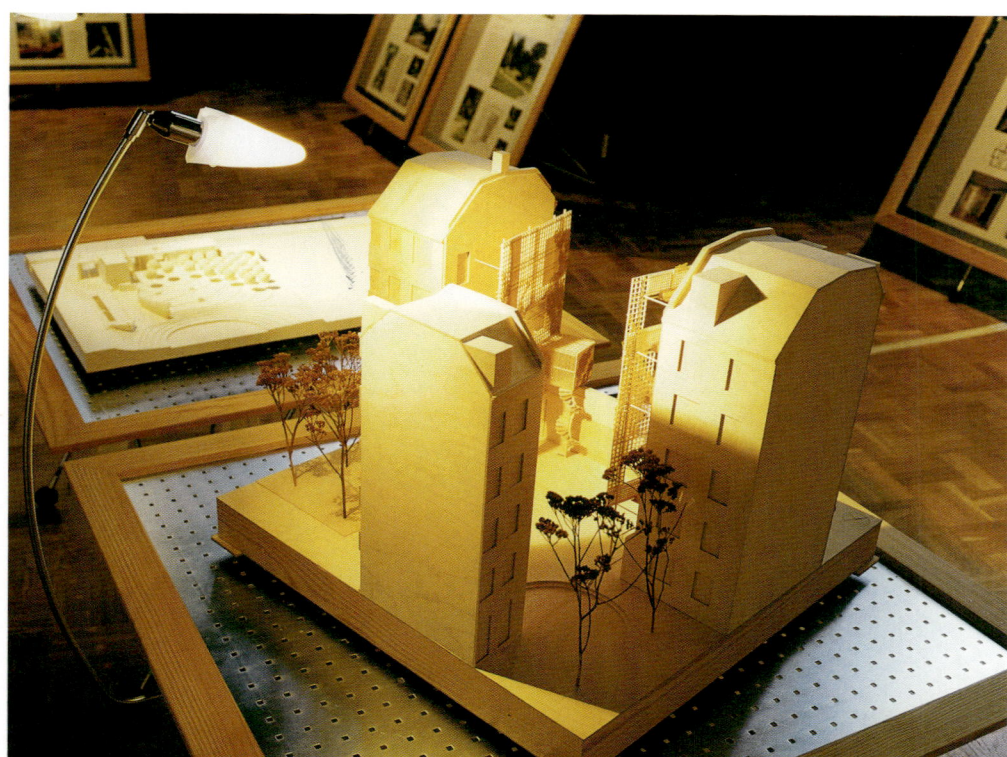

PROJECT:
THE DANISH WAVE
DENMARK, AUSTRALIA, BRAZIL, CHINA AND JAPAN

WHERE:
Denmark, Australia, Brazil, China, and Japan

WHEN:
1999 - 2002

CLIENT:
the Danish Cultural Institute and the Danish Centre for Architecture

MARKET SECTOR:
architecture and design

DESIGNER OF STAND:
Kvorning design team

GENERAL CONSTRUCTER:
4 key designers

CONSULTANTS:
various

MANUFACTURERS:
various

MATERIALS:
stainless steel and larch wood

AREA:
500 m²

BUDGET:
€ 300,000

PROJECT DURATION:
4 years

OPENING:
spring 1999

'HIGH PRAISE AND A PAT ON THE BACK FOR DANISH ARCHITECTURE AND DESIGN...'
(BERLINGSKE TIDENDE, DENMARK)

For the major cultural export project 'The Danish Wave', which began in Australia in 1998-99, Kvorning Design & Communication designed and co-ordinated a 500 m² travelling exhibition of Danish architecture and design. The display system, made of stainless steel and larch wood, was custom made for the exhibition. The display modules could be arranged in various combinations to form such display furniture as large, slanting display boards; high and low podia; or showcases. An important element of the exhibition was a 30 m² aerial photo of Copenhagen, on which the locations of more than 40 architectural projects could be found.

In addition, the exhibition presented a number of noteworthy examples of Danish graphic, industrial, and furniture design as well as a select segment featuring unique Danish handicrafts.

After visiting five cities in Australia in 1999, The Danish Wave travelled to The 4th International Architecture Biennale in Sao Paulo, Brazil, where it took first place out of 395 international exhibitions.

The exhibition has also travelled throughout China, and most recently has been shown in Japan.

KVORNING DESIGN & COMMUNICATION GRAND STAND

PROJECT:
INTERNATIONAL ARCHITECTURE BIENNALE THE DANISH PAVILION, VENICE, ITALY

WHERE:
8th International Architecture Biennale, Venice, Italy
WHEN:
2002
CLIENT:
Danish Ministry of Culture and Copenhagen X
MARKET SECTOR:
architecture
DESIGNER OF STAND:
Kvorning design team
DESIGN TEAM:
5 key designers
GENERAL CONSTRUCTER:
various in Denmark and Italy
CONSULTANTS:
various
MANUFACTURERS:
various in Denmark and Italy
MATERIALS:
Lexan plastic plates, steel, patina-surfaced planks
AREA:
450 m²
BUDGET:
€ 330,000
PROJECT DURATION:
100 days
OPENING:
summer 2002

'SOME OF THE MOST REFINED EXHIBITION TECHNOLOGY AND ONE OF THE MOST WELL-BALANCED AND CONFIDENTLY PRODUCED PRESENTATIONS AT THE BIENNALE...'
(ARKITEKTEN – DENMARK'S OFFICIAL ARCHITECTURE MAGAZINE)

'From Dusk to Dawn' was Denmark's official contribution to The 8th International Architecture Biennale, held in Venice in 2002. The exhibition, housed in Denmark's permanent exhibition pavilion on the Biennale grounds in Giardini, used the two main themes of NOW and NEXT to illuminate both Copenhagen's existing architecture and a handful of noteworthy new projects, due to be sprouting up over the next few years.
A characteristically large arch traversed the pavilion diagonally, dividing the room into two spaces: NOW and NEXT. Along this long footbridge rose a translucent wall with several cutaway sections. These formed portals to NEXT and to the capital's new architecture projects.
When illuminated, the bridge – rising slightly over the floor and laid with wide, patina-surfaced planks – reflected both Copenhagen's and Venice's maritime heritages. The bridge, the wall, and the lighting combined to give the effect of the passage from evening into night. The exhibition's content consisted chiefly of short, introductory texts; large, appealing photos; animated projections; 1:1 mock-ups and models on light podia; working ateliers; and web-cam connections to construction sites. A 14-metre-long, 3-metre-high projection screen in three sections was placed in the main room of the exhibition pavilion.
More info: www.biennale.dk

grand_stand **KVORNING DESIGN & COMMUNICATION**

KVORNING DESIGN & COMMUNICATION GRAND STAND

				PROJECT:
				MINIMAL CONSTRUCTIONS
				COPENHAGEN, DENMARK
				CHINA

WHERE:	**DESIGN TEAM:**	**BUDGET:**	
Fashion show, Bella Center,	2 key designers	€ 110,000	
Copenhagen, Denmark;	**GENERAL CONSTRUCTER:**	**PROJECT DURATION:**	
ModularShading, China	various	Copenhagen project: 10 days in	
WHEN:	**CONSULTANTS:**	1992 and 10 days in 1993	
1992 - 1993; 2003 - 2004	Ture Wester, engineer	China project: permanent	
CLIENT:	**MANUFACTURERS:**	**OPENING:**	
Craftsmen's Guild of Copenhagen	various	Copenhagen project: spring 1992	
MARKET SECTOR:	**MATERIALS:**	and 1993	
various	sail structure and steel	China project: planned to open in	
DESIGNER OF STAND:	**AREA:**	2003 or 2004	
Kvorning design team	varies		

SAIL-STRUCTURES IN MEGA-SIZE!

Kvorning Design & Communication has had several projects working with large indoor and outdoor sail-structures.

These large, light constructions always make for an effective and spectacular substitute for traditional exhibition stands and Kvorning uses its experience to design these structures so that they make as much of an impact as possible.

One of the structures shown, which was on display in Copenhagen's Bella Center, was over 25 metres tall and covered an area of approximately 300 m². The structure, formed by stretching a sail between hanging steel tubes, served as the focal point of a week-long fashion exhibition.

ModularShading is a newly-developed system of sail-structures. The sketch shown is from a major international project planned for 2003-04. More info: www.modularshading.com

grand stand **KVORNING DESIGN & COMMUNICATION**

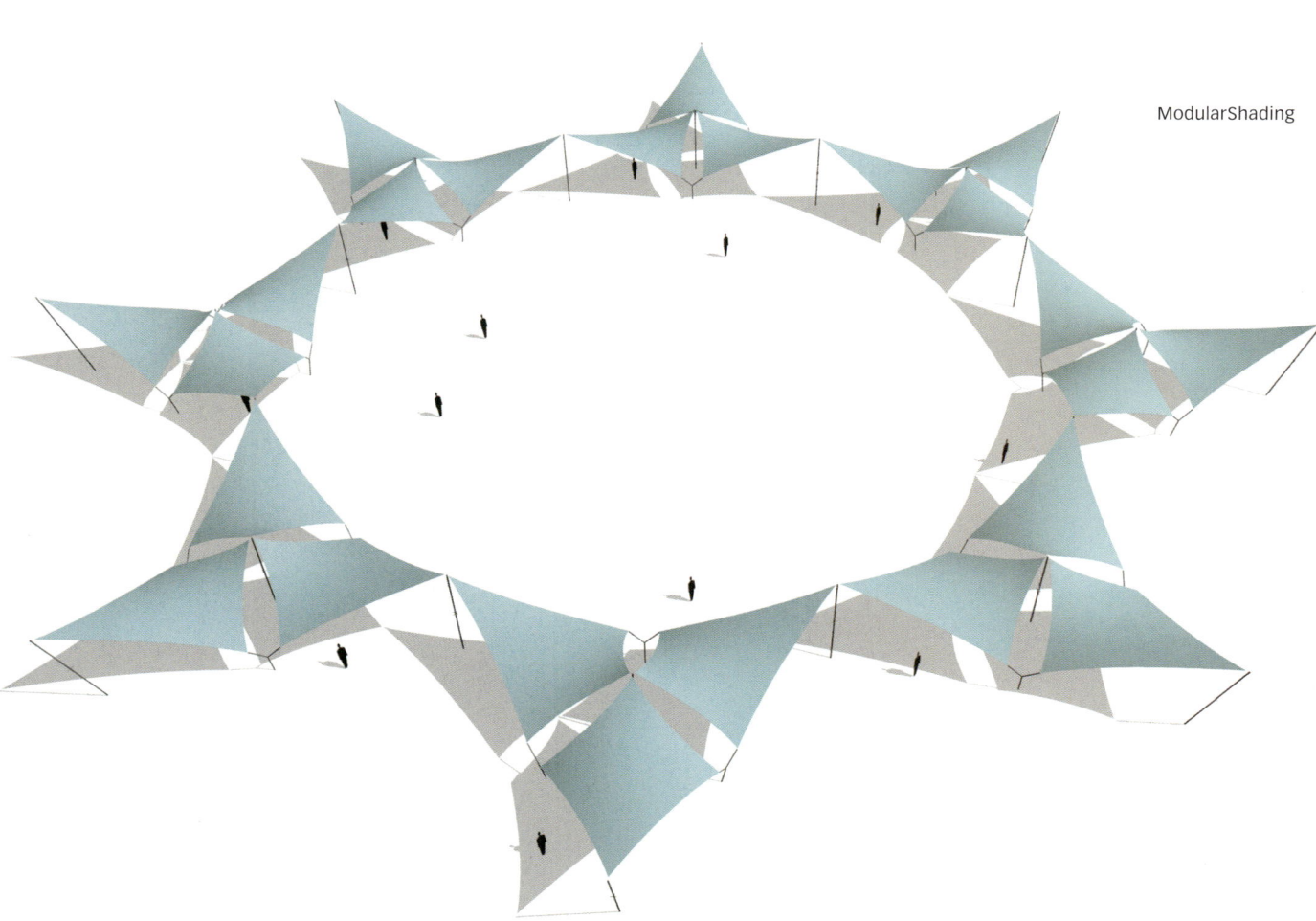

ModularShading

129
GRAND STAND

PROJECT:
IN PLACE OF DOMINIQUE PERRAULT COPENHAGEN, HELSINKI AND TALLINN

WHERE:
Copenhagen, Denmark
Helsinki, Finland
Tallinn, Estonia

WHEN:
1999 - 2001

CLIENT:
Danish Centre for Architecture and Dominique Perrault

MARKET SECTOR:
architecture

DESIGNER OF STAND:
Kvorning design team

DESIGN TEAM:
2 key designers

GENERAL CONSTRUCTER:
various

CONSULTANTS:
Jorgen Kjer

MANUFACTURERS:
various

MATERIALS:
projectors, mirrors and podia

AREA:
300 m²

BUDGET:
€ 60,000

PROJECT DURATION:
aprox. 30 days per location

OPENING:
winter 1999

'IT IS A FANTASTIC AND WONDERFUL EXPERIENCE TO ENTER INTO THE EXHIBITION HALL...' (BYGGERI 1999, TRADE JOURNAL FOR DANISH CONSTRUCTION)

In co-operation with Dominique Perrault Design Studio, Kvorning designed and co-ordinated an exhibition of the works of Perrault, the French architect and designer, for Copenhagen's Danish Centre for Architecture. The exhibition was staged in a series of blacked-out rooms, in which over 2,400 slides were projected onto white podia from 30 ceiling-mounted projectors. Several other unexpected details, including animations of Perrault's signature and quotations on the walls, rounded out the exhibition's lighting effects.

Now a travelling exhibition, the project has been on display in Helsinki, Finland and Tallinn, Estonia. For the travelling version, Kvorning developed a special system that was installed in sections into the ceilings of the exhibition halls. Mirrors were used to focus the projections onto the floor where visitors walked from one project to another in a kaleidoscopic rhythm.

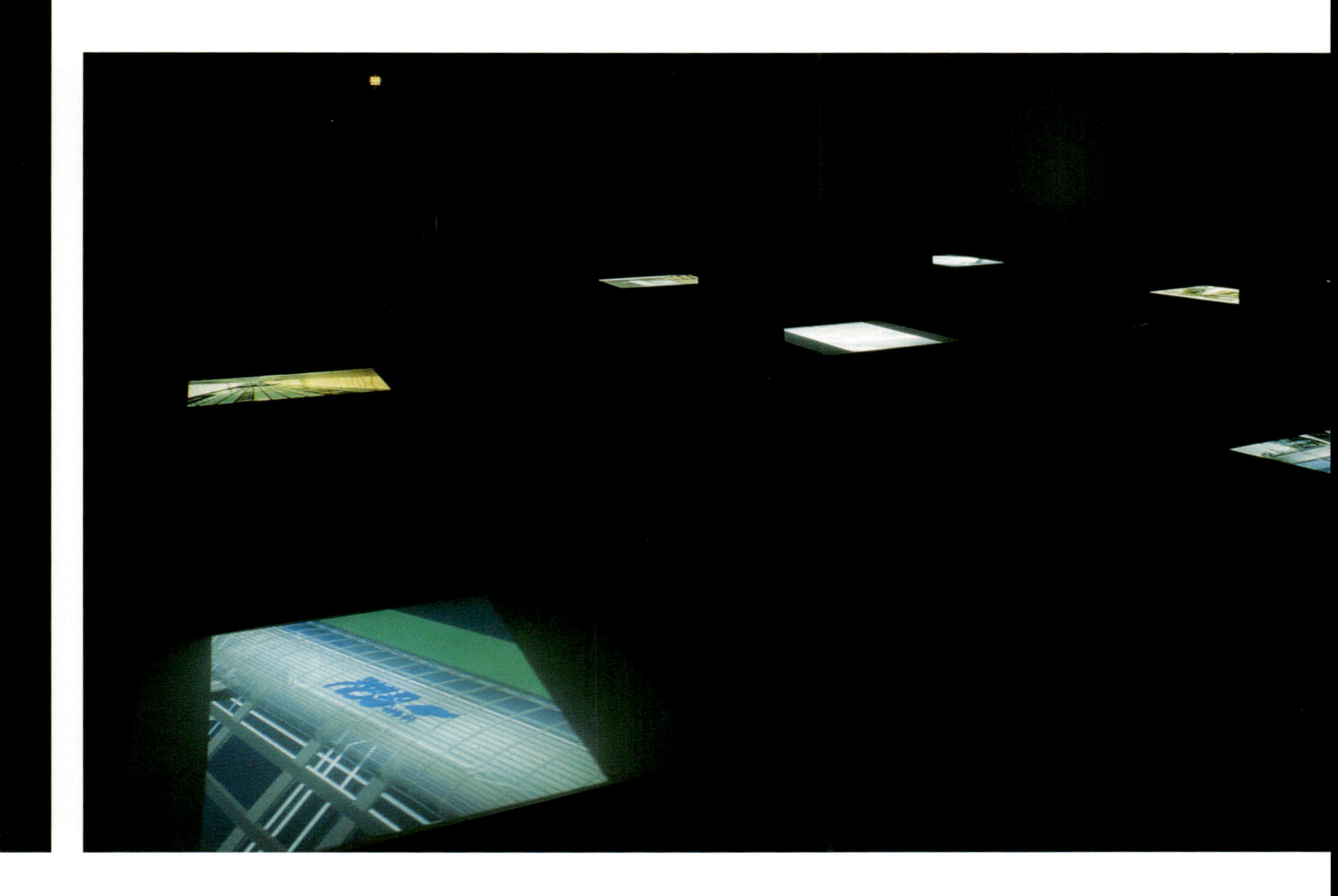

KVORNING DESIGN & COMMUNICATION GRAND STAND

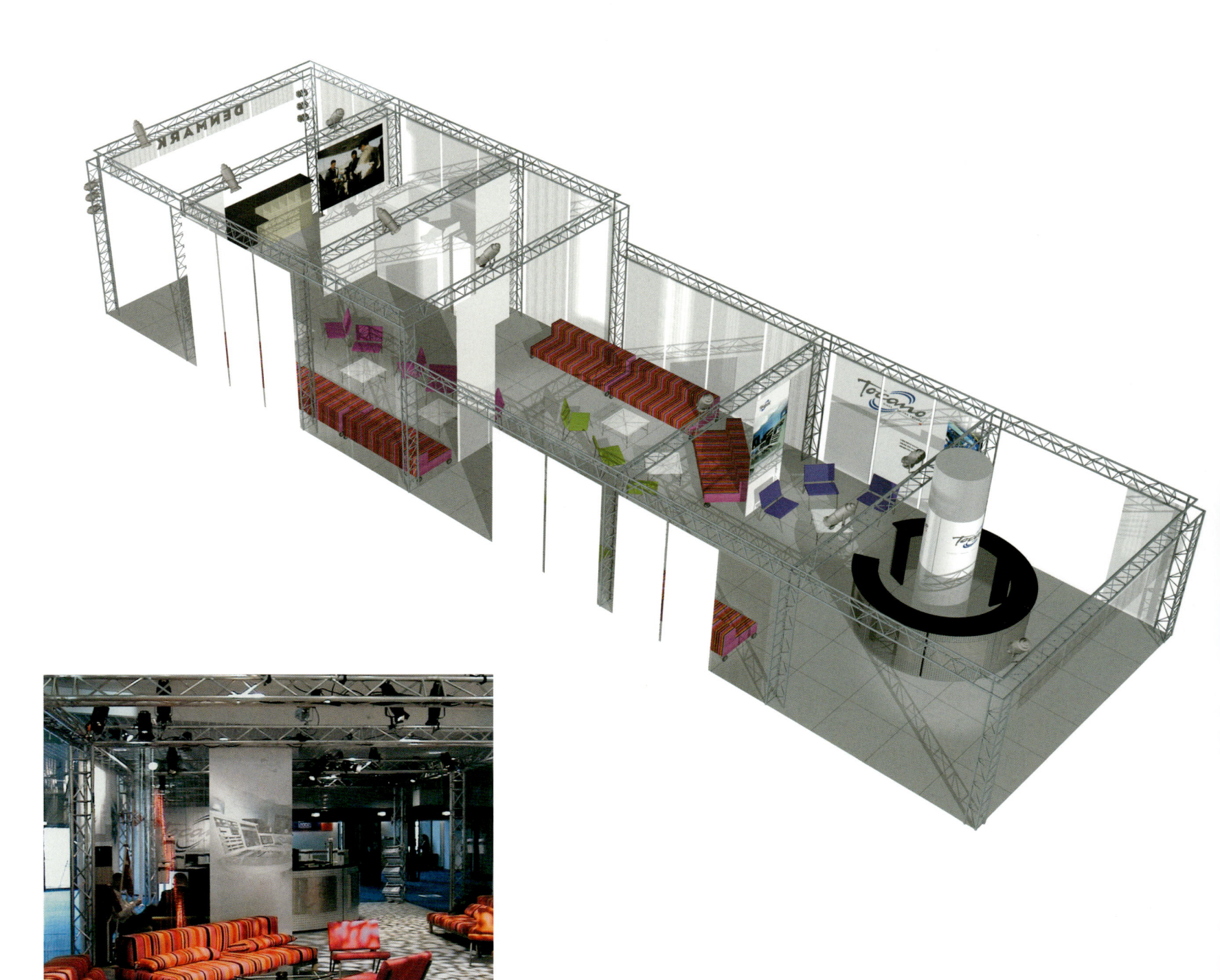

Midem 2002

132
grand stand **KVORNING DESIGN & COMMUNICATION**

PROJECT:
MIDEM 2002 + 2003
CANNES, FRANCE

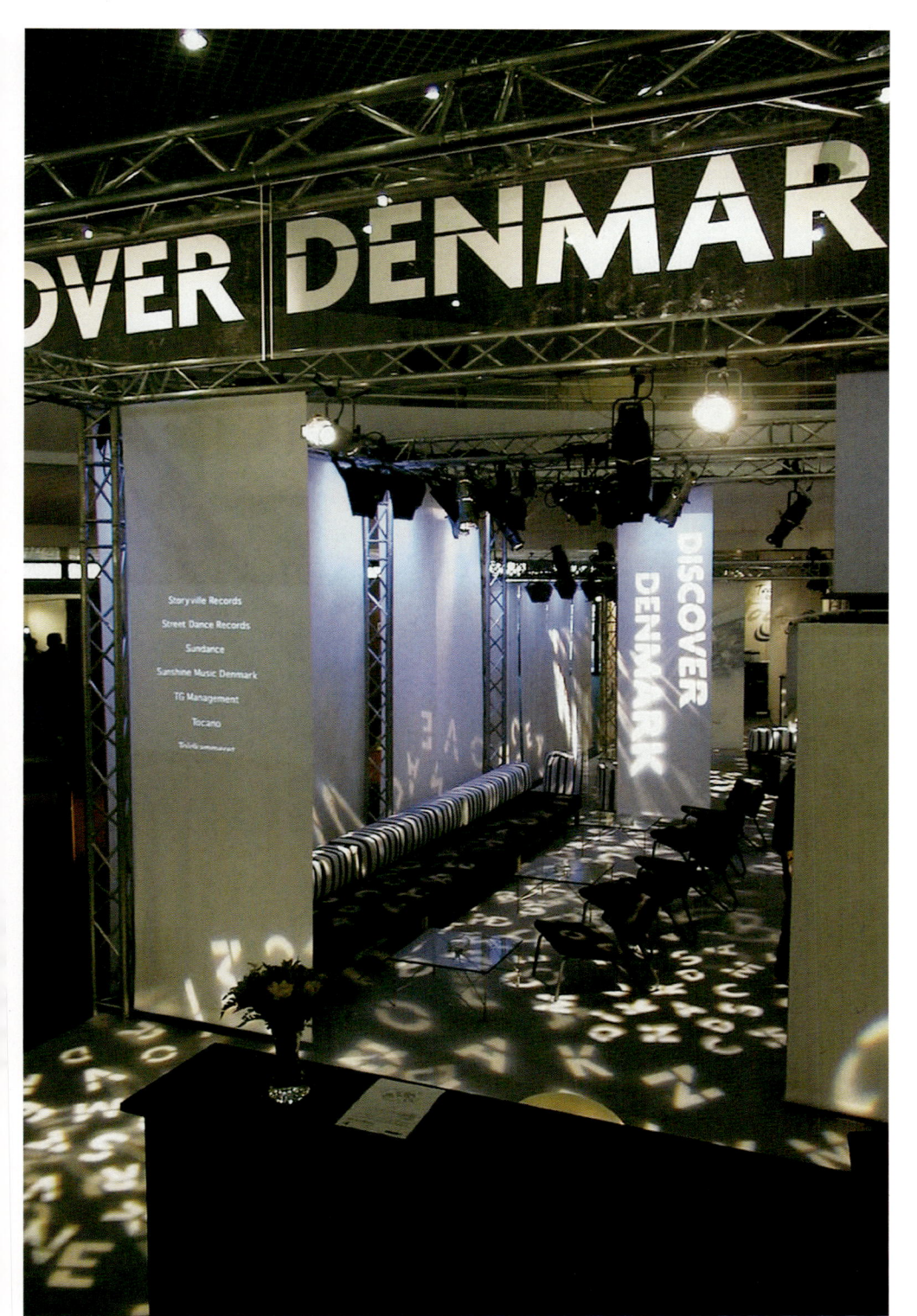

WHERE:
Midem, Cannes, France
WHEN:
2002 and 2003
CLIENT:
Danish Ministry of Culture and MIC – Danish Music Information Centre
MARKET SECTOR:
music industry
DESIGNER OF STAND:
Kvorning design team
DESIGN TEAM:
4 key designers
GENERAL CONSTRUCTER:
various
CONSULTANTS:
various
MANUFACTURERS:
various
MATERIALS:
rig-system, stainless steel mesh and drop paper banners
AREA:
200 m²
BUDGET:
€ 80,000
PROJECT DURATION:
10 days
OPENING:
January 2002 and 2003

'DENMARK WENT ALL OUT AND CAME IN STRONG AT MIDEM 2003...' (MBI, MUSIC BUSINESS INTERNATIONAL, ENGLAND)

Every January, the international music industry meets in Cannes at MIDEM, the world's largest international music trade fair. Since 1992, Kvorning Design & Communication has designed and co-ordinated the exhibition stand for Denmark's music organisations and record labels. The stand basically serves as a meeting place that provides people from the music industry with a relaxing place to meet and negotiate the purchase and sale of Danish music. Over the past few years, the stand has come to serve as the representation for more than 50 record labels and typically has more than 100 exhibitors associated with it.

In connection with the exhibition, Denmark often arranges live music at the stand or at venues in Cannes. Several of the bands performing in these concerts have gone on to become international successes.

The exhibition stand itself is constructed as a rig-system with walls of stainless steel mesh. The stand's stage lighting and specially-designed furnishings are frequently regarded as one of the fair's most spectacular elements.

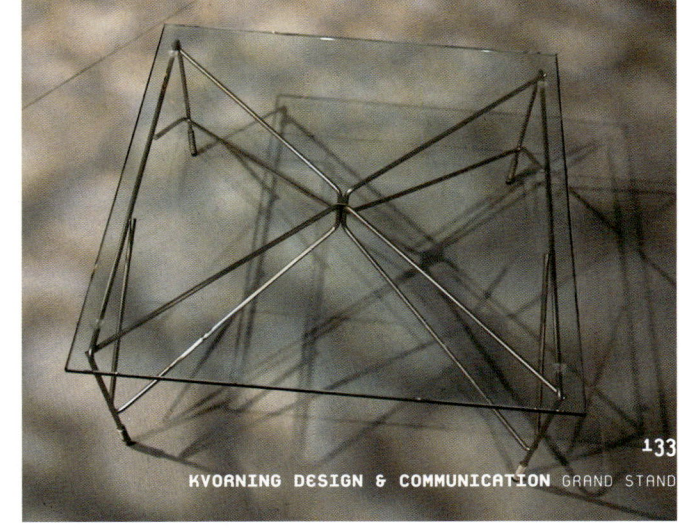

Midem 2003

KVORNING DESIGN & COMMUNICATION GRAND STAND

LIGHT WEIGHTS
WORLDWIDE

NAMES OF PROJECTS:
Light Weights:
BUG Systems
Spaces of Time
Opening Hours
Carl Nielsen

CLIENT:
Danish Music Information Centre and Danish Center for Accessibility
+ various

DESIGNER OF STAND:
Kvorning design team

Kvorning has developed a series of specially-designed exhibition systems, primarily for use in travelling exhibitions. Though these lightweight and flexible systems are custom-made, their construction takes into account the possibility of mass production for larger orders.

BUG Systems consists of two floor displays – BUG and BIG BUG, the wall mountable WALL BUG, and two exhibition tables, BUGSY 35 and BUGSY 55 – both of which can be fitted with glass display cases. More info: www.bugsystems.com

Spaces of Time is the title of a photo exhibition focusing on 16 Danish composers. The travelling exhibition is constructed of Lexan plastic and stainless steel and has been on display in several European capitals.

Opening Hours is an exhibition that focuses on handicapped access to museums. In keeping with the theme of the exhibition, both the design and the content of the exhibit take special consideration of the needs of handicapped patrons. The system itself is constructed of lightweight aluminium plates with an internal honeycomb structure.

An exhibition focusing on the Danish composer **Carl Nielsen** has toured Europe for more than 10 years. The travelling exhibition is ultra-lightweight, consisting of two 6-millimetre-thick Lexan plastic plates, which unfold to form a sturdy display.

134
grand stand **KVORNING DESIGN & COMMUNICATION**

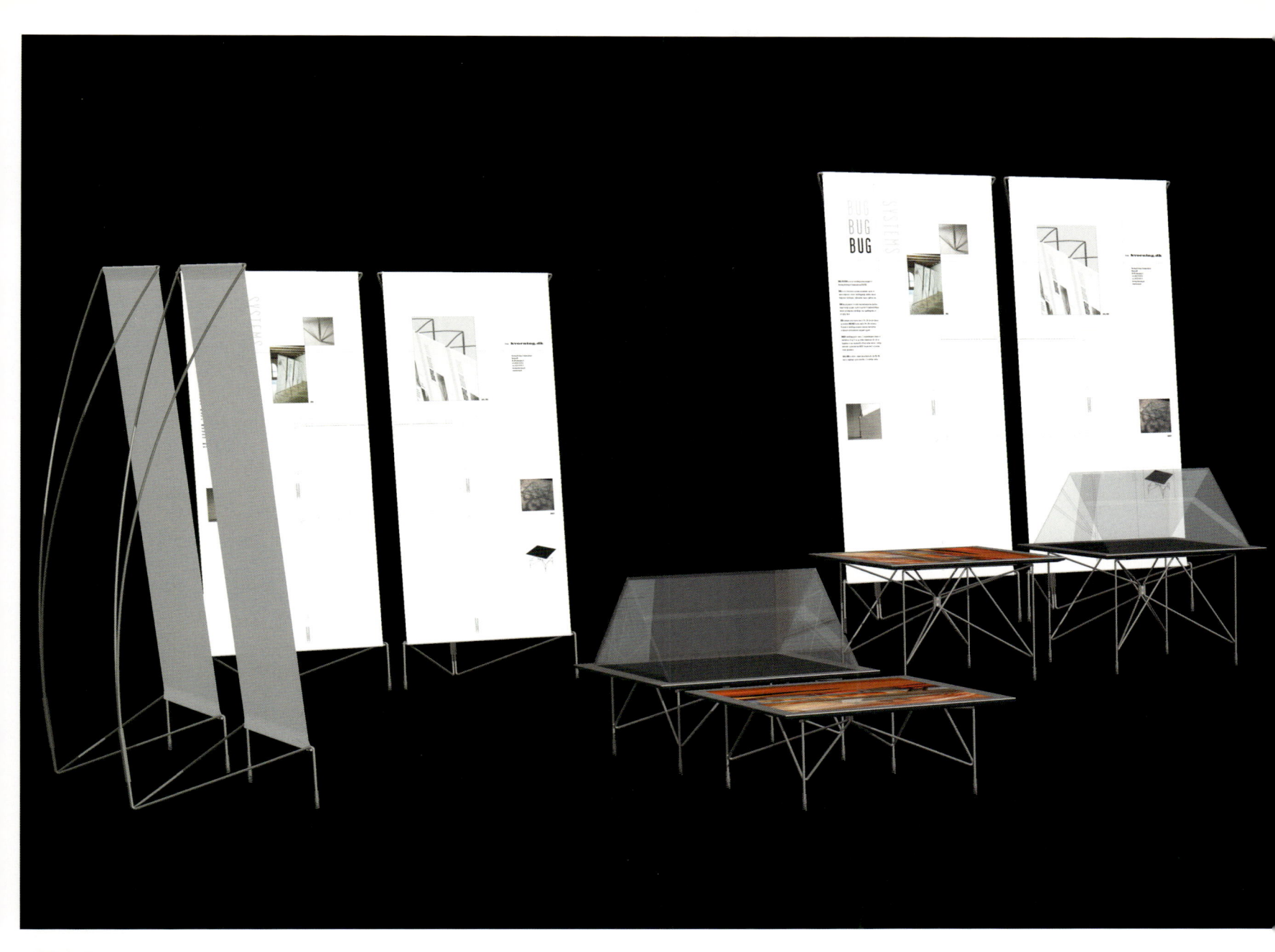

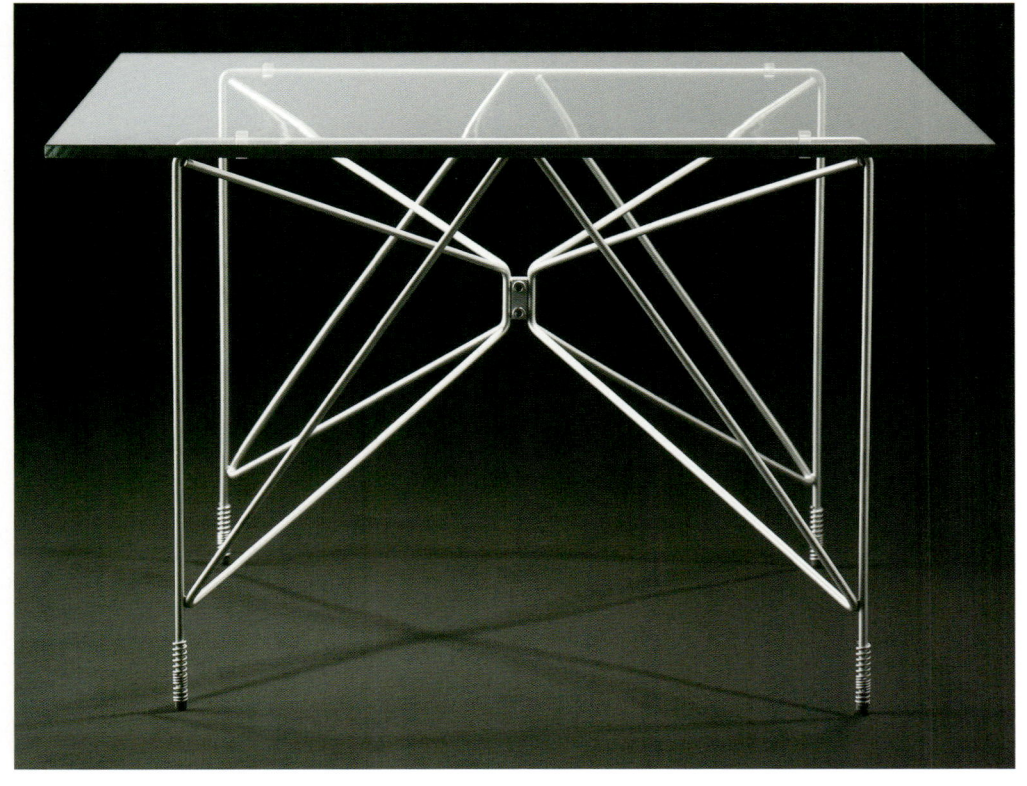

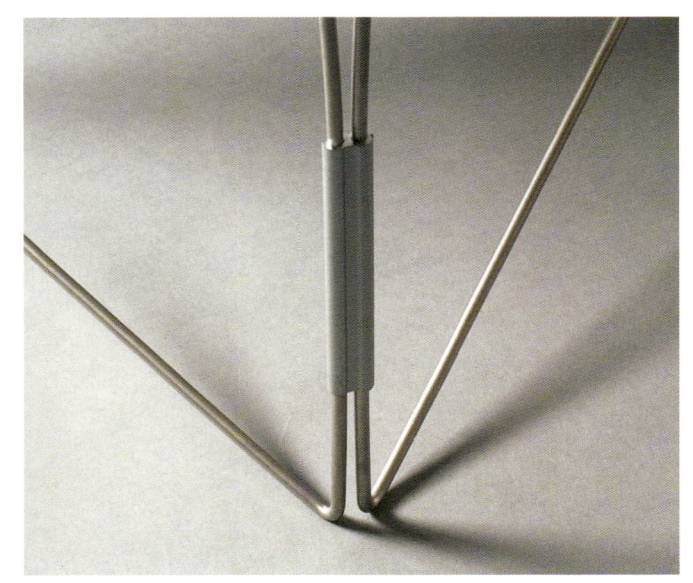

KVORNING DESIGN & COMMUNICATION GRAND STAND

COMPANY NAME:
KVORNING DESIGN & COMMUNICATION

HEAD OFFICE:
Nyhavn 63D
DK-1051 Copenhagen K
Denmark

PHONE:
+45 33 93 93 53

FAX:
+45 33 93 93 75

E-MAIL:
kvorning@kvorning.dk

WEBSITE:
www.kvorning.dk

MANAGEMENT:
Arne Kvorning, manager

CONTACTS:
Arne Kvorning, arne@kvorning.dk

STAFF:
5 - 10 + freelance staff

KEY DESIGNERS:
Arne Kvorning
Pia Bajlum
Sofie Wiik McGwin
Michael Poulsen
Pernille Aakjaer

FOUNDED:
1992

MEMBER OF:
- DAL/AA The Federation of Danish Architects
- MDD Danish Designers
- ICOM

COMPANY PROFILE:
Kvorning Design & Communication offers consulting services in design, identity, exhibitions and communications for public organizations and private companies.
Quality, dedication, continuity of communication and service are the key words – from idea flow and design development to project co-ordination, production and follow-up.
Kvorning has co-ordinated and completed projects in more than 30 countries worldwide.

CLIENTS:
- Academic Press, Copenhagen
- Copenhagen City
- Copenhagen X
- DMF-Danish Musicians' Union
- Icopal A/S
- Karen Blixen Museum
- MIC-Danish Music Information Centre
- The Danish Centre for Architecture
- The Danish Cultural Institute
- The Danish Jewish Museum
- The Danish Ministry of Culture
- The Danish Ministry of Foreign Affairs
- The Danish Ministry of Housing
- The National Museum, Copenhagen
- The Royal Danish Academy of Fine Arts

SERVICES:
- Exhibition design – permanent, temporary and travelling exhibitions, design of display and exhibition equipment, light and sound, budget and production management, practical co-ordination, transportation and set-up.
- Graphic design – design and identity programs, magazines and annual reports, sales and information material, CD production, packaging, book production, and more.
- Communications, marketing and PR services
- Product design, display systems, showcases, lighting and fittings.
- Web design, user interface, technique, operation and maintenance.
- Interactive solutions, hands-on displays and more.
- Architecture and interior design.

AWARDS:
- **1st Prize:** Best exhibition at the 4th International Architecture Biennial in Sao Paulo, Brazil 2000
- **1st Prize:** Logo for Save the Children Association, introduced worldwide

OPERATES:
Worldwide

LAND DESIGN STUDIO

LONDON, UK

land design studio

grand stand **LAND DESIGN STUDIO**

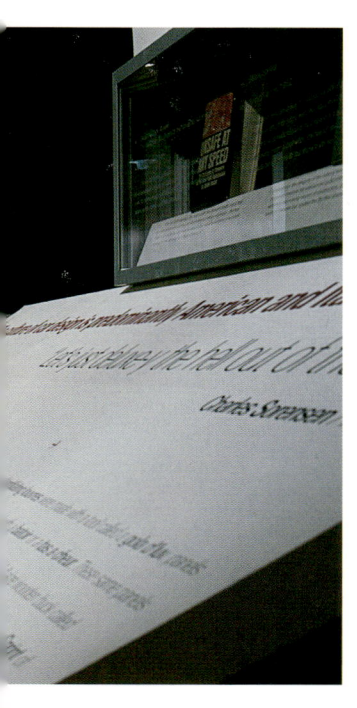

PROJECT:
MOVING OBJECTS
LONDON, UK

WHERE:
Royal College of Art, London, UK

WHEN:
1999

CLIENT:
Royal College of Art, Ford Motor Company

DESIGNER OF STAND:
Land Design Studio

DESIGN TEAM:
John Blanchard, Joe Burrin, BCD

FABRICATOR:
Mansfield

AREA:
1,750 m²

BUDGET:
£ 500,000

PHOTOGRAPHER:
Nick Wood

One of the primary objectives for this project was to fundamentally alter the perception of the RCA's existing gallery spaces. Notions of movement and distortion were important factors in this creative approach which, in turn, allowed for a subtle manipulation of the exhibits and gallery spaces. Land approached the project with a clear narrative in mind, which ultimately shaped and defined the sequence of galleries. Installations included oversized body panelling and candy coloured, dissected car-body shells. The exterior of the RCA applied powerful, lenticular imaging to the main fenestration. A coherent visitor movement system soon developed through the ground floor and basement levels of the RCA. A gallery dedicated to 'Road Culture' became the foundation for the ensuing exhibition. Other spaces dealt with topics such as: 'Vehicle Anatomy, Art or Science?', 'Interior and Exterior Styling, Colour and Gender & Environment'. Full-scale concept models were reserved for the final climax which transformed the Henry Moore Gallery into a stylised multi-storey car park.
A substantial book designed by Big Corporate Disco was published in association with the exhibition.

LAND DESIGN STUDIO grand stand

PROJECT:
PLAYZONE AT THE MILLENNIUM DOME GREENWICH
GREENWICH, UK

WHERE:
Millennium Dome, Greenwich, UK

WHEN:
2000

CLIENT:
New Millennium Experience Company

DESIGNER OF STAND:
Land Design Studio

DESIGN TEAM:
Robin Clark, James Dibble, Peter Higgins, Shirley Walker, Buro Happold, Atelier 10, Simple Productions

FABRICATOR:
FRPL Construction Management

COMPUTER MODELLING:
Anthony Pearson

AREA:
1,454 m²

BUDGET:
£ 12,000,000

PHOTOGRAPHER:
Nick Wood

At the Dome, Land's background in designing for 'narrative' gave them the opportunity to create a responsive architectural structure. Land created a site-specific structure with an area of 1,454 m² that sat over 900 m² of retail space. The intriguing form responded to the view of the passerby on the primary elevations. The distinctive 'snouts' evolved from the direct requirement for content back-projection facilities; this cantilevered 'flying lease' effectively extended the footprint by 480 m². With potentially 3,500 visitors per hour, sequencing was a crucial issue. The entrance provided a controlled queuing area with preview entertainment. Once inside, there was an option to overview the PlayZone from a 'fast track', or to extend the visit to about 30 minutes by participating or spectating at close hand. The organising principle of the content was the desire to create a highly inter-active experience. The selection of new media installations form a showcase for future play. Here digital technology was curated through a worldwide search of practitioners, with some content being directly developed by Land. The opportunity to commission the content, scenographic environment and architectural envelope simultaneously produced a truly integrated solution which was delivered as a complete design and build package.

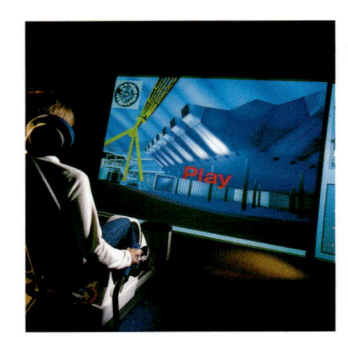

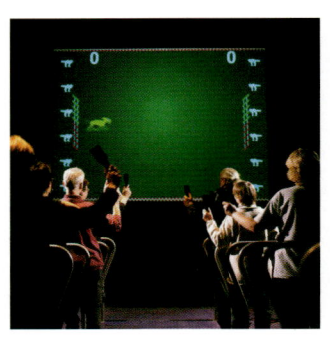

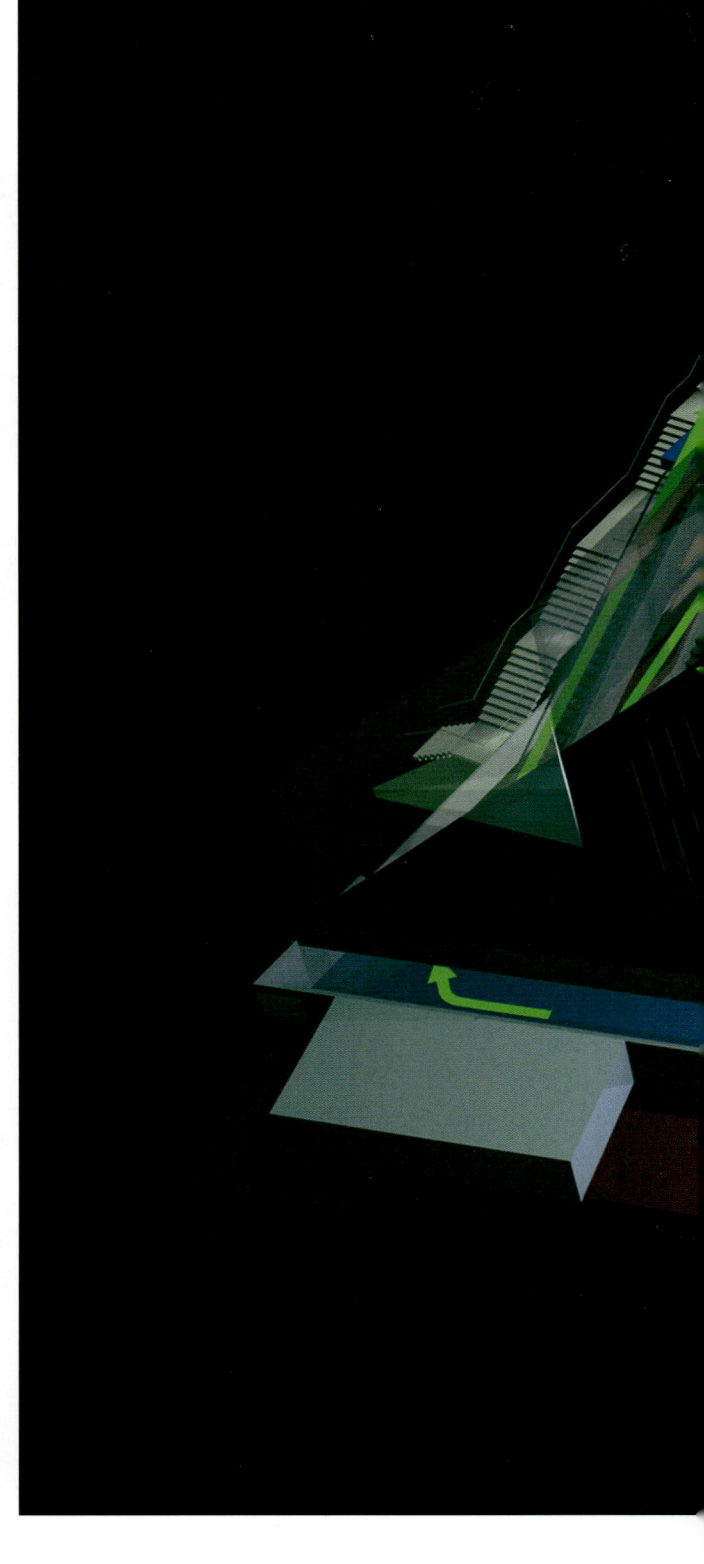

grand stand

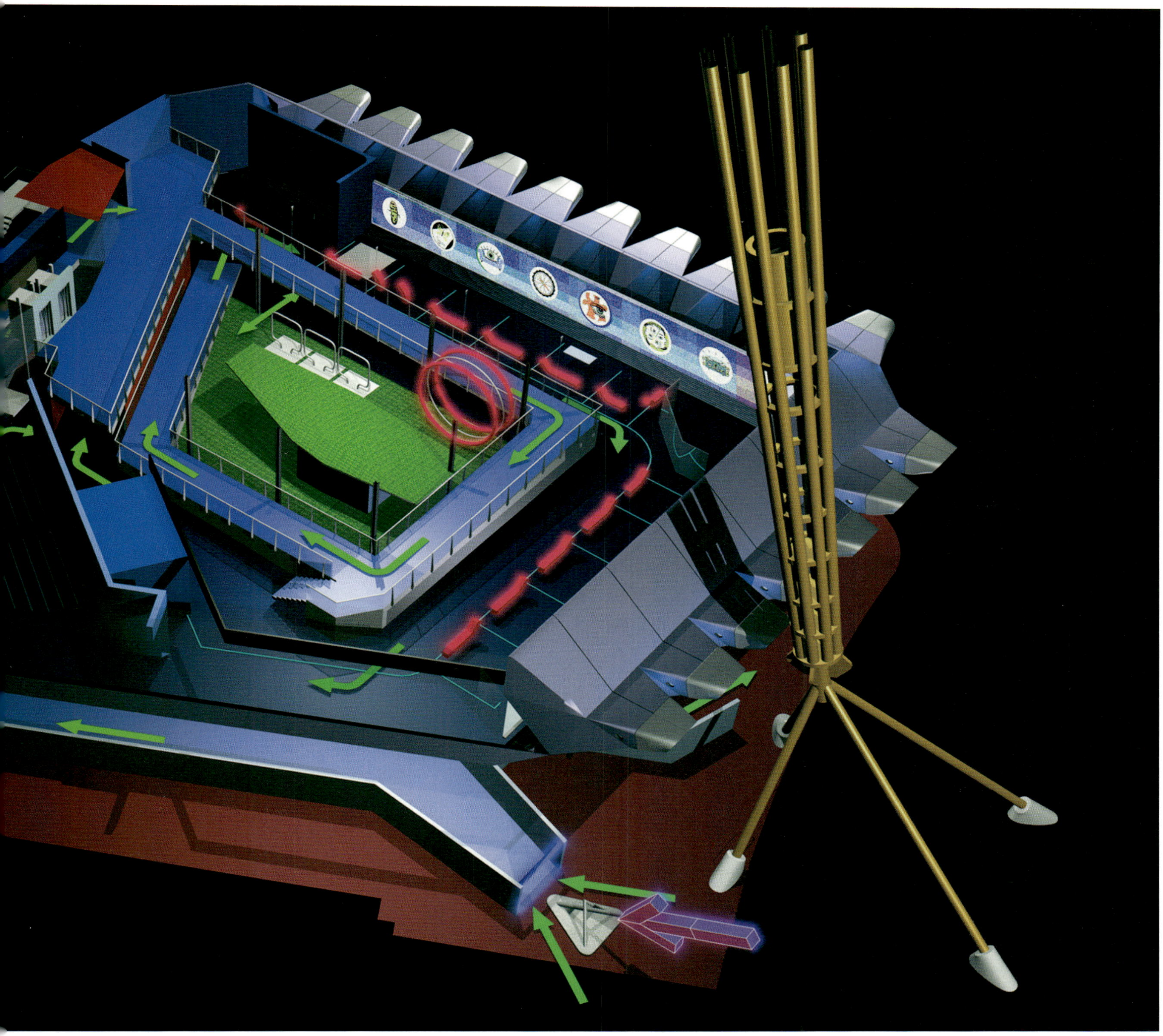

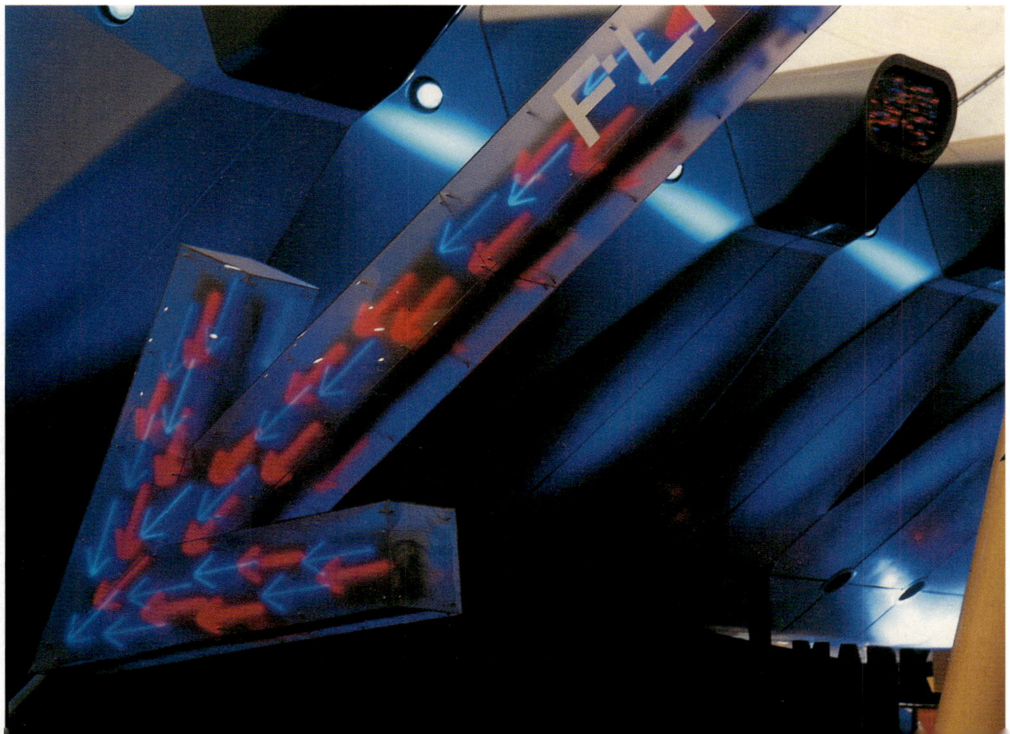

PROJECT:
FUTURES GALLERY
BIRMINGHAM, UK

WHERE:
Thinktank, Birmingham, UK
WHEN:
2001
CLIENT:
Thinktank
DESIGNER OF STAND:
Land Design Studio
DESIGN TEAM:
John Blanchard, James Dibble, ISO
FABRICATOR:
Edmonds, Harris Blyth
AREA:
775 m²
BUDGET:
£ 1,300,000
PHOTOGRAPHER:
Land Design Studio

This 775 m² gallery is one of four components that constitute the Thinktank (the Birmingham Museum of Science and Discovery) at Nick Grimshaw's Millennium Point in Birmingham. The complex challenge of presenting concepts of future science and technology was overcome by creating dynamic streaming audio/video, text and image on large format 3 x 2 metre screens. This helps the visitor understand the process of research and development of current innovation.

The architecture and ambience is created by the information media, with the budget spent on software rather than steel and glass. Visitors are able to access information embedded in the main screens which may be downloaded onto foreground flatscreens for more personalised investigation. Selected tangible objects, such as herding robots or a voice-activated car dashboard, are located in the midground, and help complete the process of engaging the visitor.

As a concept, this 'walk-in-website' has an extended potential that supports the real-time, real-space experience. The ambition was for the visitor to continue the experience outside of the Gallery by investigating an extended hierarchy of information in their own time and space, through an authored Thinktank website. This concept has yet to be realised.

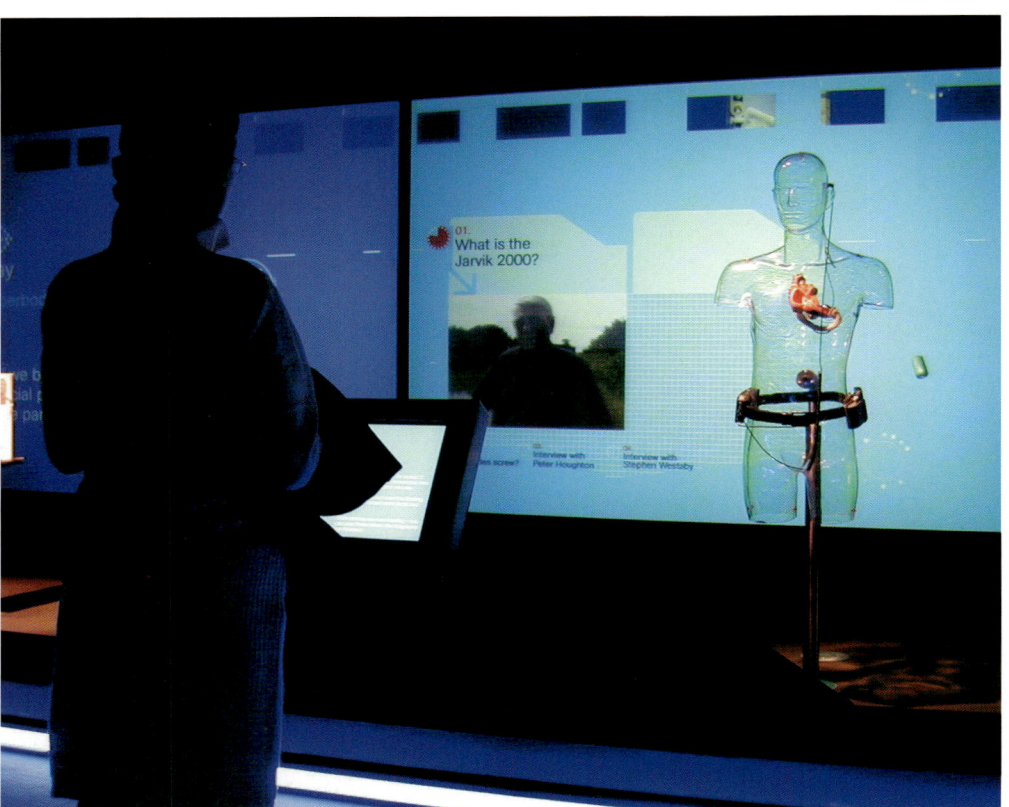

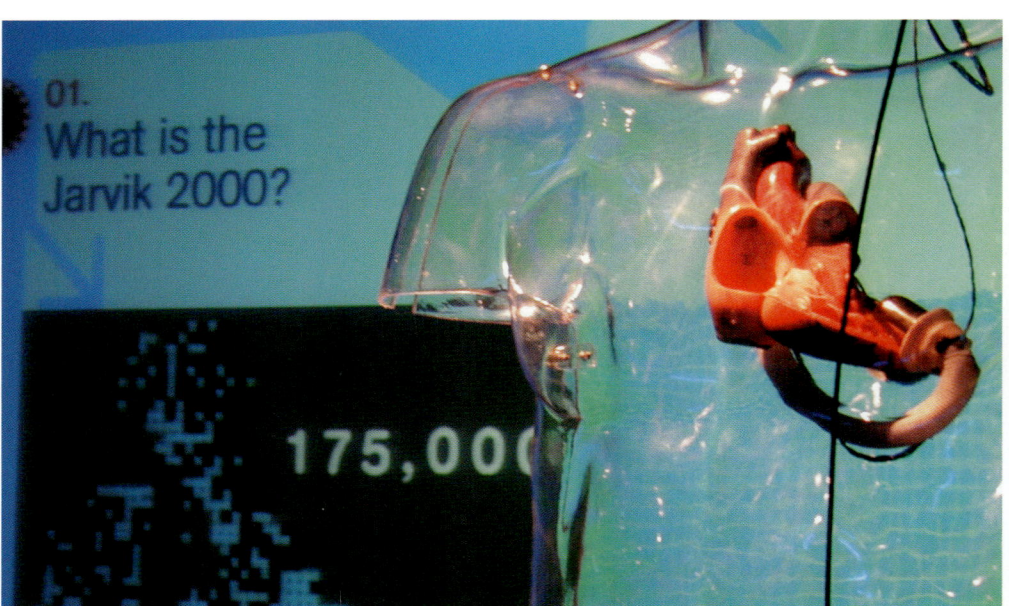

PROJECT:
THE FAMOUS GROUSE EXPERIENCE
CRIEFF, PERTHSHIRE, UK

WHERE: Crieff, Perthshire, UK
WHEN: 2002
CLIENT: Highland Distillers
DESIGNER OF STAND: Land Design Studio
DESIGN TEAM: Robin Clark, Peter Higgins, Art + Com
FABRICATOR: FRPL Construction Management
AREA: 200 m²
BUDGET: £ 2,000,000
PHOTOGRAPHER: Land Design Studio

The complete re-development of this Visitor Centre was undertaken by Land in 2000. The strength of the original guide-led manufacturing process was maintained whilst the construction of a new pavilion enabled Land to provide a nosing demonstration and a pre-show with a spectacular finale.
A refurbished 18th century cottage provided the ideal opportunity to create a memorable interactive experience set within a sophisticated sensory environment. The concept is drawn from the leitmotif of the award-winning TV commercial. Seismic floor sensors combined with a series of six computer-processed data projectors enable groups to splash through digital water, crack digital ice and fly across ever-evolving digital Scottish landscapes.
Once the eight minute show is complete, the movement sequence delivers the pulsed group directly into the refurbished shop and restaurant.

LAND DESIGN STUDIO grand stand

148

grand stand **LAND DESIGN STUDIO**

PROJECT:
DINOBIRDS
LONDON, UK

WHERE:
London, UK
WHEN:
2002
CLIENT:
Natural History Museum
DESIGNER OF STAND:
Land Design Studio
DESIGN TEAM:
Ross Hopcraft, Robert Carter
FABRICATOR:
Decor & Display Contracts
MATERIALS:
Parallam timber frame
AREA:
280 m²
BUDGET:
£ 400,000
PHOTOGRAPHER:
Philip Vine

Land Design Studio was appointed by the Natural History Museum (NHM) following the discovery of a spectacular series of fossils in a limestone quarry in China. These rare discoveries convincingly demonstrate the evolution of the dinosaur into the bird. This controversial thesis has been debated within the scientific community for some time and provoked the need for an exhibition to rationalise and describe the investigative process. Since the inception of free museum entry, there has been the overwhelming need for National Museums to create high-quality, touring exhibitions. In response, Land produced a low-cost, modular system that satisfies this utilitarian need by creating a variety of immersive environments with communication media worthy of a permanent installation. Touring exhibitions need significant periodic re-evaluation, and Land enjoyed the opportunity to work with the NHM on this prestigious event for the third time in nine years.

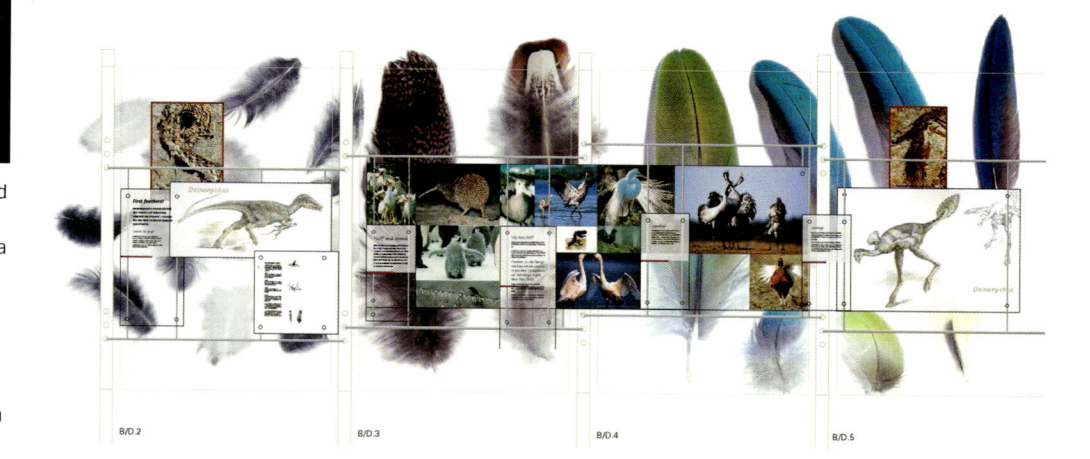

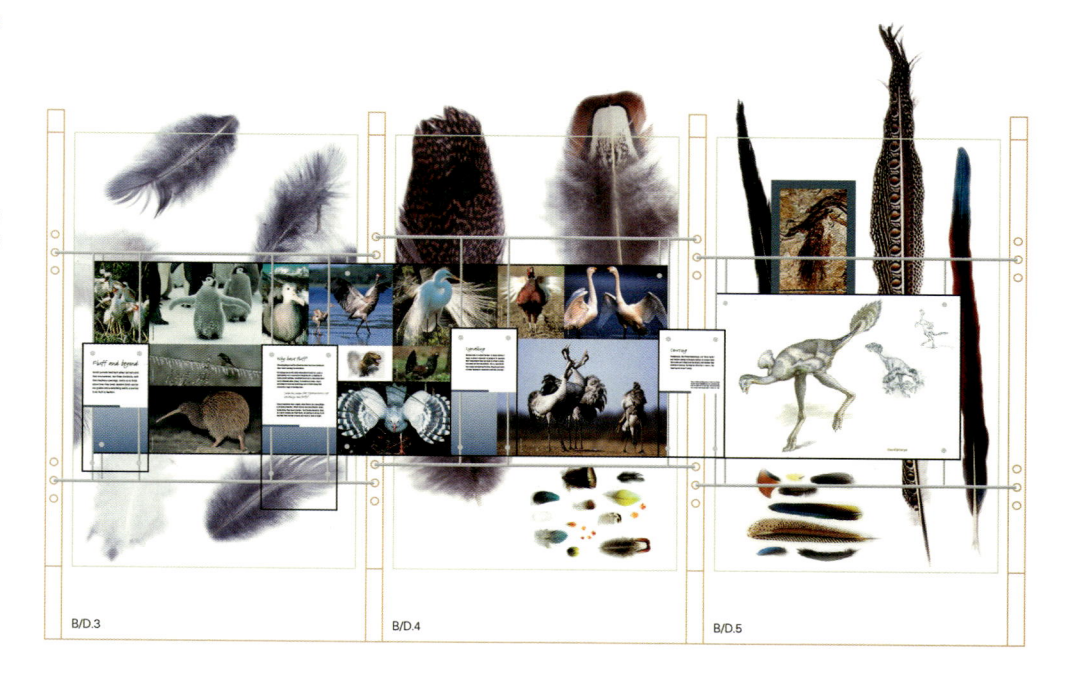

LAND DESIGN STUDIO grand stand

PROJECT:
SONY-ERICSSON
ORLANDO, FL, USA

Designed as a monument within the CTIA annual convention exhibit hall, the Sony-Ericsson exhibit stands in stark contrast to the overall visually hyper-kinetic atmosphere. The S+E letters, which purposefully define the exhibit structure, visually symbolize the two industry titans' positions of strength and optimistic outlook. The shared geometry of the letters allows for interlocking of their forms along the centerline of the exhibit, resonating the commitment of the newly formed venture.

The sweep of the two-level design accommodates the dual program of the exhibit: product demonstration and reception on the first level, and private conference on the second. Elevated almost two feet above the convention floor, the main level gives visitors the impression they are entering a significant event space. The linear slotted ceiling above tightens the sense of space, creating a focused environment for previewing small-scale state-of-the-art electronic products. Circular acrylic discs showcase high-tech devices against the curved wall behind, and bent planes with circular accents form demonstration counters. Connected by an upper reception bridge, the two-sided second-level conference spaces were designed for meetings and private presentations. The color palette, like the forms of the exhibit, is purposefully simple and direct for bold visual impact. Predominately white, all other accent colors echo the company's new identity and view to future prosperity.

156
grand stand **LORENC+YOO DESIGN**

LORENC+YOO DESIGN grand stand

PROJECT
SONY-ERICSSON
ORLANDO, FL, USA

WHERE:
CTIA Cellular Telephone & Internet Association, Orlando, USA

WHEN:
March 2002

CLIENT:
Sony-Ericsson, North America

DESIGNER OF STAND:
Jan Lorenc, Chung Youl Yoo

DESIGN TEAM:
Sakchai Rangsiyakorn, Steve McCall, Susie Caldwell Norris, David Park, Ken Boyd

PROJECT PRODUCER/DIRECTOR:
Journey Communications, Beth Cochran, Wayne PA

GENERAL CONSTRUCTOR:
Geograph Industries, Harrison OH

CONSULTANTS:
lighting: Ramon Luminance Design, Atlanta GA

MANUFACTURERS:
SET, Indianapolis IN, Structural system, stressed skin panels

MATERIALS:
plastic laminate, anodised aluminium, acrylic
specialty lighting and furniture including: Globus chair, Ball chair, Bluebelle chair, Deculpo table, Spin chair, Bombo bistro table and bar stools, Geometrix track lighting, Nelson Saucer pendant, cilindre pendant, NEC flat screen monitors

AREA:
464.5 m² (5,000 square feet)

BUDGET:
$ 1,600,000

PROJECT DURATION:
design and fabrication 9 months

OPENING:
March 2002

Perspective sketch @ "What we're going to do" Exhibit — conceptual sketch

LORENC+YOO DESIGN grand stand

160

grand stand **LORENC+YOO DESIGN**

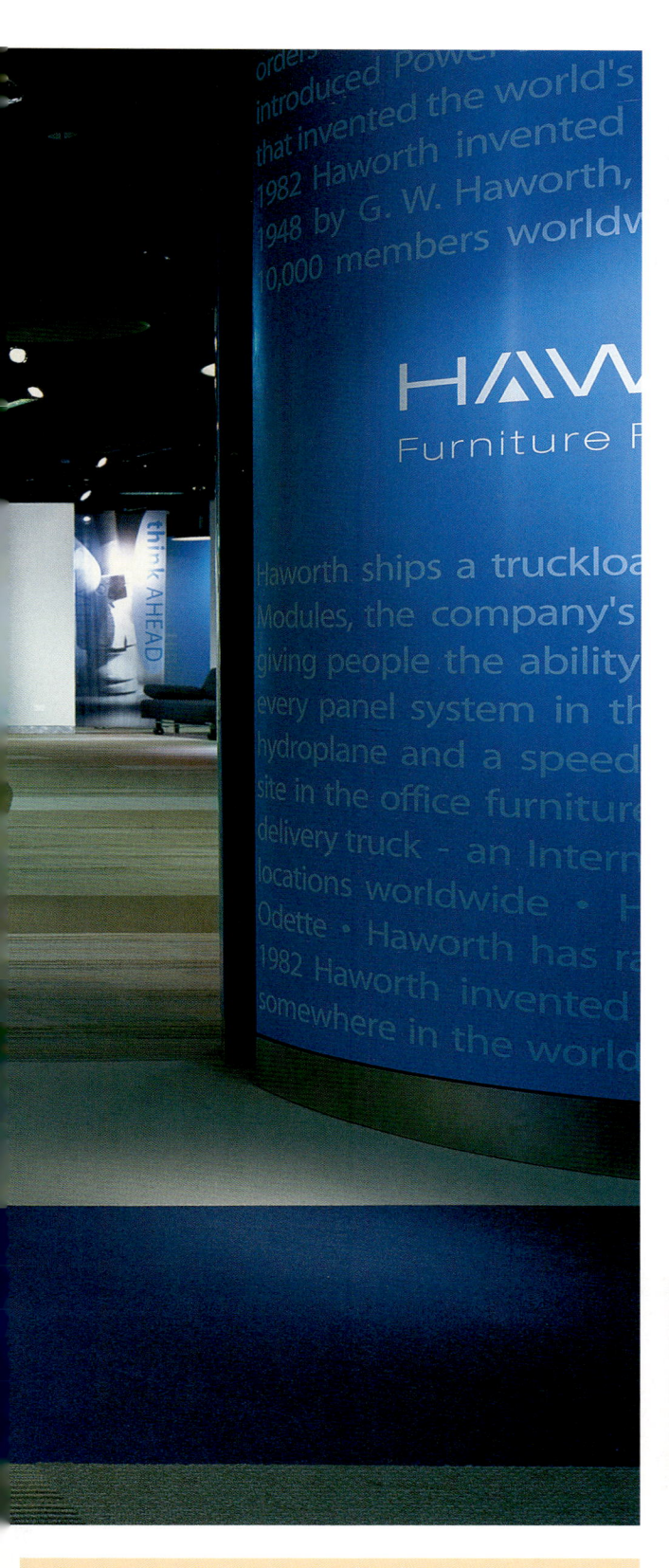

PROJECT:
HAWORTH FURNITURE COMPANY
NEOCON, CHICAGO, IL, USA

Animation is a primary theme. Oval printed graphic images are mounted across the storefront in a 'dancing' pattern, while an abstracted globe features a deconstructed video monitor displaying a continuous loop illustration of worldwide business locations. Additional large-scale graphic banners syncopate and organize the overall array of furniture on display.
A dramatic sweeping wall of color with overscaled letters spelling the company name draws visitors into the space. Adding further drama, the seating display wall at the opposite side of the space is angled on both horizontal and vertical axes. Graphic images create a strong interpretive element upon the wall surface. Rounding out the composition is a quiet zone with case study stories including client and project photographs arranged on a system of three-dimensional matrix panels.
Creating a strong bond among all elements is the bright fresh color scheme. Grounded with pure white, the spring green and sky blue colors are consistent throughout graphics, columns, feature walls and product labels.

WHERE:
Neocon, Chicago, USA
WHEN:
10 - 12 June 2002
CLIENT:
Haworth., Design and Marketing Team
DESIGNER OF STAND:
Jan Lorenc, Mark Malaer
DESIGN TEAM:
Lorenc+Yoo Design:
Sakchai Rangsiyakorn, Steve McCall, Ken Boyd, Susie Caldwell Norris, Janice McCall
Haworth: Ken Krayer, Tracy Reed, Julie Blanton, Beth Parenteau, Marla Horton-Skym

GENERAL CONSTRUCTOR:
Xibitz, Grand Rapids MI
CONSULTANTS:
lighting: Illuminart, Ypsilanti MI
MANUFACTURERS:
Haworth furniture, Interface carpet
MATERIALS:
custom vinyl, custom-printed nylon fabric scrim, cold-form steel, stainless steel, MDF, acrylic
AREA:
1,950.9 m² (21,000 square feet)
PROJECT DURATION:
design and fabrication 6 months
OPENING:
10 June 2002

PROJECT:

ZAMIAS

LAS VEGAS, NV, USA

WHERE:
ICSC (International Council of Shopping Centers) Leasing Mall, Las Vegas, USA

WHEN:
19 - 22 May 2001

CLIENT:
Zamias Services, Reading PA

DESIGNER OF STAND:
Jan Lorenc, David Park

DESIGN TEAM:
Steve McCall, Veda Sammy, Susie Caldwell Norris, Janice McCall

PROJECT PRODUCER/DIRECTOR:
Journey Communications, Beth Cochran, Wayne PA

GENERAL CONSTRUCTOR:
Geograph Industries, Harrison OH

CONSULTANTS:
lighting: Ramon Luminance Design, Atlanta GA

MATERIALS:
aluminum, acrylic, Zolatone painted sonatubes, MDF with plastic laminate, fabric ceiling, cut-out sintra, custom lighting, custom tables, seating, conference room, and cabinetry

AREA:
483.1 m² (5,200 square feet)

BUDGET:
$ 90/square feet

PROJECT DURATION:
design and fabrication 6 months

OPENING:
May 2001

The sophisticated layout conveys the sense that retail marketplaces are descendents of the agora, or marketplace, established in ancient Greece. The main conference room serves as the 'temple' while additional meeting rooms serve as 'shops', each with a product collage display presenting a retail analogy. Carpet inlays tie the seating and colonnade into the overall composition. The exhibit establishes and develops a strong 'contemporary renaissance' image in concert with a complete array of graphic materials aimed at potential and existing clients. The exhibit design presents Zamias Services. as a company firmly grounded in tradition with its eye squarely focused on the future. This 'modern-classic' theme creates for visitors the impression of walking through a classical marketplace, surrounded by display windows filled with items for sale, while a graphic 'frieze' tells the company's story. Along with meeting spaces, lounge seating and interpretive display panels, there is a service area for 'The Pig & Whistle' restaurant, café seating and two private offices.

LORENC+YOO DESIGN grand stand

PROJECT:
LIFETIME MOVIE NETWORK
ANAHEIM, CA, USA

WHERE:
Western Cable Show, Anaheim, USA
WHEN:
January 1998
CLIENT:
Lifetime Movie Network
DESIGNER OF STAND:
Jan Lorenc
DESIGN TEAM:
Chung Youl Yoo, Steve McCall,
David Park, Gary Flesher,
Janice McCall,
Martha Bracey Henson
GENERAL CONSTRUCTOR:
MDM Scenery Works, Atlanta GA
CONSULTANTS:
lighting: Ramon Luminance Design,
Atlanta GA, Factor, Graphics,
Atlanta GA
MANUFACTURERS:
Live Wire chairs, Montreal, Canada
MATERIALS:
various wood veneers,
actual studio equipment
AREA:
232.3 m² (2,500 square feet)
BUDGET:
$ 650,000
PROJECT DURATION:
design and fabrication 12 months
OPENING:
January 1998

One corner of the exhibit space resembles a mini-studio complete with public and private areas, with peepholes into each. An upswept, curving cherry veneer wall supports messages and monitors which serve as a backdrop for the camera boom crane; in front is a protective blue-gray steel railing. On the other side of the wall are two semi-private areas: one is an L-shaped workroom whose outside walls facing the corridor are lined with Lifetime posters; the other is a wedge-shaped conference room bounded by translucent acrylic set in curved purple mullions, supported by a double layer of floating fabric scrim and a cherry-wood oculus. Another corner holds a 'living room' mock studio set, plus a monumental 'hearth' with some 150 Lifetime video cassettes and one large television screen. Freestanding obelisks are topped with light lenses fastened by metal straps which also embrace multi-sided poster displays. Nourishment and literature are offered at the cappuccino stand which reflects the form of the feature wall behind the crane. A rarity among booths usually designed with transience in mind, the set clearly displays a mind-set that expresses the rich life of interiors – a mindset, of course, that Lifetime wanted to express.

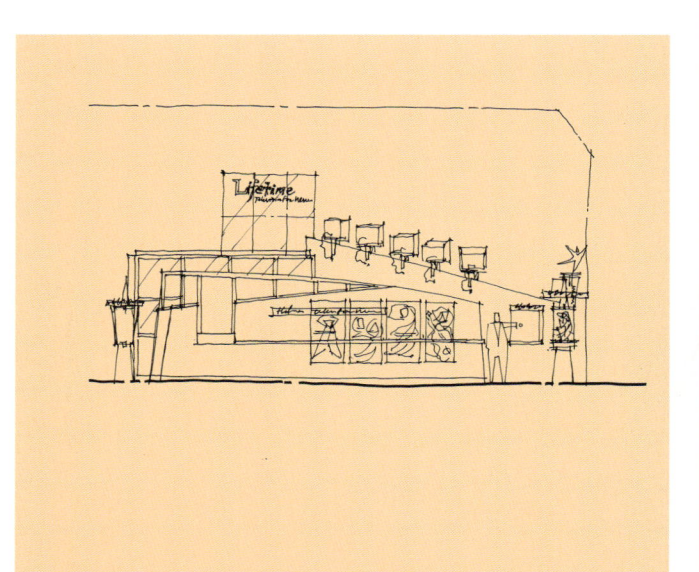

164
grand stand **LORENC+YOO DESIGN**

fetime
Elevatin
COMPE LING
Uplifting
Lifetime
LIFETIME
MOVIE NETWORK

PROJECT:
WORDSPRING DISCOVERY CENTER
ORLANDO FL, USA

WHERE:
WordSpring Discovery Center, Orlando, USA

WHEN:
November 2002

CLIENT:
Wycliffe Bible Translators

DESIGNER OF STAND:
Jan Lorenc, Chung Youl Yoo

DESIGN TEAM:
Steve McCall, Susie Caldwell Norris, David Park, Ken Boyd, Sakchai Rangsiyakorn, Gary Flesher

GENERAL CONSTRUCTOR:
1220 Exhibits, Nashville TN

CONSULTANTS:
lighting: Illuminart, Ypsilanti MI; Audio-Visual, Platt Design Group, Pasadena CA

MANUFACTURERS:
custom fabrication

MATERIALS:
natural hardwoods, corrugated metal, glulam beams, woven wood slats, whole logs, stucco, a kayak from New Guinea

AREA:
418.1 m² (4,500 square feet)

BUDGET:
$ 1,200,000

PROJECT DURATION:
design and fabrication 36 months

OPENING:
November 2002

The Wycliffe story is communicated through six separate areas of sculpted, sequentially-organized space. The areas are revealed in progression and include: Introduction, The Bible, Language, Modern Translation, The Process, and Involvement. For consistency from one area to the next, an overhead horizontal title band follows the perimeter walls within each space, forming a unifying datum line.

Streams of scrambled letters and text in different languages create ribbons of words that flow to the introductory gathering space and on to a global showcase of indigenously clothed and authentically sculpted human figures. Each band presents a different translated language. The language, population, location, and translation status are displayed in front of each figure and visitors may hear the language spoken from audio cones located above.

A circular theater is crafted from horizontal wood planks which resemble a village hut. The Language Area is centered upon an abstract wooden language tree. Over three thousand oval-shaped leaves hang from the tree, each containing the name of one language.

The entire exhibit communicates simultaneously with the scholar, the casual browser, and with children. Interactive provisions for kids throughout the exhibit encourage learning about other children and their languages around the globe.

grand stand **LORENC+YOO DESIGN**

LORENC+YOO DESIGN grand stand

COMPANY NAME:
LORENC+YOO DESIGN

HEAD OFFICE:
109 Vickery Street
Roswell, Georgia, 30075-4926
USA

PHONE:
+1 (770) 645 2828

FAX:
+1 (770) 998 2452

E-MAIL:
jan@lorencyoodesign.com

WEBSITE:
www.lorencyoodesign.com

OTHER LOCATIONS:
Philadelphia, USA
Seoul, Korea

MANAGEMENT:
Jan Lorenc
Chung Youl Yoo
Mark Malaer

CONTACTS:
Jan Lorenc

STAFF:
USA: 12
Korea: 2

KEY DESIGNERS:
Jan Lorenc
Chung Youl Yoo
Mark Malaer
David Park
Ken Boyd
Steve McCall
Gary Flesher

FOUNDED:
1978

MEMBER OF:
- SEGD
- AIA
- ICSC
- ASTC
- ACM

COMPANY PROFILE:
Lorenc+Yoo Design works with a variety of international clients on a diverse series of project types including trade show design, museum planning and exhibition design, interior design, furniture design, signage design and event design. The firm's staff of architects, interior designers, industrial designers, graphic designers, furniture designers, and journalists collaborate with the goal of creating a seamless environment with a unified narrative.

CLIENTS:
- Sony-Ericsson
- Haworth Furniture Company
- Children's Museum of South Carolina
- Gaylord Entertainment
- Lifetime Television
- Georgia-Pacific Corporation
- MCI-Worldcom
- Wycliffe Bible Translators
- Coca Cola Company
- E*Trade
- IBM
- Simon
- Bank of America
- North Carolina State University
- Lotte-Korea, Japan
- L'Oreal, Paris
- World Golf Village
- Urban Retail Properties
- General Growth Properties

SERVICES:
- Trade Show Design and Project - Management
- Museum Design
- Visitor Center Design
- Corporate Legacy Museum Design
- Signage Design
- Site Sculpture and Art
- Shop Design
- Theme Park/Event Design

AWARDS:
SEGD - Society for Environmental Graphic Design
- Jan Lorenc chosen for SEGD board of directors
- 2002 - First Union Exhibit - **Silver Award**
- 2001 - Jan Lorenc chosen to head International Design Competition Jury
- 2000 - Birmingham Airport Flight Sculpture
- 1999 - Donut King
- 1998 - Jan Lorenc selected as one of 25 Monuments to the Profession.
- 1998 - **Best Banner** at 25th Anniversary Convention Washington, DC 1998
- 1993 - **Merit Award** - Meridian
- 1990 - **Silver** - Mailboxes
- 1990 - **Silver** - Mailboxes Show
- 1990 - **Bronze** - MCI Construction Barricade
- 1987 - **Honor Award** - Meridian
- 1987 - **Award of Excellence** - Wildwood

Exhibitor Magazine
- 2003 - **Silver Award** - Sony-Ericsson
- 2002 - **Silver Award** - Palladium
- 2001 - **Silver Award** - Phillips Edison
- 1999 - **Silver Award** - Lifetime
- 1995 - **Silver Award** - Habitat for Humanity

ASLA - American Society of Landscape Architects
- 1993 - ASLA Georgia Chapter Oxmoor
- 1994 - Sandy Springs Revitalization
- 1998 - ASLA Illinois Chapter: Prairie Stone

Atlanta Urban Design Commission
- 1997 - Woodruff Arts Center
- 1992 - Nexus Arts Center

American Institute of Architects
- 1998 - Georgia Pacific Denver

Creative Club of Atlanta Show South
- 2002 - Sony-Ericsson
- 1995 - Georgia-Pacific Corporation - Georgia Center for Children - Bazaar Bizosso
- 1983 - Habitat for Humanity Pavilion - Wildwood

- Print Casebooks - Best in Environmental Graphics 1989, 1991, 1993, 1994
- Print Casebooks - Best In Exhibition Design - 1994
- ID 1994 Competition - Bazaar Bizosso

Georgia Institute of Technology - College of Architecture.
- 2000 - 2003 - Jan Lorenc chosen for Advisory Board for the College of Architecture Department of Industrial Design

STEP Inside Design-100 Competition
- 2003 - Sony-Ericsson

Signs of the Times
- 2003 - First place Orlando City Gate/Millenia
- Electric Signs 1987, 1988, 1990

Signs of the Times
- Commercial 1986, 1990

Graphis Design 2001
- McWane Center - Birmingham, AL
- Lifetime Exhibit - Anaheim, CA
- PREIT Exhibit - Las Vegas, NV
- ZAMIAS Exhibit - Las Vegas, NV

Graphis Design 2000
- Georgia Pacific - Denver
- Donut King - Atlanta

Graphis Design 1999
- Cool Springs - Nashville

Graphis Design 1997
- Georgia Pacific - Atlanta

Graphis Design 1996
- Georgia Center for Children

Graphis Design 1995
- Palmetto Expo Center

Graphis Corporate Identity 3
- Georgia-Pacific - Atlanta

Graphis Corporate Identity 4
- McWane Center - Birmingham, AL
- Continuum Exhibit - Las Vegas NV
- Georgia-Pacific - Denver
- First Union/Zamias Exhibit - Las Vegas NV
- Lifetime/Lifetime Movie Network
- PREIT Exhibit - Las Vegas NV

Trade Fair Design Annual 2002
Avedition, Berlin :11/2002
- Paladium
- Sony-Ericsson

Trade Fair Design Annual 2000
Avedition, Berlin :11/2000
- Lifetime
- First Union at ICSC

Small Stands Germany: 2002
- Paladium
- Habitat for Humanity

You Are Here: 100 Best of SEGD
ST Press 1999
- Palmetto Expo Center

Urban Identities
Madison Square Press 1999
- Birmingham Flight Sculptures

Festival Graphics
Madison Square Press 2000
- Bazaar Bizosso

Urban Entertainment Graphics
Madison Square Press 1997
- Malibu Grand Prix
- Habitat for Humanity
- Bazaar Bizosso

OPERATES:
Worldwide

STRATEGIC PARTNERSHIPS:
Journey Communications
295 East Swedesford Road
Wayne, Pennsylvania 19087, USA
beth@journeycommunications.com
www.journeycommunications.com

LORENC+YOO DESIGN KOREA:
CDR/Box&Cox,
4F, Bukang Building,
Nonhynn-dong, Kangnam-gu
Seoul, Korea
Tel: +82 2 541 5290
Fax: +82 2 541 2590
www.boxcox.com
jyoun@boxcox.com

MIGLIORE + SERVETTO ARCHITETTI ASSOCIATI
MILAN, ITALY

ABOUT

migliore+servetto

Ico Migliore and Mara Servetto graduated from the architecture faculty at Turin Polytecnic and became assistant professors of Achille Castiglioni at the Faculty of Architecture, Milan University. They went on to work in Milan in the field of architecture and exhibition design. Their exhibit designs are testing grounds for new communicative techniques closely linked to experimental uses of lighting and materials. They have designed exhibitions and installations for Giorgio Armani, Krizia, Pirelli, Tod's-Ferrari, Diego della Valle, Wally yacht, Boffi, Cesana and BTicino. Exhibits include 'Krizia Moving Shapes' at the Museum of Contemporary Art in Tokyo (2001), based on mobile display structures, and 'Dante Ferretti production designer' at the Academy of Motion Picture Arts and Sciences in Beverly Hills and at L.A.C.M.A. Museum in Los Angeles (2002). Their projects usually involve the overall management of the entire process, from the event concept to the organisation and planning of all phases in the realization of the event.

ICO MIGLIORE IS PROFESSOR IN EXHIBIT DESIGN AT THE FACULTY OF ARCHITECTURE, MILAN UNIVERSITY and Mara Servetto taught Industrial Design at the European Design Institute of Milan (IED). They have lectured at various universities in Italy and abroad. In 1999 they won the first prize in the invited competition 'Casa del Bianco' for a museum building; in the same year they finished the execution of Piazza Stradivari in the historical centre of Cremona Italy and in 2003 they won the ASAL awards first prize for the best exhibition design of 2002. Recently they designed the new concept store for the Iceberg Boutiques in Paris and with Philip Johnson the new flag ship store FAY for Diego della Valle in Milan. For Toroc they developed sports facilities projects for the Turin Olympic Games 2006. In 1998, a book on their work was published by L'Archivolto: *Ico Migliore and Mara Servetto: Work Journal and Fibreglass*.

FLUID AT ZERO GRAVITY Designing or setting up an event entails redefining a given space in which the temporary design of the 'setting' is a dynamic driving-force determining what people think and do within a densely-written 'script'. This design shifts from defining not just the setting but also the complex script of the total event, enabling designers to create in a given place a whole range of levels of perception and patterns of use. In terms of communication, this is why exhibit design is the best way of relating a work of art (or a piece of merchandise) to an audience. Given the ever-rising tide of images and messages coming from exhibitions, trade fairs and installations, the quality of an exhibit design increasingly determines the quality and

---

PROJECTS:
MIGLIORE + SERVETTO ARCHITETTI ASSOCIATI

PROJECT PAGE 172:
BTICINO EXHIBITION CONCEPT
EUROPE

PROJECT PAGE 174:
DRAWING DREAMS – DANTE FERRETTI
BEVERLY HILLS, USA

PROJECT PAGE 176:
TOD'S FERRARI EXHIBITION
MILAN, ITALY

communicative power of an event; and the main subject of the event is no longer the exhibit itself, still less its structuring, but the totality of the cognitive experience it is able to generate through dynamic relationships between the various actors – audience, exhibits, subject – involved in it.

EXHIBIT DESIGN ACTS ON THE PHYSICAL SPACE ASSIGNED TO IT USING COMPONENTS OF VARYING DENSITIES, such as dynamism/sequencing, interaction/movement, light/effects, graphics/image, density/emptiness, time/distance. Essentially, then, the exhibit is a fluid at zero gravity that can be designed in the three spatial dimensions, plus the fourth dimension, which is time. (...) Actual construction apart, the objective is, therefore, to produce something like a conceptual map of 'magnetic fields of attraction' designed to define the 'right time' and 'distance between things'.

THE DESIGN MUST BE ABLE TO TRANSFORM 'DORMANT' SPACES (ready-built structures, existing spaces in buildings, urban spaces) into places, potential supermarkets supplying culture and feeling. (...) Designers also define levels of learning and interpretation by determining how long it takes to tour the place, and how full spaces relate to empty ones. Like an individual letter in relation to the page design and narrative structure of a text, each element in an exhibit design has its own features but the completeness and meaning of the parts comes from the totality alone because the way the exhibits relate to one another is what gives them their meaning.

AN EXHIBITION OR DISPLAY IS A 'LANDSCAPE WITH A SHIFTING HORIZON' to which a multiplicity of objects and ideas are added, stratifying to form a totality which people interact with at different speeds and use in different ways, and in which the exhibit – artwork, merchandise, information – has to emerge clearly from the complexity of the whole.

(From Abitare N°426 - May 2003)

COMPANY STATEMENT MIGLIORE + SERVETTO

"A DYNAMIC RELATIONSHIP BETWEEN THE EXHIBITION AND THE VISITOR THROUGH THE LIGHT AND THE TECHNOLOGY"

PROJECT PAGE 178:
KRIZIA MOVING SHAPES
MOT, TOKYO, JAPAN

PROJECT PAGE 181:
KRIZIA WORLD
MILAN, ITALY

PROJECT PAGE 182:
'THE MAKING OF' PIRELLI CALENDAR 2002
MILAN, ITALY

MIGLIORE + SERVETTO ARCHITETTI ASSOCIATI grand stand

PROJECT:
BTICINO EXHIBITION CONCEPT
EUROPE

WHERE, WHEN AND AREA:
Saie due, Bologna, Italy,
March 2002, 220 m²
Lighting and Building, Frankfurt,
Germany, April 2002, 100 m²
Mediel, Naples, Italy,
May 2002, 200 m²
Interieur, Kortrijk, Belgium,
October 2002, 70 m²
Smau, Milan, Italy,
October 2002, 200 m²
Intel, Milan, Italy
May 2003, 2400 m²

CLIENT:
BTicino

DESIGNER OF STAND:
Ico Migliore and Mara Servetto

DESIGN TEAM:
Hwang Seon Mi, Frederik
De Wachter, Alessandro Costariol,
Laurent Léon, Cheng Yu Ming

GRAPHICS:
Ico Migliore, Alessandro Costariol
and Massimo Pitis,
Italo Lupi (Intel 2003)

GENERAL CONSTRUCTOR:
Eurofiere, Turin,
Eurostands, Milan (Intel 2003)

MATERIALS:
glass, mirrored walls
polycarbonate and laquered wood,
brushed steel, backlit printed PVC
screen, electro-luminescents

PROJECT DURATION:
various

PHOTOGRAPHER:
Donato di Bello, Milan
Wolf & Wolf, Gent (Interieur 2002)

In the stand for Intel 2003, an entrance ramp placed next to the reception leads to the central exhibition area, a kind of single large square with a floor that gradually slopes from an altitude of +1.30 to an altitude of 0.00. Inside this ideal square the presence of other containers, featuring products, graphic design and dynamic animation, aims to offer a clear insight into the quality of BTicino products, in spite of the complexity of its output and history.
A mirror runs along the entire rear wall, making the space appear twice as large, duplicating the image of the other nine tall self-supporting elements in which the BTicino products are grouped by categories or families.
Nine large round screens (dia 270 cm) with continuous projection, placed in front of each element, tell the story of the products through a projection of images and graphics, while a screen measuring 24 x 2.5 metres, covering an entire wall, features a series of animated motifs and images. The animations, almost like real physical elements in the exhibition interior, move in a computerized and synchronized manner through the different screens, rendering the product communication very dynamic.
On the right side of the space there are three lateral rooms that offer tests and interactive experiences, allowing greater concentration and a more in-depth knowledge of the new systems and products.

Since 2002, the Migliore + Servetto studio has managed the image of BTicino in relation to exhibition interiors, with various projects. In particular, for presenting the domestic My Home system, it has created an exhibition interior concept which involves the visitor in a direct and exhaustive experimentation. For the Saie due stand, in an open and accessible space without obligatory itineraries, single domestic environments are reproduced in the form of essential elements and quotations, on a slightly reduced scale. These elements, scattered freely in the space, superimposed in different perspectives, create a plurality of possible domestic landscapes. For the purposes of offering a more strictly product-related communication, on the contrary, as in the Interieur stand, tall, striking luminous elements characterize the interior.

MIGLIORE + SERVETTO ARCHITETTI ASSOCIATI grand stand

PROJECT:
TOD'S FERRARI EXHIBITION
MILAN, ITALY

WHERE:
ex - officine Riva Calzoni, Milan, Italy
WHEN:
June 2001
CLIENT:
Tod's - Ferrari
DESIGNER OF STAND:
Ico Migliore and Mara Servetto
DESIGN TEAM:
Marcella Bonacina, Roberto Siena, Lyu Hyung Min
GENERAL CONSTRUCTOR:
Allestimenti Benfenati, Milan
MATERIALS:
backlit screens: opalescent PVC
volumes: black laquered wood
images: printed on stretched cotton
suspended display cabinets: laquered wood and polycarbonate
floor: painted concrete
platforms: laquered wood
AREA:
2,700 m²
PROJECT DURATION:
2 months
OPENING:
26 June 2001
PHOTOGRAPHER:
Donato di Bello, Milan

This is a fluid and expansive design that defines the disposition of the exhibits and other elements of the exhibition in relation to the place. The public is allowed free movement among the various magnetic poles of the exhibition. On the rear wall, two large screens show a range of film trailers on world of cars, curated by Lucchino Gastel.
At the entrance to the exhibition, close-ups of Tod's products by Giovanni Gastel hang from three large black volumes.
In the main room, tall display units, with light strips in the upper part, are suspended above floor level and placed along an irregular grid. Below their bases, different coloured lighting indicates three different exhibition themes. Screened by polycarbonate sheeting, the units display Tod's products and materials together with Ferrari-related objects. Dynamic projections and video projections of personalities from the world of cinema and automobiles constitute an integral part of the exhibition design. Standing on platforms located at the four sides of the exhibition, teams of craftsmen offer a live demonstration of the different stages in product-making.

177
MIGLIORE + SERVETTO ARCHITETTI ASSOCIATI grand stand

PROJECT:
KRIZIA MOVING SHAPES
MOT, TOKYO, JAPAN

WHERE:
Museum of Contemporary Art of Tokyo - MOT, Tokyo, Japan
WHEN:
November - December 2001
CLIENT:
Krizia
DESIGNER OF STAND:
Ico Migliore and Mara Servetto
DESIGN TEAM:
Frederik De Wachter,
Hwang Seon Mi, Marcella Bonacina
GRAPHIC DESIGN:
Italo Lupi
FASHION CURATOR:
Gabriella Pescucci,
assisted by Shizu Omachi
GENERAL CONSTRUCTOR:
Tecnolegno, Cormano, Milano
VIDEO AND ELECTRONIC SYSTEM:
Eletech, Seveso, Milano
MATERIALS:
portals: polished steel,
motorised volumes: steel structure and tensed gauze,
suspended volumes: steel structure and printed textile
polycarbonate panels covered with polarised film
projection screen: white clothing
walls at the rear: specchio piuma
AREA:
1,000 m²
PROJECT DURATION:
6 months
OPENING:
20 November 2001
PHOTOGRAPHER:
Studio M2, Tokyo

The design is conceived as a circular itinerary that passes through the different theme areas of the exhibition. Each of these areas is characterised by a different setting.
The exhibition design is filled with large and simple displays that animate the museum space.
The furnishing of the space is coherent with the large, spacious exposition hall of the museum. The large spaces underscore the dynamic of the design, which is no longer experienced as a static entity, but as a moving spectacle. This was realised with the help of the right lighting and motorised technical elements.
The first exhibition area contains a large wall devoted to knitwear. This is followed by a rectangular room where six tall structural steel portals, regularly placed at the centre, contain six groups of fashions arranged in themes and suspended above floor level. Beyond this, a gallery displays a Krizia-related strip-cartoon designed by Guido Crepax.
The gallery leads to the main room where large suspended volumes move upwards and downwards progressively revealing seven different families of clothing.
In the last area, dynamic graphics are projected upon a large screen made of white knitwear. Juxtaposing the projection are eight suspended polycarbonate sheets covered by a specially polarised film that allows the clothing to be viewed only from certain points. In this way, fashions are alternately revealed and concealed to the passing visitor.

grand stand **MIGLIORE + SERVETTO ARCHITETTI ASSOCIATI**

MIGLIORE + SERVETTO ARCHITETTI ASSOCIATI grand stand

PROJECT:
KRIZIA MOVING SHAPES
MOT, TOKYO, JAPAN

180
grand stand **MIGLIORE + SERVETTO ARCHITETTI ASSOCIATI**

PROJECT:
KRIZIA WORLD
MILAN, ITALY

WHERE:
Spazio Krizia, Milan, Italy
WHEN:
Milan fashion week, June-July 1999
CLIENT:
Krizia
DESIGNER OF STAND:
Ico Migliore and Mara Servetto
DESIGN TEAM:
Giancarlo Baroni, Lyu Hyung Min
GRAPHICS:
Ico Migliore and Marcella Bonacina
GENERAL CONSTRUCTOR:
Gefit, Milan
MATERIALS:
transparent PVC spheres,
(dia 150 -180 cm)
aerial support (suspension) system:
steel cables with motor system
AREA:
550 m²
PROJECT DURATION:
2 months
OPENING:
30 June 1999
PHOTOGRAPHER:
Lorenzo Scaccini, Milan

The design integrates the selection of fashions on show with the presence of public in a single staging.
In addition to the aesthetic qualities of both textiles and clothing, the design of the stand also reflects their quality of lightness and dynamic wearability. Twenty-five transparent bubbles are hung in a regular grid within a surreal black space. Inside of each bubble, a different item of clothing is suspended and lit from below. A motor system controls the vertical movement of the bubbles according to a pre-established pattern. This movement is further enhanced by the horizontal fluctuation of the bubbles caused by the public's movement within the stand.
Bright projections of pictures, fashions, textiles and graphic elements on walls and floor add a further dynamic element to this space.
However much the designs float in the air, they are still clearly visible for the public. Without being able to touch them, people can observe them from all sides down to the finest details.

MIGLIORE + SERVETTO ARCHITETTI ASSOCIATI grand stand

PROJECT:
'THE MAKING OF' PIRELLI CALENDAR 2002
MILAN, ITALY

WHERE:
Teatro Armani, Milan, Italy

NAME OF PROJECT:
'The Making of' Pirelli calendar 2002 by Peter Lindbergh

WHEN:
October 2001

CLIENT:
Armani, Pirelli

DESIGNER OF STAND:
Ico Migliore and Mara Servetto

GRAPHICS:
Migliore + Servetto, Architetti Associati

DESIGN TEAM:
Anna Mantero

GENERAL CONSTRUCTOR:
Allestimenti Benfenati, Milan

MATERIALS:
images on transparent polyester, original prints on aluminium plate

AREA:
450 m²

PROJECT DURATION:
1 month

OPENING:
1 October 2001

PHOTOGRAPHER:
Donato di Bello, Milan

A series of images printed on polyester, placed transversally so that each image visually overlaps with others, provides a broad and variable picture of the overall work of the Pirelli calender 2002's designer, Peter Lindbergh.
On the left side of the room, a display of the original prints, curated by the photographer, allows for a detailed viewing of each single image.
The use of natural light underlines the transparency of the suspended panels and permits an overall view of the space. On the rear wall, natural light has been artificially intensified in order to emphasise the overlapping effect of the panels, as on an exaggerated lightbox.
On the left side of the room, photographs are lit by a system of pointers anchored to the ceiling. These perfectly frame each single image and create a series of planes of light markedly detached from the wall that allow for a high quality vision of each sigle photographic image.

grand stand MIGLIORE + SERVETTO ARCHITETTI ASSOCIATI

MIGLIORE + SERVETTO ARCHITETTI ASSOCIATI grand stand

COMPANY NAME:
MIGLIORE + SERVETTO
ARCHITETTI ASSOCIATI

HEAD OFFICE:
Viale Col di Lana 8
20136 Milan
Italy

PHONE:
+39 02 89 42 01 74

FAX:
+39 02 45 49 02 51

E-MAIL:
mail@miglioreservetto.com

WEBSITE:
www.miglioreservetto.com

MANAGEMENT:
Ico Migliore
Mara Servetto

CONTACTS:
Seon Mi Hwang

STAFF:
12

KEY DESIGNERS:
Ico Migliore
Mara Servetto

FOUNDED:
1997

COMPANY PROFILE:
Including an international team of architects and graphic designers, studio M+S (aa) concentrates on exhibition design and architecture. The exhibition design projects aim to create a strong dialogue between the exhibits and the visitor. The firm seeks to provide of a full-circle experience of discovery and involvement through the use of lighting and new communication technologies such as animated graphics and dynamic projections, together with a strong application of new materials. Ico Migliore is professor of Exhibition Design at the Faculty of Architecture of Milan.

CLIENTS:
- Giorgio Armani
- Tod's
- Krizia
- Iceberg-Gilmar Div. Ind.
- Hogan
- Time Warner Company
- Cesanamedia
- City of Cremona
- BTicino
- Comitato Olimpico Torino 2006
- Inter-F.C: Internazionale Milano
- Pirelli
- Cesana
- Cinecittà Holding
- Boffi
- Fay
- Wallpaper Magazine

SERVICES:
- Architecture
- Exhibition and stand design
- Event design
- Retail design
- Graphic design

AWARDS:
- 1st prize ASAL 2002 for the best exhibition design of 2002
- 1st Prize Competition on invitation Casa di Bianco Exhibition and Commercial Building, Cremona, 1999
- 1st prize Competition on invitation 'Uciwa funs', Fukuoka, Japan, 1996

OPERATES:
Worldwide

OIL FOR 3D COMMUNICATIONS

AMSTERDAM, THE NETHERLANDS

ABOUT

oil for 3d communications

According to the Amsterdam firm Oil for 3D Communications, exhibition and event design is highly marketing-oriented. The message needs to be coherent. In practice, determining the right strategy seems to be the hardest task. Clients love to hide behind their signs and displays, but underestimate their audience by doing so. According to Oil, visitors want to be surprised in a simple and intelligent fashion. To achieve this, a client needs to completely reveal himself.

OIL FOR 3D COMMUNICATIONS WAS FOUNDED IN 1996 and has five employees, of whom three are designers. The firm is clear about its position in the market: Oil begins where the advertising agency stops. Oil can easily compete with architecture firms or advertising agencies, who, although they often make beautiful exhibits, generally underestimate the communicative aspect. A stand should in fact be considered a three-dimensional billboard, since it is about communication in a spatial environment. Design is meant to serve the message.

IN THE OPINION OF OIL, THE BIGGEST STUMBLING BLOCK is the client, since it often takes so much effort to make them understand the point of stands and trade shows. Clients generally prefer to manifest themselves as uncontroversially as possible. They are afraid that their exhibit will be too distinctive, and that visitors will say so. Clients often prefer to hide behind their signs and product displays. But that is, in fact, not the solution. This is where Oil believes the process actually starts: telling the client what not to do. For example, it is best not to blow up the whole brochure and stick it on the walls, or to simply blow up the ad. Instead, the client needs to open himself up and find the courage to put himself on the line together with the design firm. It is important to convince the client that everything revolves around what the trade-show attendee wants! How does he actually experience the stand, what is his impression? Often, a visitor has walked a great distance before reaching the stand in question.

FOR EVERY PROJECT, OIL LIKES TO START FRESH and with an open mind, in order to clarify what the company stands for. The client might see that a design is beautiful or has a certain feel to it, but expressing the true character of the company is a completely different story. What is at the heart of the desired communication? At the end of the day, the message has to be powerful and unambiguous, with one clear voice. It is of crucial importance to find out what the current position of the company is and how it perceives its future development; if necessary, the entire marketing strategy will be read to discover this. The oil-rig in Oil's logo stands as a metaphor for their work method: analogous to the process of drilling for oil, they often need to

PROJECTS:
OIL FOR 3D COMMUNICATIONS

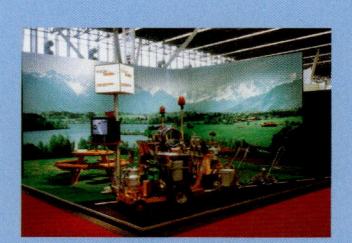

PROJECT PAGE 188:
LET'S GO
INTERTRAFFIC, AMSTERDAM,
THE NETHERLANDS

PROJECT PAGE 190:
THE FACE OF A NEW COMPANY
IGC, AMSTERDAM,
THE NETHERLANDS

dig deeply before something valuable comes to the surface. Generalities simply do not suffice.

IN THE STAND DESIGNS THAT OIL MADE FOR NEW SKIES – a European company that sells satellite connections – the development of the company is clearly visible. Every stand reflects a different marketing strategy: from the development of a recognisable identity through 'branding' to the presentation of a service-oriented company with a well-established reputation. For this later phase, Oil came up with a light and airy exhibit incorporating the symbolism and rhetoric of an airline company ('first class connections'), where service comes first. People were received directly at the stand by two hostesses, who offered coffee from their serving carts and also handed out brochures and small gifts. This was also in response to the many kilometres the visitors had in some cases already walked by the time they reached the stand. These people were exhausted, had sore feet and were not interested in complicated stories.

OIL TRIES TO HELP THE CLIENT UNDERSTAND that it is important to surprise the intended audience in an intelligent fashion. Exhibits should offer a certain level of entertainment if people are to remember them. It is the client's decision to what extent and in what manner they want to surprise the visitors, be it in a subdued fashion or by really pulling out all the stops like New Skies in their most recent stand, where people were seduced with optical effects. The design consisted of a simple rectangular box, with enormous prints of the New York skyline applied on the inside of the long sides. By putting on 3D glasses, the visitor felt he was actually on a rooftop in New York looking down at the skyscrapers. The space was dissected by a long reception table set against a mirror. Whoever walked into the booth perceived the table as twice as long, thanks to the mirror. With simple instruments a strong effect is achieved.

P. BIESEMAN, ACCOUNTANT OIL COMPANY STATEMENT

"OH, IF ONLY THERE WERE NO DESIGNERS, IT WOULD MAKE LIFE SO MUCH EASIER"

PROJECT PAGE 192:
NEW HORIZONS
IBC, AMSTERDAM,
THE NETHERLANDS

PROJECT PAGE 194:
FIRST CLASS CONNECTIONS
IBC, AMSTERDAM,
THE NETHERLANDS

PROJECT PAGE 196:
PICNIC ON TOP OF THE WORLD IBC, AMSTERDAM,
THE NETHERLANDS

PROJECT PAGE 198:
THE ORANGE EXPERIENCE
CONVENTION FACTORY,
AMSTERDAM, THE NETHERLANDS

grand stand **OIL FOR 3D COMMUNICATIONS**

PROJECT:
LET'S GO
INTERTRAFFIC, AMSTERDAM,
THE NETHERLANDS

WHERE:
Intertraffic, Amsterdam,
The Netherlands
WHEN:
April 2002
CLIENT:
Basler Lacke and Wyssbrod
MARKET SECTOR:
road marking paint and machines
DESIGNER OF STAND:
Oil
DESIGNER:
Tjø van Zuijlen
GENERAL CONSTRUCTOR:
Wim Hees Interbouw, Aalsmeer,
The Netherlands
PRINTER:
Vertical Vision, Weesp,
The Netherlands
MATERIALS:
printed wallpaper, artificial grass,
picnic furniture
AREA:
42 m²
PROJECT DURATION:
5 days

Remarkable plainness and Swiss hospitality make an effective presentation. Two Swiss companies combined to participate in a traffic technology trade fair in The Netherlands. One of them improved its road marking machines, the other came up with a new paint. With their innovative products they are both ready for the big job. So why not raise a glass of wine and drink success, together with your visitors, on a lovely alpine meadow?

189

OIL FOR 3D COMMUNICATIONS grand stand

PROJECT:
THE FACE OF A NEW COMPANY
IBC, AMSTERDAM,
THE NETHERLANDS

WHERE:
IBC, Amsterdam, The Netherlands
WHEN:
September 1999
CLIENT:
New Skies Satellites
MARKET SECTOR:
satellite communication provider
DESIGNER OF STAND:
Oil
DESIGN TEAM:
Paul Pennock, Tjø van Zuijlen
GENERAL CONSTRUCTOR:
Dehullu Project, Ochten,
The Netherlands
MATERIALS:
various, from conventional to high tech plastics and stretch fabric
AREA:
50 m²
PROJECT DURATION:
5 days

Being a newcomer in the technically focused market of satellite communication, New Skies needs a distinguishing face. Adding a third dimension to the corporate identity does the trick. The design communicates New Skies' activities and spirit of worldwide communication through space, but with an unusual approach. The stand is built around a collection of caricature-like pieces of furniture. Together they create an extra-ordinary atmosphere of friendlines, accessibility, elegance.

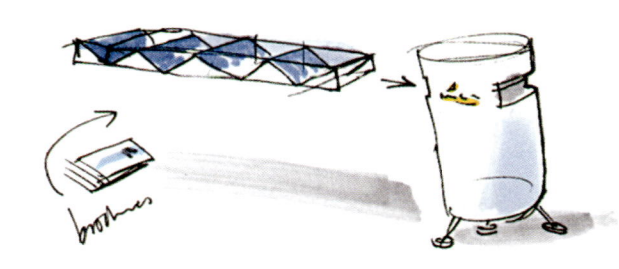

OIL FOR 3D COMMUNICATIONS grand stand

NEWskies
SATELLITES
NSS 7
The Atlantic broadband neighborhood
new networks
satellites
group

PROJECT:
NEW HORIZONS
IBC, AMSTERDAM,
THE NETHERLANDS

WHERE:
IBC, Amsterdam, The Netherlands
WHEN:
September 2000
CLIENT:
New Skies Satellites
MARKET SECTOR:
satellite communication provider
DESIGNER OF STAND:
Oil
DESIGN TEAM:
Paul Pennock, Tjø van Zuijlen
GENERAL CONSTRUCTOR:
Formule C, Weesp, The Netherlands
CONSULTANTS:
metal constructions: Henneke Metal Works, Zaandam, The Netherlands
PRINTER:
Vertical Vision, Weesp, The Netherlands
MATERIALS:
aluminium, stretch fabric and acrylic
AREA:
100 m²
PROJECT DURATION:
5 days

New Skies is a promising satellite enterprise, offering its clients the prospect of new services, new technology and new products. Solidified satellite beams dominate the image of this presentation. Together they form a cosmopolitan skyline. Each beam reaches out to a different part of the earth, printed on the carpets of the sitting areas, allowing visitors to take a seat in their favourite part of the world. The towers are made of light metal construction kits and are being used at exhibitions all over the world. Together with the rest of the modular furniture, new presentations with an equally clear effect can easily be composed.

OIL FOR 3D COMMUNICATIONS grand stand

PROJECT:
FIRST CLASS CONNECTIONS
IBC, AMSTERDAM,
THE NETHERLANDS

WHERE:
IBC, Amsterdam, The Netherlands

WHEN:
September 2001

CLIENT:
New Skies Satellites

MARKET SECTOR:
satellite communication provider

DESIGNER OF STAND:
Oil

DESIGN TEAM:
Paul Pennock, Tjø van Zuijlen

GENERAL CONSTRUCTOR:
Formule C, Weesp, The Netherlands

CONSULTANTS:
ExpoTech lighting, Amsterdam,
The Netherlands

PRINTER:
Vertical Vision, Weesp,
The Netherlands

MATERIALS:
aluminium, printed open screen,
fabric, conventional and theatre
lighting

AREA:
110 m²

PROJECT DURATION:
5 days

For a satellite enterprise the sky is a busy place. But how do you visualize a concept like that? Participating in this trade fair gave Oil the challenge of selecting the right companies communicating by satellite. Therefore the theme – first class connections – is fit for dual interpretation. In this stand, the references to aviation create a feel of large-scale international business. The design is based on sky and lightness. The fabric choices and a subtle light arrangement create an atmosphere of thin air. Aeroplane trolleys distribute information, drinks and give-aways.

grand stand **OIL FOR 3D COMMUNICATIONS**

NEWskies
SATELLITES
NEWskies
SATELLITES
first class
connections
performance
internet access
NSS-7
the atlantic
first class
connections
welcome

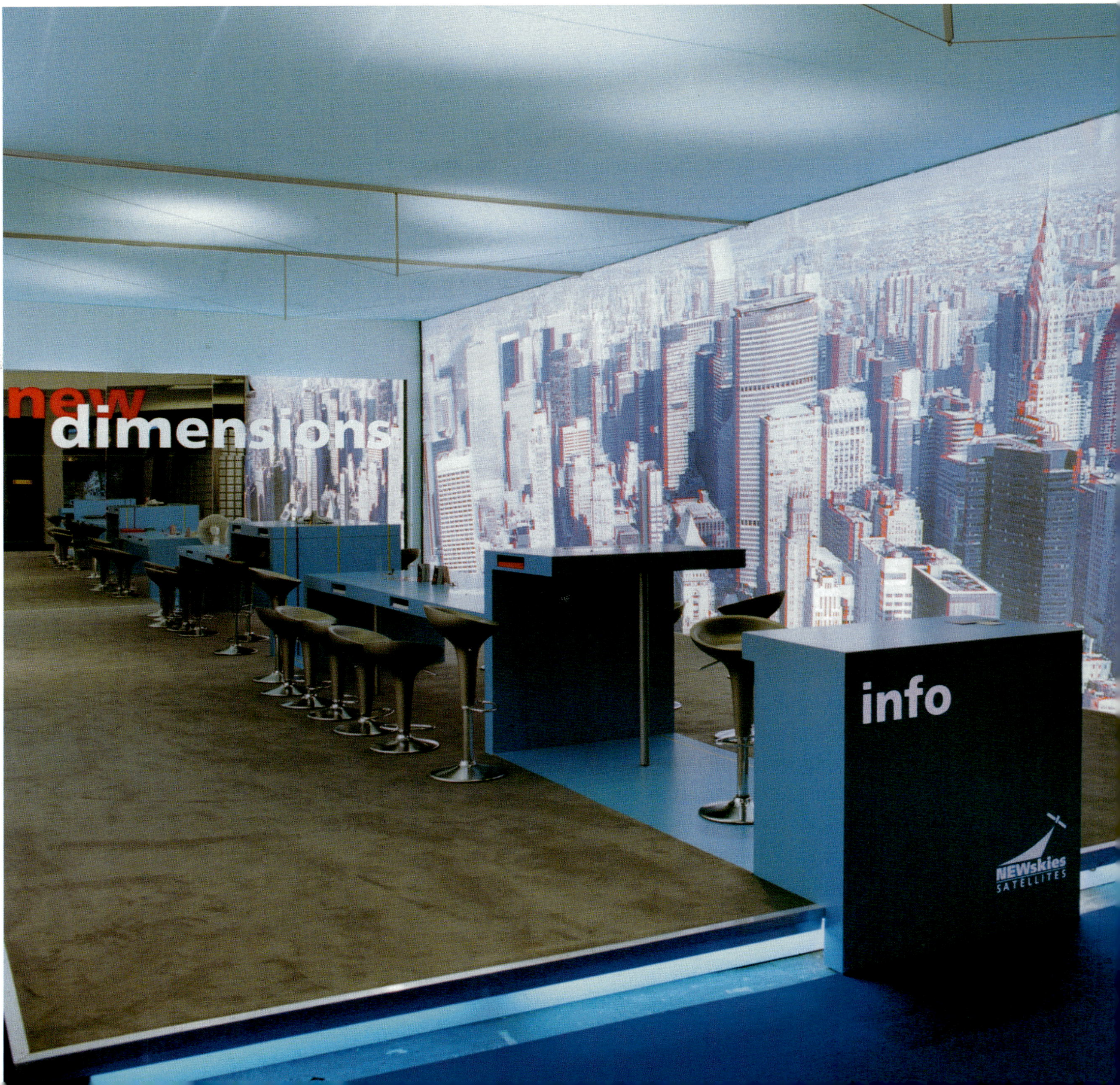
new
dimensions
info
NEWskies
SATELLITES

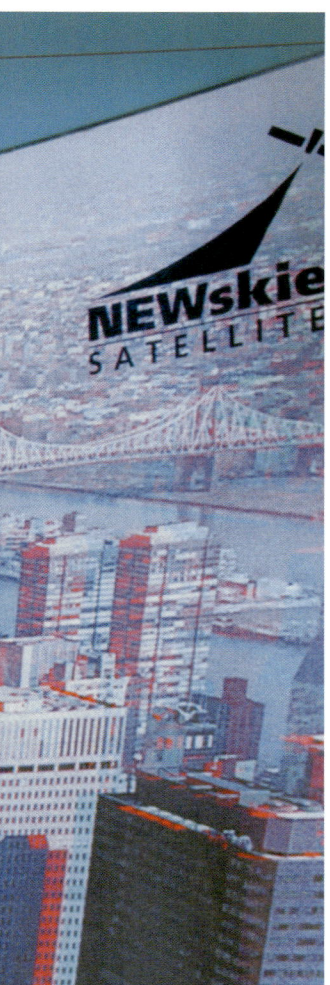

PROJECT:
PICNIC ON TOP OF THE WORLD IBC, AMSTERDAM, THE NETHERLANDS

WHERE:
IBC, Amsterdam, The Netherlands
WHEN:
September 2002
CLIENT:
New Skies Satellites
MARKET SECTOR:
satellite communication provider
DESIGNER OF STAND:
Oil
DESIGN TEAM:
Paul Pennock, Tjø van Zuijlen, Lawrence Kwakye
GENERAL CONSTRUCTOR:
Formule C
CONSULTANTS
graphics: Pinsharp, UK
PRINTER:
Exposize, Eindhoven, The Netherlands
MATERIALS:
printed bisonyl, light boxes
AREA:
98 m²
PROJECT DURATION:
5 days

During one of the major trade fairs for the broadcast industry, New Skies invited all 'global communicators' for a picnic. The food came from the various countries in which New Skies is doing business. The world is represented on a table on which New Skies' satellite network is displayed. Wearing 3D glasses, one can imagine being on the roof of a skyscraper in a metropolitan setting. A modest design and a simple 3D effect turn the stand into an unexpected and remarkable experience. Moreover a relatively small area sudddenly looks quite spacious.

197
grand stand

198
grand stand **OIL FOR 3D COMMUNICATIONS**

PROJECT:

THE ORANGE EXPERIENCE

CONVENTION FACTORY, AMSTERDAM, THE NETHERLANDS

WHERE:
The Orange experience, roadshow throughout The Netherlands

WHEN:
January - March 2003

CLIENT:
Orange

MARKET SECTOR:
wireless telecommunications

DESIGNER OF EVENT:
Oil

DESIGN TEAM:
Lawrence Kwakye, Paul Pennock, Tjø van Zuijlen

GENERAL CONSTRUCTOR
Formule C, Weesp, The Netherlands

CONSULTANTS:
various

MATERIALS:
various

AREA:
3,600 m²

PROJECT DURATION:
5 days

Some brands are so special that they need to be experienced with all the senses. The launch of Orange in The Netherlands was supported by a series of events for their partners, business contacts, distributors and retailers. An atmosphere with the look, feel and values of the Orange identity familiarised them wih the brand. A first, 'soft' introduction was made in a living room-like environment in a truck that visited the target group. After that, the Orange relations were invited to an event that revealed content, products and services. By continually addressing people in an unexpected manner, the distinguishing aspects of Orange were made tangible.

OIL FOR 3D COMMUNICATIONS grand stand

COMPANY NAME:
OIL FOR 3D COMMUNICATIONS

HEAD OFFICE:
Cornelis Schuytstraat 2
1071 JH Amsterdam
The Netherlands

PHONE:
+31 (0)20 626 25 26

FAX:
+31 (0)20 626 25 66

E-MAIL:
info@oil.nl

WEBSITE:
www.oil.nl

MANAGEMENT:
Paul Pennock

STAFF:
6

KEY DESIGNERS:
Paul Pennock
Tjø van Zuijlen
Lawrence Kwakye

FOUNDED:
1996

MEMBER OF:
BNO, Association of Dutch Designers

COMPANY PROFILE:
Purpose: to design surroundings so that they represent the message a client wants to get across. Communication made tangible.
Foundations: various design disciplines. With curiosity as a binding factor. Together our foundations for developing concepts for threedimensional communication.
Result: unexpected, but careful answers to communication needs.

CLIENTS:
- New Skies Satellites
- Orange
- Vialis Traffic and Mobility

SERVICES:
- Exhibition and stand concept and design
- Event concept and design
- All other kinds of 3D design
- Graphic design
- Multi media

OPERATES:
Worldwide

PROMHOUSE
ALMERE, THE NETHERLANDS

grand stand

PROJECT:
HANS BARTELDS ZAAL
UTRECHT, THE NETHERLANDS

WHERE:
Utrecht, The Netherlands
WHEN:
December 2002
CLIENT:
Amev
(division of the Fortis group)
MARKET SECTOR:
finance
DESIGNER:
Promhouse Exhibition Design + Strategy
GENERAL CONSTRUCTOR:
Amev Facilitair Bedrijf
LIGHTING DESIGN:
Promhouse Exhibition Design + Strategy
GRAPHICS:
Promhouse Exhibition Design + Strategy
MATERIALS:
cabinets: spray-painted MDF
furniture: Artifort
displays: custom made, spray-painted MDF, glass
floor: carpet
walls: graphics, custom-made bookshelves, 'parking spaces' for showcases, sanded-glass sunblinds
ceiling: custom-made cassette system with integrated lighting and air conditioning
AREA:
115 m²
DURATION OF PROJECT:
March - December 2002

The room is dedicated to Hans Bartelds' achievements for Amev, a division of the Fortis group. Images on the walls represent the current employees of the company and the showcases contain objects telling the story of his career. The colours reflect and represent the Amev corporate identity. The showcases can be 'parked' in the walls to create clear space for official ceremonies.

PROMHOUSE grand stand

grand stand **PROMHOUSE**

PROJECT:
INTERNATIONALE FUNK AUSSTELLUNG 2001
BERLIN, GERMANY

WHERE:
Internationale Funk Ausstellung, Berlin, Germany

WHEN:
25 August - 2 September 2001

CLIENT:
Super Audio CD (cooperation between Philips & Sony)

MARKET SECTOR:
consumer electronics

DESIGNER:
Promhouse Exhibition Design + Strategy

GENERAL CONSTRUCTOR:
Van den Oever Expo Groep

LIGHTING DESIGN:
Aukes Theatertechniek

GRAPHICS:
Promhouse Exhibition Design + Strategy

MATERIALS:
floor: white laminate floor panels
interior walls: white laminate panels
exterior walls: Plexiglas SACD boxes in a steel structure
walls listening areas: coloured velour padded panels
counters: white laminate, stainless steel
lighting: stage colours, colour frame strips & Gobo projectors

AREA:
220 m² ground floor & 102 m² upper floor

DURATION OF PROJECT:
first concept developed March 2001

This project aimed to create a platform which increase awareness of the SACD. The structure consisted of a steel structure with 200,000 empty SACD boxes. The Plexiglas walls were used as a surface for projected images and messages and were constantly changing colour.

PROMHOUSE grand stand

PROJECT:
EUROSHOP 2002
DUSSELDORF, GERMANY

WHERE:
Euroshop 2002, Düsseldorf, Germany
WHEN:
23 - 27 February 2002
CLIENT:
Vink Holding
MARKET SECTOR:
semi-finished plastics
DESIGNER:
Promhouse Exhibition Design + Strategy
GENERAL CONSTRUCTOR:
Beemsterboer
LIGHTING DESIGN:
Promhouse Exhibition Design + Strategy
GRAPHICS:
Promhouse Exhibition Design + Strategy
MATERIALS:
An open curved steel construction combined with the material of the client
floor: a floating floor uplit from below made of yellow laminated floor panels
product units samples from Vink: steel carriers with semi-finished plastic samples of Vink
lightboxes: Vink lightboxes with product information
furniture : yellow-black laminate bar and tables
lighting: yellow tube lights under the floor and as ceiling
AREA:
127.5 m²
PROJECT DURATION:
4 months

The curved segments have the shape of a tunnel, encouraging visitors to walk inside and continue towards the other side of the stand. By fully incorporating the material of Vink Kunststoffen in the stand, we have generated maximum exposure of the physical product Vink can offer. At the same time, because people tend to wander around the stand, there is the optimum chance for communication. The open parts allow visitors feel at ease.

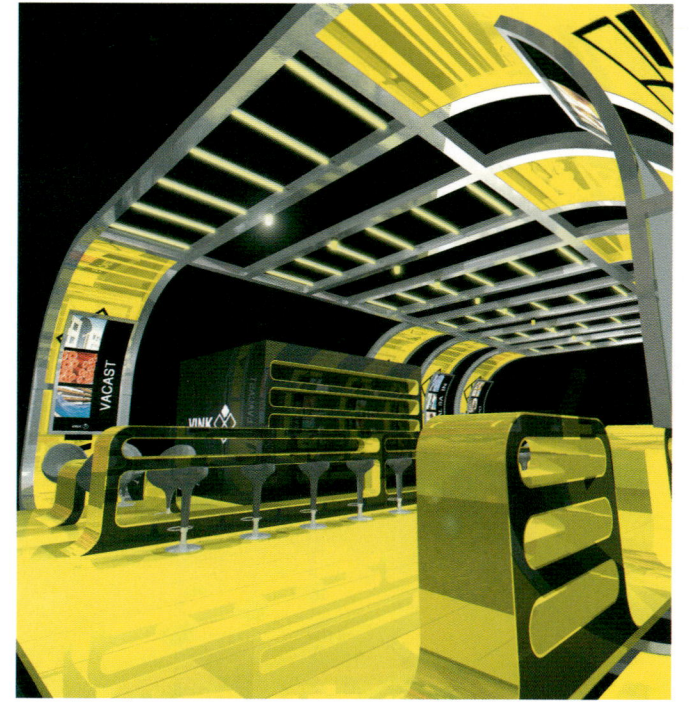

208
grand stand **PROMHOUSE**

PROMHOUSE grand stand

grand stand PROMHOUSE

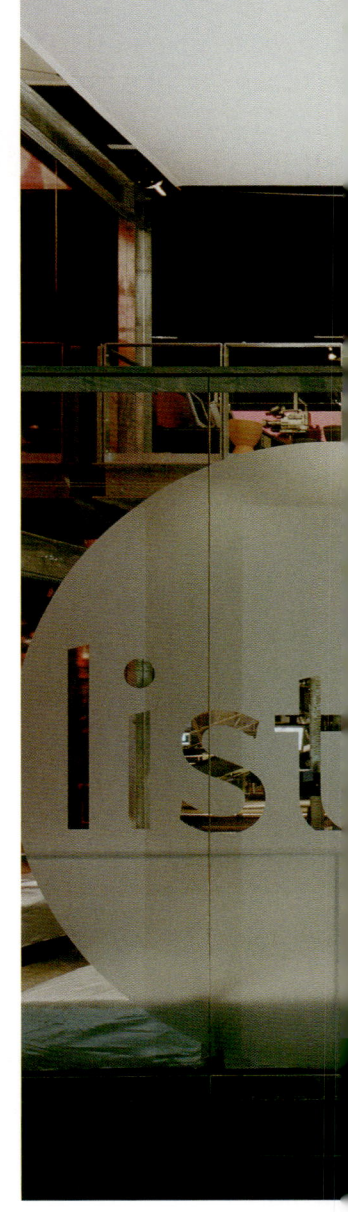

PROJECT:
**INTERNATIONAL BROAD-
CASTING CONVENTION 2001**
AMSTERDAM, THE NETHERLANDS

WHERE:
International Broadcasting
Convention 2001, Amsterdam,
The Netherlands
WHEN:
14 - 18 September 2001
CLIENT:
SONY Business Europe
MARKET SECTOR:
professional broadcast
DESIGNER:
Promhouse Exhibition Design +
Strategy
GENERAL CONSTRUCTOR:
Hypsos
LIGHTING DESIGN:
Promhouse Exhibition Design +
Strategy
GRAPHICS:
Promhouse Exhibition Design +
Strategy
MATERIALS:
floor: genuine hall floor
basic structure: galvanised steel
all walls: thoughened glass panels
displays: custom made, steel epoxy
coated and spray-painted MDF
AREA:
836 m² ground floor &
360 m² upper floor
DURATION OF PROJECT:
7 months

Maximum transparency represents the Sony desire for both openness and dialogue with customers. Prints of the human brain symbolise the sharing of knowledge. The upper level is reserved for product demonstrations.

PROJECT:
**INTERNATIONAL BROAD-
CASTING CONVENTION 2002**
AMSTERDAM, THE NETHERLANDS

Building on 2001's transparency and openness, the design provides a 'platform' for visitors and, crucially, dialogue. Innovative applications are showcased in sunken 'hotspots', retaining the overall feel of spaciousness and openness.

WHERE:
International Broadcasting Convention 2002, Amsterdam, The Netherlands

WHEN:
13 - 17 September 2002

CLIENT:
Sony Business Europe

MARKET SECTOR:
professional broadcast

DESIGNER:
Promhouse Exhibition Design + Strategy

GENERAL CONSTRUCTOR:
Beemsterboer

LIGHTING DESIGN:
Promhouse Exhibition Design + Strategy

GRAPHICS:
Promhouse Exhibition Design + Strategy

MATERIALS:
floor, walls: wooden construction, laminate finish
meeting rooms: galvanised steel and glass panels
displays: epoxy-coated steel, spray-painted MDF

AREA:
836 m² ground floor

DURATION OF PROJECT:
1 month

PROMHOUSE grand stand

energis
e-business + telecoms solutions
energis
e-business + telecoms solutions
energis

IP VPN
ADSL
Corporate Voice
0800 IP
Managed Webhosting
Streaming Media
BUY IT
direct
BUY IT

PROJECT:
THE INTERNETWORKING EVENT 2002
AMSTERDAM, THE NETHERLANDS

WHERE:
The InterNetworking Event 2002, Amsterdam, The Netherlands
WHEN:
3 - 5 April 2002
CLIENT:
Energis
MARKET SECTOR:
Telecommunication
DESIGNER:
Promhouse Exhibition Design + Strategy
GENERAL CONSTRUCTOR:
Beemsterboer
LIGHTING DESIGN:
Promhouse Exhibition Design + Strategy
GRAPHICS:
Promhouse Exhibition Design + Strategy
MATERIALS:
floor: wooden construction, white laminate finish, carpet
walls: epoxy-coated steel construction with fluorescent panels
furniture and displays: custom made, steel, Plexiglas, illuminated base
AREA:
90 m² ground floor
DURATION OF PROJECT:
1 year

Promhouse translated the new Energis corporate identity into a stand design that enhances the brand feeling not just for those outside but also for the company members. Images and messages are projected onto fluorescent panels that are recognisable from a distance. Colours, layout and fonts are chosen carefully to support the key messages. Flexible yet always recognisable, the image remains consistent even in the smallest presentation.

PROMHOUSE grand stand

COMPANY NAME:
PROMHOUSE EXHIBITION DESIGN + STRATEGY

HEAD OFFICE:
Ambachtsmark 83 + 84
1355 EG Almere
The Netherlands

PHONE:
+31 (0)36 531 36 66

FAX:
+31 (0)36 531 76 41

E-MAIL:
info@promhouse.com

WEBSITE:
www.promhouse.com

MANAGEMENT:
Jos Beijen
Ton Wittebol

CONTACTS:
Jos Beijen
Ton Wittebol

STAFF:
15

KEY DESIGNERS:
Jos Beijen
Beate Palluck
Mark van Luyk
Ton Wittebol

FOUNDED:
1991

CLIENTS:
- AMEV
- Blaze Technologies
- BT Ignite
- Dentsu/Canon Europe
- Energis
- Fortis Bank
- Industrie Maurizio Peruzzo
- Lucent Technologies
- Mitsubishi Paper
- O_2 Netherlands
- Philips International
- Scitex Vision
- Sony Business Europe
- Vink Kunststoffen

SERVICES:
- Exhibition Design & Strategy
- Retail Design & Concepts
- Communication Design & Strategies
- Event Design

OPERATES:
Worldwide

RAUMSCHIFF

HAMBURG, GERMANY

raumschiff

ABOUT raumschiff

In recent years, the team of the Hamburg firm Raumschiff (German for 'spaceship') arrived at an innovative approach to company presentations. The principle of non-classical communication is at the core of the efforts of business economist Jogi Jörn and designer Christian Kaul to put successfully into practice maximum brand and product perception by means of multi-facetted communication measures. Raumschiff places great importance on creating an effective, unique trade fair presence; however, they also stress the need not to limit the company or product presentation to this level, but also to create sufficient space for new conceptual structures.

RAUMSCHIFF BEGINS ITS SEARCH FOR A SUITABLE CONCEPT for a brand's presentation by determining where the emphasis can best be placed. It does this by considering the widest potential array of possible 'platform solutions'. Accordingly, their repertoire of ideas is not limited to the formulation of a stand's design, but rather, they strive to find the optimal context of presentation specifically for the product involved. But since Raumschiff defines itself as a communication agency, the search for a concept starts, as a rule, free of any notions of a spatial nature. They arrive at a set of conceptually rich ideas which will assure the perfect communication of the product statement and translate it into a completely thought-out exhibition concept. In turn, Raumschiff's designers create their design by transforming these communication insights into three dimensions.

RAUMSCHIFF BEGAN WHEN AN INTERDISCIPLINARY TEAM OF DESIGNERS, concept designers, interaction artists, architects, programmers, engineers, marketing specialists and consultants succeeded in accomplishing the difficult task of bringing together the typically separate worlds of communication design and the creative solutions of a future-oriented agency for spatial design. In this way a complex background, rich in disciplines, served as the birthplace of projects characterised by both accessibility and lasting retention value, and which established innovative presentation platforms such as fully-equipped promotional vehicles which function as mobile advertisement ambassadors.

NO LESS EXCITING ARE THE CONCEPTS WHICH THE FIRM has realised for theme and science parks, trade marketing, road shows, trade fairs and events, concepts which always embody the goal of integrative communication. Striking, minimalistic, sensitive and subtle, Raumschiff's installations never come across as heavy or cumbersome. And despite this reserve, their concepts grab hold of visitors with their communicative power and an impressive retention

PROJECTS:
RAUMSCHIFF

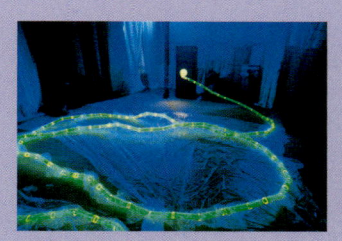

PROJECT PAGE 220:
ENBW PRODUCT PRESENTATION
STATE OF BADEN WURTTEMBERG, GERMANY

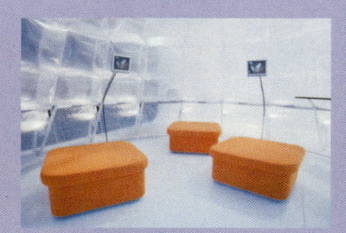

PROJECT PAGE 223:
FUTUREROOM INSTALLATION
EUROSHOP, DUSSELDORF, GERMANY

PROJECT PAGE 224:
HAIRWORLD 2000
BERLIN, GERMANY

PROJECT PAGE 226:
HYATT EUROPEAN PRESENTATION
BERLIN, GERMANY

value, often surprising them with their clever, playful effects.

FOR EACH PROJECT, THE TEAM'S RICHLY INVENTIVE INTERACTION ARTISTS create in their own idea workshop imaginative, intelligent solutions with the help of state-of-the-art technical know-how. One of the design agency's unique features is its vast arsenal of previously developed interaction concepts. These permit the creation of illusions which can give prospective customers the impression of being a part of the installation. These techniques enable them to package a message in such a way that it remains in the mind of visitors long after them visit. Interactive game modules and exhibits amaze and fascinate with their technical refinement, sparking the observer's curiosity as to the high-tech secrets behind the scenes. Who wouldn't get curious if a feather on a monitor reacted to a person blowing on it? In this way the points to be communicated to visitors of a trade fair or promotion are given clear visual articulation in an entertaining manner through an intuitive and direct interaction, typically based on a real action which causes an immediate virtual re-action.

BUILDING ON THE TECHNICAL SYSTEM SOLUTIONS DEVELOPED for individual product presentations and marketing projects, the firm established an additional field of operation: Futureroom Promotion Systems. Futureroom develops and distributes high quality multi-functional systems for promotions, (special) events, and point-of-sale presentations. Raumschiff's successful individual productions served as the launch pad for this free-standing distributor of economical product design series in easy-to-use quality, with a contemporary appearance and functionality.

A LOOK AT FUTUREROOM'S WIDE RANGE OF PRODUCTS REVEALS such original products as a multi-functional, inflatable PVC dome, a remote-controlled, illuminated service station or modern plastic membrane architecture as roofing for event locations. Futureroom offers the customer effective exhibition architecture, destined to contribute to the total success of a project's promotional effectivity. With all its projects, it is Raumschiff's aim to pursue innovative directions, to create new communication-based spaces and concepts.

COMPANY STATEMENT RAUMSCHIFF

"LOADING BRANDS WITH EMOTION AND CREATING UNIQUENESS IS THE NAME OF THE GAME"

PROJECT PAGE 227:
GAUSS EUROPEAN PRESENTATIONS
VARIOUS LOCATIONS

PROJECT PAGE 228:
DANFOSS TEST STATION
NORDBORG, DENMARK

PROJECT PAGE 230:
SCHILL & SEILACHER PRODUCT PRESENTATION
HAMBURG, GERMANY

PROJECT PAGE 231:
BLUE BULL
VIENNA, AUSTRIA

grand stand **RAUMSCHIFF**

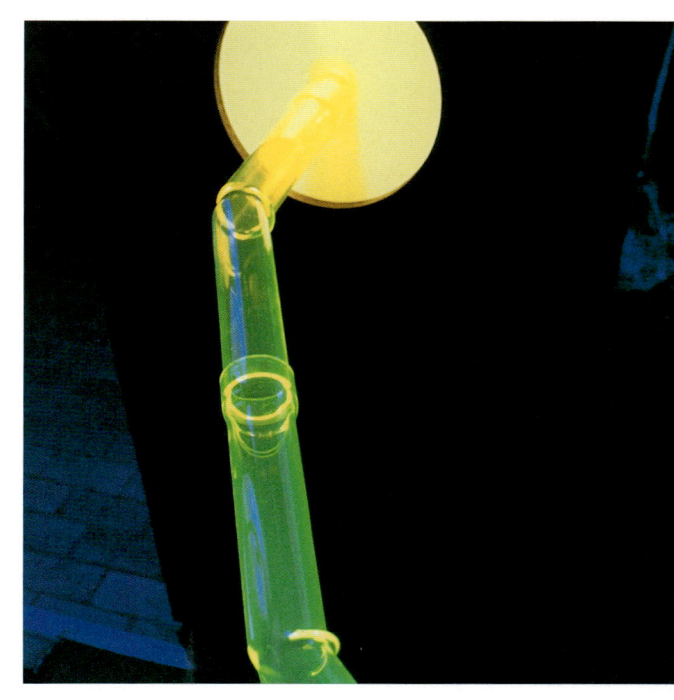

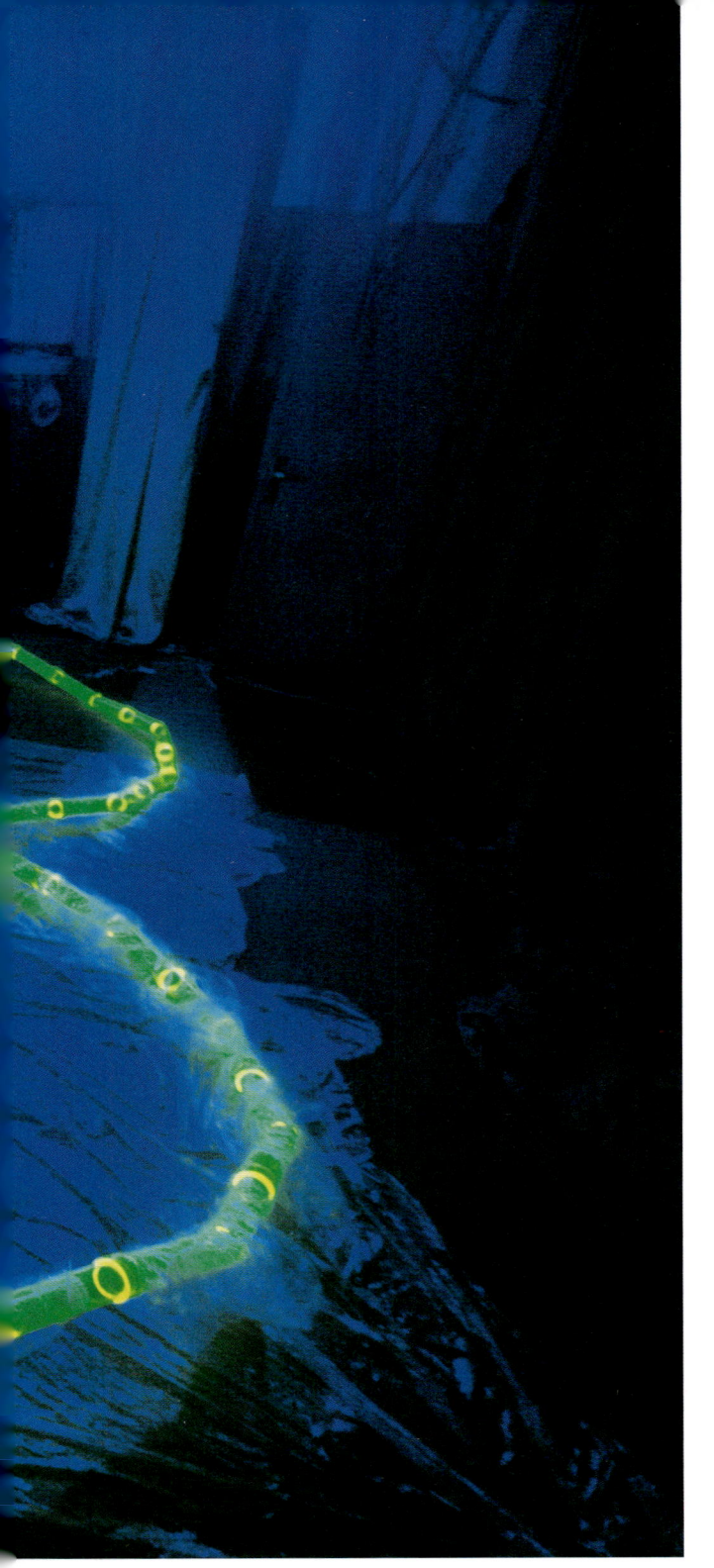

PROJECT:
ENBW PRODUCT PRESENTATION
STATE OF BADEN WÜRTTEMBERG, GERMANY

WHERE:
EnBW product presentation, Baden Württemberg, Germany
WHEN:
2000
CLIENT:
EnBW
MARKET SECTOR:
energy
DESIGNER OF STAND:
Uli Winters
DESIGN TEAM:
Markus de Seriis, Steven Cichon
GENERAL CONSTRUCTOR:
Quasar, Wiesbaden, Germany
MATERIALS:
steel, Plexiglas, PVC
AREA:
120 m²
BUDGET:
€ 70,000 for production/logistics excl. fair costs
PROJECT DURATION:
3 months

For an event being organised by Energie Baden-Württemberg, Raumschiff is in the process of developing six modules, which together will comprise an interactive total environment. The object of the installation is to translate into visual form, and give emotional content to, the different categories of energy consumption, such as warmth, cold, and technical gases. Raumschiff created six play situations in which visitors were directly oriented with the features of the individual categories of energy consumption in an emotionally charged manner. For example, a 'hook-up' was awarded to participants who succeeded in preventing the 4 metres high inflatable snowman from 'melting' by turning the cold-lamp crank vigorously enough.   >>

PROJECT

ENBW PRODUCT PRESENTATION
STATE OF BADEN WÜRTTEMBERG,
GERMANY

Prizes were awarded as well to those who succeeded in getting their energy and that of their team-mates to flow into a steam table, and in so doing, starting up a steam engine simply by placing a hand on it. In addition, a self-propelled robot was developed which functioned as a roving bar, inviting visitors to partake of a drink.
The distinctive Raumschiff design integrates this 'emotional experience' into an architectonic framework. As a result, the Mindblow-Set, in which participants inflate a helium balloon by concentrating, became a hit at the fair, having high entertainment value not only for the participants but for the large audiences it attracted. The concepts to be communicated were translated by means of the emotional involvement stimulated.

grand stand **RAUMSCHIFF**

PROJECT:
FUTUREROOM INSTALLATION
EUROSHOP, DÜSSELDORF, GERMANY

WHERE:
Euroshop, Düsseldorf, Germany
WHEN:
2002
CLIENT:
Futureroom, Hamburg
MARKET SECTOR:
promotion systems
DESIGNER OF STAND:
Christian Kaul
DESIGN TEAM:
Theresa Becker, Niels Flade
MATERIALS:
wood, aluminium, PVC
AREA:
63 m²
BUDGET:
€ 42,000 for production/logistics excl. fair costs
PROJECT DURATION:
6 weeks

The Futureroom installation for the 2002 Euroshop trade fair in Düsseldorf clearly reflected an orientation toward intelligent and futuristic design, but its open form enabled it to highlight the products on display – namely Futureroom's intelligent high-end promotion solutions – without distracting from them. Raumschiff constructed the installation measuring 7 x 9 metres from one single element: a concave surface which, similar to a photographer's backdrop, has a geometrically neutralising effect, making it possible to place products before a kind of indefinite, undefined space. The installation is painted completely in white, thus maximising the contrast with the silver and orange colours of the products.
A spherical sound environment enabled visitors to be entirely enclosed in the Futureroom World.

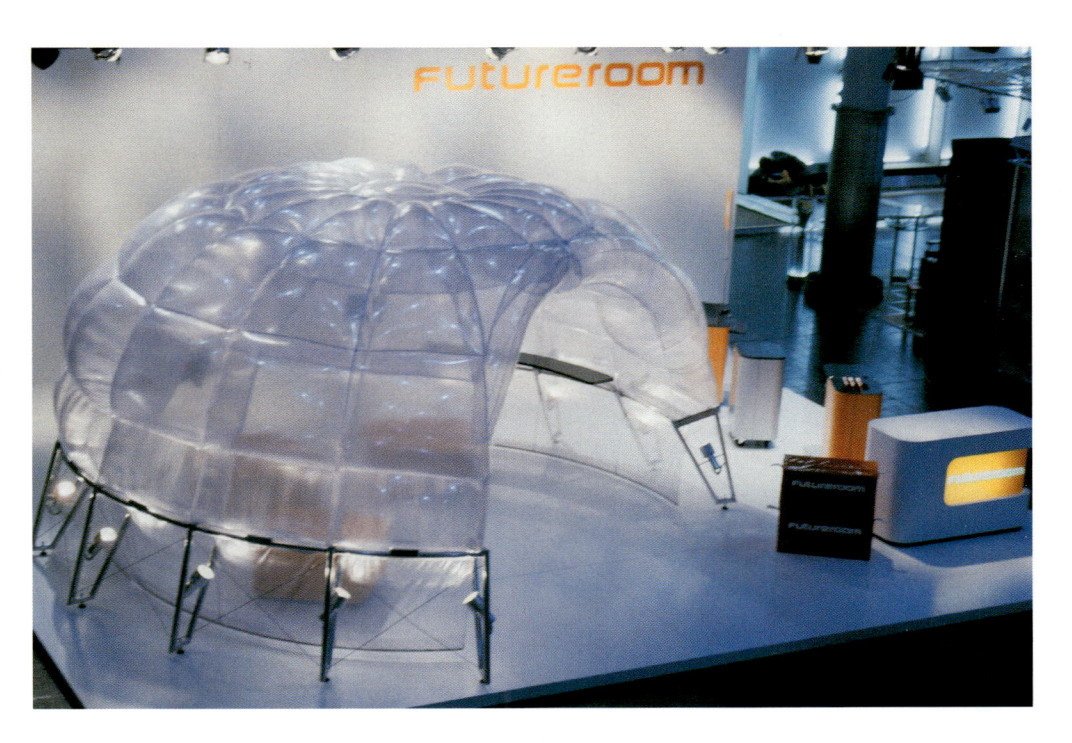

RAUMSCHIFF grand stand

grand stand **RAUMSCHIFF**

PROJECT:
HAIRWORLD 2000
BERLIN, GERMANY

WHERE:
Hairworld 2000, Berlin, Germany
WHEN:
2000
CLIENT:
Schwarzkopf Professional
MARKET SECTOR:
Cosmetics
DESIGNER OF STAND:
Christian Kaul
DESIGN TEAM:
Niels Flade, Alexander Keip
GENERAL CONSTRUCTOR:
Michael Vagedes, Hamburg, Germany
MATERIAL:
wood, Plexiglas, gauze, metal
AREA:
1,250 m²
BUDGET:
€ 600,000 for production/logistics excl. fair costs
PROJECT DURATION:
1 year

This 1,250 m² installation was the highlight of the Hairworld 2000 trade fair in Berlin.
Perfect lighting and a harmonious yet variegated design concept organised the individual categories and production lines in a clear and unambiguous manner. However, despite the mass of the product presentations involved, Raumschiff achieved a lightness and transparency welcomed as an innovation at the fair.
From the floor cushions of the chill-out areas, on which one could relax and watch the non-stop show, to the spacy white-and-silver dance and stage areas and the production worlds (called *Media* and *Interactive*): everywhere, the visitor could see, smell and experience the individual products and innovations. Clear colour zones and large printed motifs guided the visitor through the world of Schwarzkopf Professional.

225
RAUMSCHIFF grand stand

PROJECT:
HYATT EUROPEAN PRESENTATION
BERLIN, GERMANY

WHERE:
Hyatt European Presentation,
Berlin, Germany
WHEN:
2000
CLIENT:
Hyatt International Hotels & Resorts
MARKET SECTOR:
hotels
DESIGNER OF INSTALLATION:
Christian Kaul
DESIGN TEAM:
Alexander Keip
MATERIALS:
wood, glass, natural stone, foam elements
AREA:
60 m²
BUDGET:
€ 50,000 for production/logistics excl. fair costs

Brightly coloured glass surfaces in the floor stand for the Hyatt Group's three hotel types. The communication areas are demarked by means of painting-like suspended wall elements. The amorphous cushion modules, a modern transformation of the luxurious cushion wall motif, play a central role in the presentation. In combination with a severe, classic use of form, this yields an installation with both modern flair and elegance.

grand stand **RAUMSCHIFF**

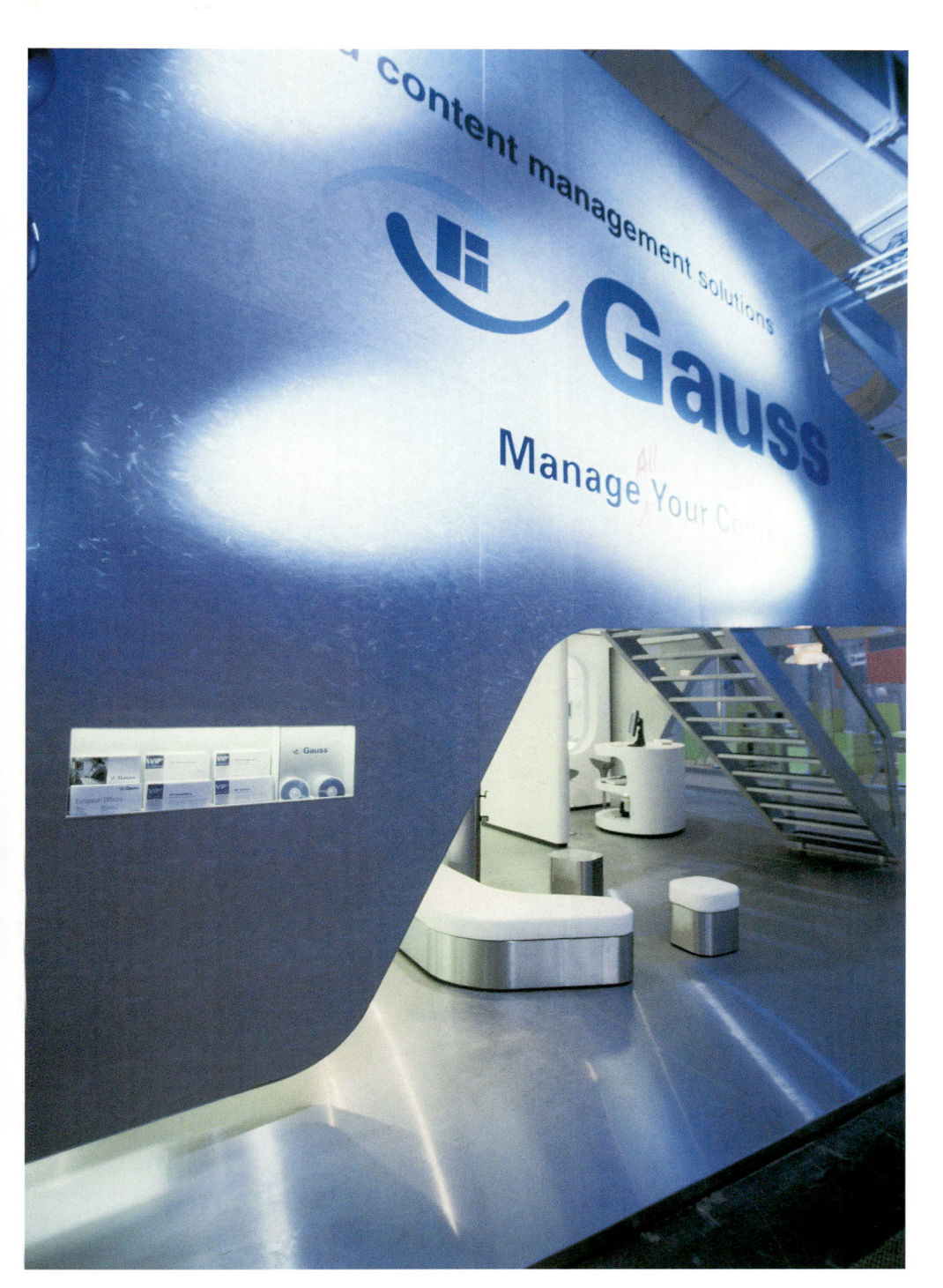

PROJECT:
GAUSS EUROPEAN PRESENTATIONS
VARIOUS LOCATIONS

WHERE:
various locations, including: Hannover (CeBIT), Berlin, Germany, Stockholm and London

WHEN:
2001

CLIENT:
Gauss Interprise, Hamburg

MARKET SECTOR:
content management software

DESIGNER OF STAND:
Alexander Keip

DESIGN TEAM:
Niels Flade, Stefan Ehrhardt

MANUFACTURERS:
Metron, Germany

MATERIALS:
PVC, metal, foils,

AREA:
60 - 180 m²

BUDGET:
€ 700,000 for production/logistics excl. fair costs

PROJECT DURATION:
1 year

Gauss Interprise develops content management software featuring organisation and filter functions. In translating Gauss' software products into visual form, Raumschiff drew inspiration from intercellular processes in the field of biochemistry. For example, the installation's amorphous shell represents a semi-permeable membrane which, similar to the Internet, makes selective information exchange possible. This organic design is complemented by the external skin's moiré foil which resembles the sparkling liquid substance of cell structures. The visitors become 'carriers', 'diffusing' from the outside to the inside, in turn winding up in the flowing forms of a white high-tech cave. Conceived as a modular system, the installation has been used for the widest possible variety of presentations in Europe.

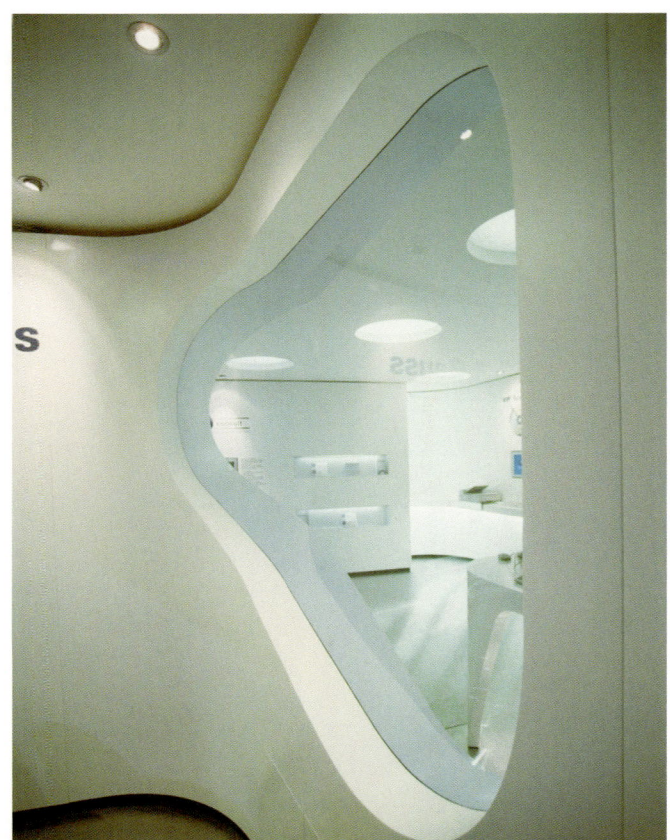

RAUMSCHIFF grand stand

PROJECT:
DANFOSS TEST STATION
NORDBORG, DENMARK

WHERE:
Nordborg, Denmark
WHEN:
2002
CLIENT:
Danfoss
MARKET SECTOR:
regulation systems
DESIGNER OF STAND:
Christoph Ebener
DESIGN TEAM:
Marcus de Seriis, Steven Cichon
GENERAL CONSTRUCTOR:
Raumschiff
MATERIALS:
metal, rubber, wood, mollitan, Plexiglas
AREA:
140 m²
BUDGET:
€ 250,000 for production/logistics excl. fair costs
PROJECT DURATION:
3 months

Raumschiff developed an experience space for children and adolescents. As one of Denmark's largest companies, Danfoss wanted to stimulate interest among young people in science and technology.

In realising this goal, Raumschiff employed its ideal fuel mixture of competence and experience in the fields of architecture and design combined with expertise in the area of interactive modules. With the help of attractive hands-on exhibits, visitors could travel into space in consistently thematic architecture and explore the fascinating world of astronomy. The highpoint of the trip was the Coriolis Room, which revolved with its visitors inside, enabling these astronauts to experience at first hand the physical peculiarities of rotating systems.

Because it could draw on all the competencies called for by such a project, Raumschiff was able to create a holistic experience-design – rather than just a space furnished with exhibits – propelling the art of the trade fair installation into a new dimension.

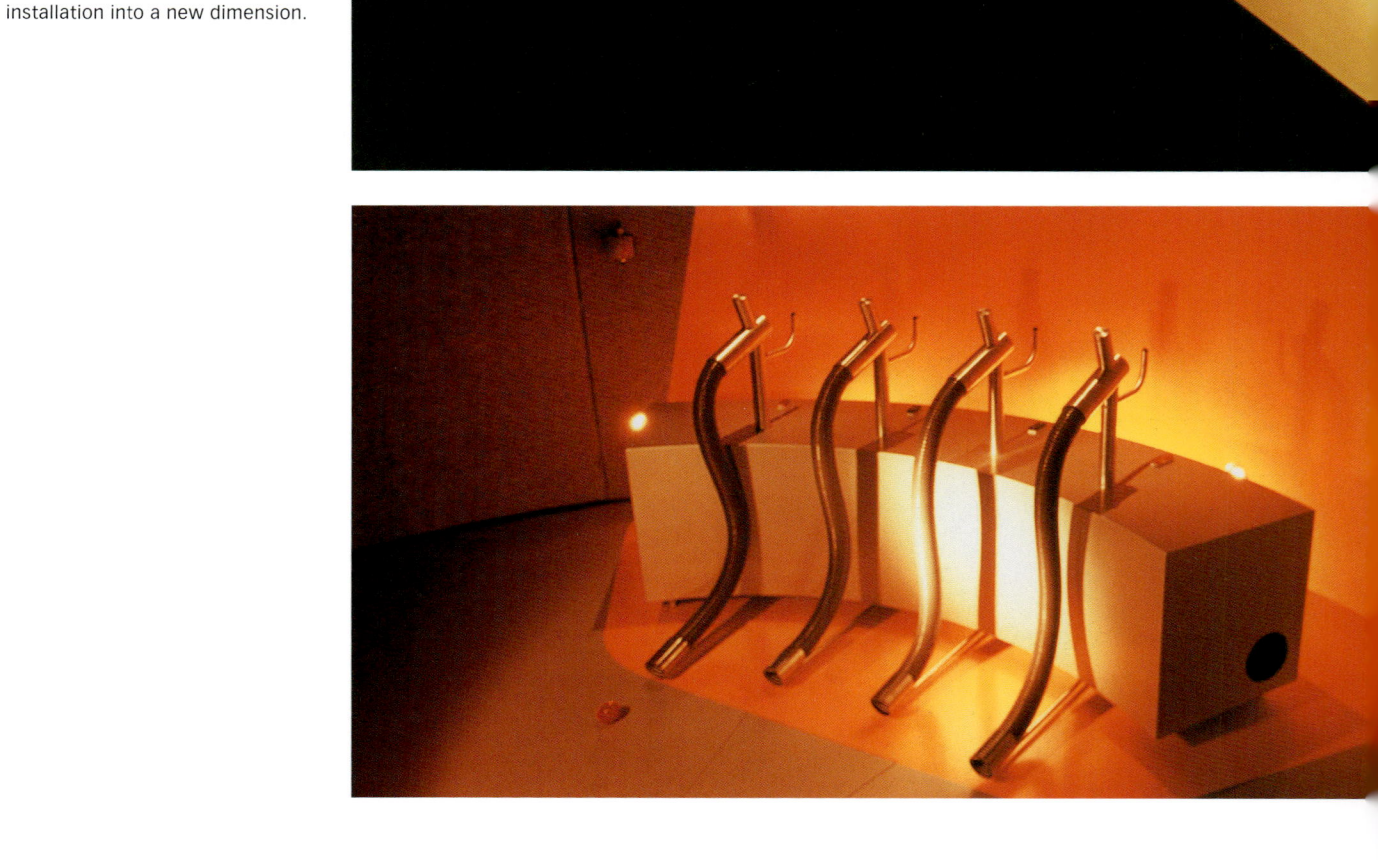

229
grand stand

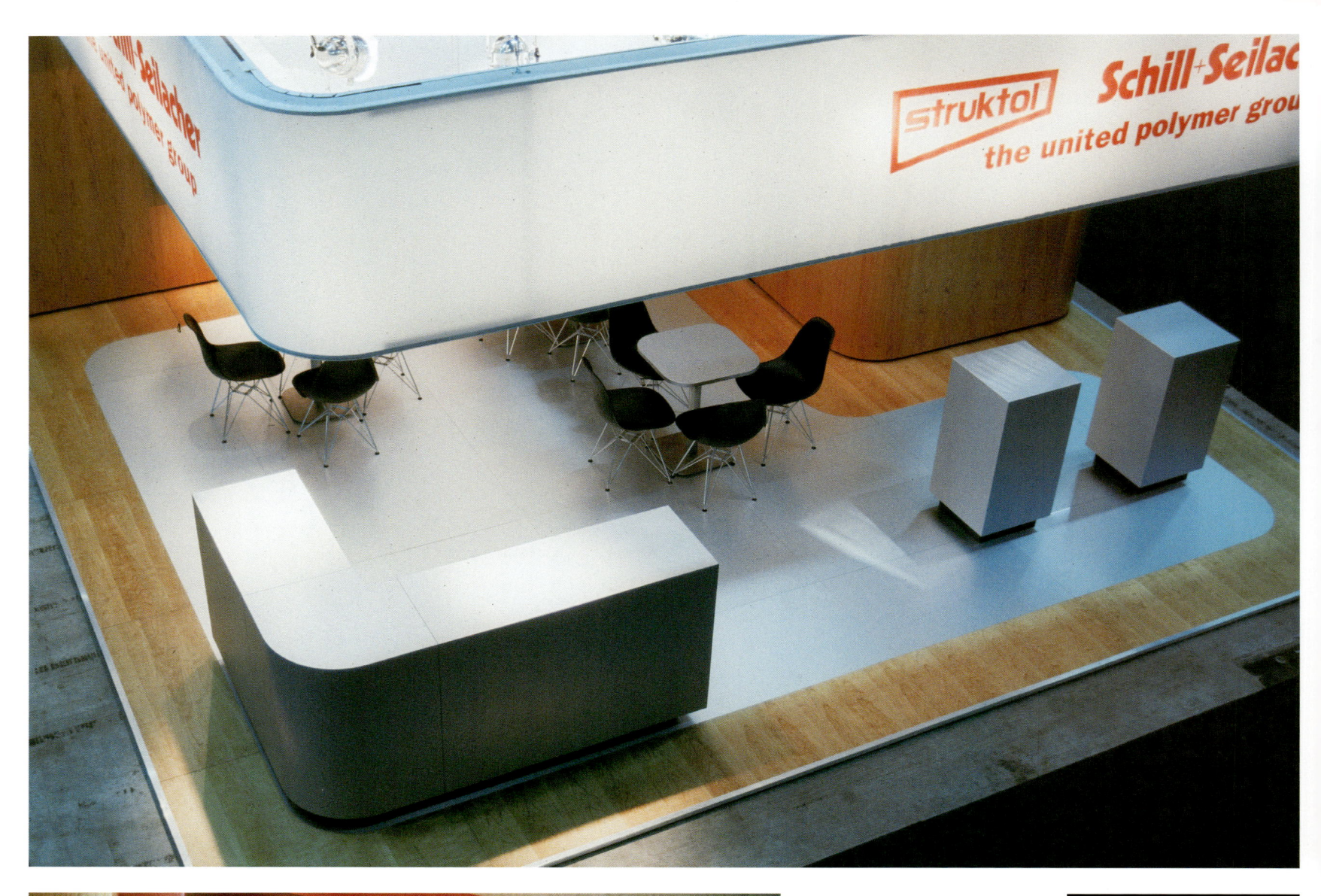

PROJECT:
**SCHILL & SEILACHER
PRODUCT PRESENTATION**
HAMBURG, GERMANY

WHERE:
Hamburg, Germany
WHEN:
2001
CLIENT:
Schill & Seilacher
MARKET SECTOR:
chemicals
DESIGNER OF STAND:
Christian Kaul
DESIGN TEAM:
Niels Flade, Alexander Keip
MATERIALS:
steel, wood, alloy, gauze, Plexiglas
AREA:
50 m²
BUDGET:
€ 65,000 for production/logistics excl. fair costs, etc.
PROJECT DURATION:
3 months

Schill & Seilacher, developers of high-quality rubber product substitutes, are a high-tech firm with tradition. The company wanted their installation to communicate both high quality and modernness of approach. The result: a modern use of form combined with timeless, classic materials. Stainless steel and walnut veneer set the tone. The entire exhibition is spanned by a back-lit canopy (a suspended construction), which frames the entire ensemble. The radiums are continued on every level, creating a homogeneous, harmonious overall effect. All-in-all a communication platform which is both solid and inviting, and where the famous Eames Fiber Chair is automatically at home.

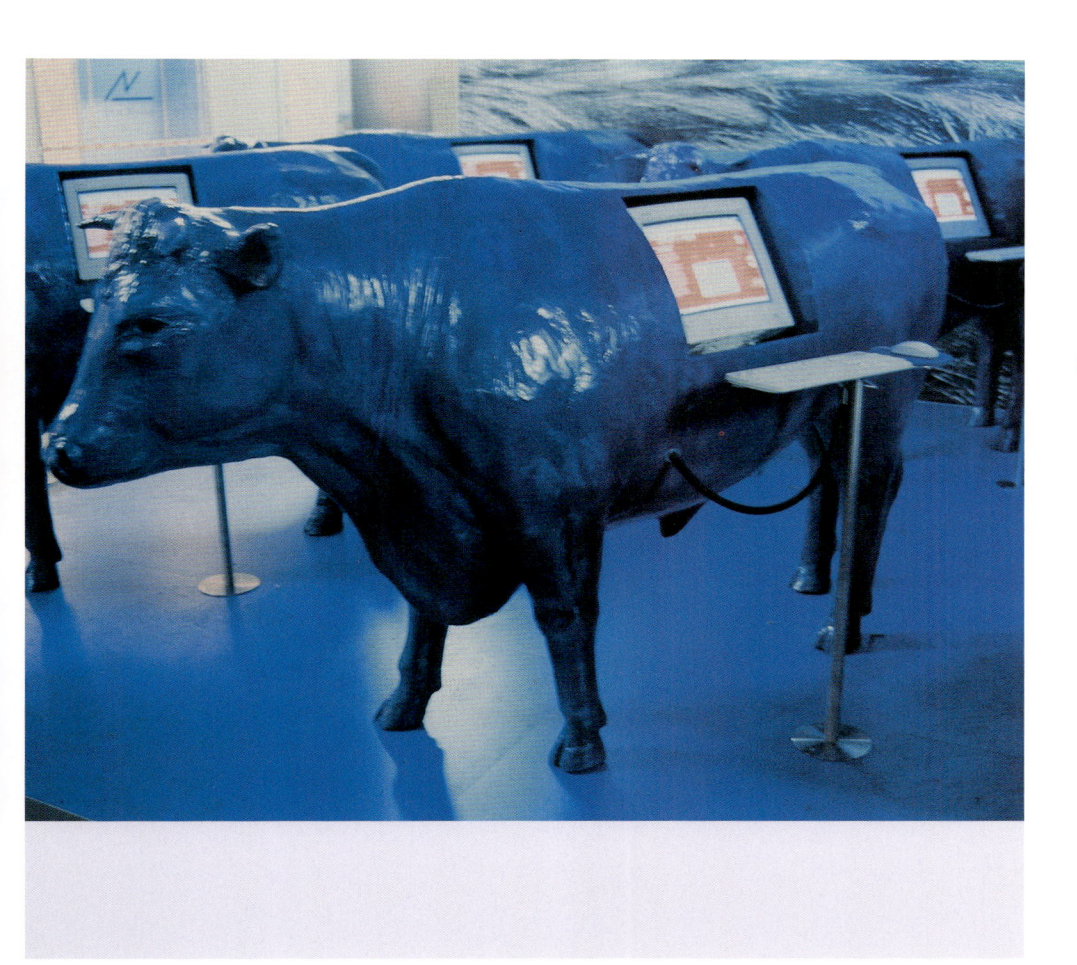

PROJECT:
BLUE BULL
VIENNA, AUSTRIA

WHERE:
Vienna, Austria
WHEN:
1999
CLIENT:
Blue Bull
MARKET SECTOR:
financial services
DESIGNER OF INSTALLATION:
Christian Kaul
DESIGN TEAM:
Niels Flade
MATERIALS:
fibreglass, wood, PVC, gauze
AREA:
40 m²
BUDGET:
€ 60,000.00 for production/
logistics excl. fair costs
PROJECT DURATION:
6 weeks

A web-based provider of financial services called Blue Bull: Raumschiff couldn't resist the impulse to start looking for bulls, place them in a pasture and colour the whole thing blue. To Raumschiff, it then seemed only logical to cover the rest of the installation in the same blue colour, including the floors, rear wall and reception desk.
The pasture was animated using superimposed beamer projections, and the bulls were cut open and turned into 'wild surf bulls'. A driving beat and sounds of bellowing bulls were added.
The installation certainly achieved more than just a demonstration of Blue Bull's functionality, and presenting their homepage and services as these novel and eye-catching surf stations produced such a positive response that, as a result of the large number of visitors attracted, the herd of bulls could at times only be heard – but not seen.

COMPANY NAME:
RAUMSCHIFF

HEAD OFFICE:
Barmbekerstrasse 3a
22303 Hamburg
Germany

PHONE:
+49(40) 278 70 60

FAX:
+49(40) 270 00 03

E-MAIL:
info@raumschiff.de

WEBSITE:
www.raumschiff.de

MANAGEMENT:
Jogi Jörn
Christian Kaul
Uli Winters
Christoph Ebener

CONTACTS:
Meike Jacobsen

STAFF:
15

KEY DESIGNERS:
Christian Kaul
Uli Winters
Alexander Keip

FOUNDED:
1997

COMPANY PROFILE:
Our target is the maximization of brand awareness. We constantly find new ways for brand presentations such as interactive concepts for science parks or fairs. We develop non-traditional platforms to achive integrated communication and real brand experience.

CLIENTS:
- GEO (Gruner + Jakt)
- Audi
- Renault
- Allianz
- Danfoss
- Premiere
- ENBW
- Bild.de
- Hyatt
- TUI
- Tomorrow Focus

SERVICES:
- Exhibition, stand design and construction
- Event and promotion design and concepts
- Communication and advertising design and concepts
- Promotion systems

OPERATES:
Europe and USA

STRATEGIC PARTNERSHIPS:
- Mansour Design, New York, USA
- SRW, Salzburg, Austria

ROTOR GROUP
ROESELARE, BELGIUM

233
grand stand

ABOUT The Rotor Group consists of Modular Lighting Instruments, Fractal Building Systems, and Rotor, the creative arm. After more than 13 years of experience, Fractal Building Systems

238
grand stand **ROTOR GROUP**

PROJECT
FREEP DEEZ EXPEDITION
KORTRIJK, BELGIUM

WHERE:
Interieur 2002, Kortrijk, Belgium

WHEN:
18 - 27 October 2002

CLIENT:
Modular Lighting Instruments

MARKET SECTOR:
lighting fixtures

DESIGNER OF STAND:
Bernard Rommens

DESIGN TEAM:
Rotor

GENERAL CONSTRUCTOR:
Fractal Building Systems

MATERIALS:
moussed PVC-canvas (floor),
poly-urethane (sphere construction)
'refrigeration-panels with
condensed air' (for the ice-walls)

AREA:
256 m²

PROJECT DURATION:
3 months (design), 1½ month
(construction), 2½ week (on site)

OPENING:
18 October 2002

239
ROTOR GROUP grand stand

PROJECT:
EUROSHOP STAND FOR FRACTAL
DUSSELDORF, GERMANY

WHERE:
Euroshop, Dusseldorf, Germany
WHEN:
23 - 27 February 2002
CLIENT:
Fractal Building Systems
MARKET SECTOR:
aluminium profiles (shopfitting/standbuilding/interior architecture)
DESIGNER OF STAND:
Yannick Florin, Peter Coussee, Jerome A.
DESIGN TEAM:
Fractal/Rotor
GENERAL CONSTRUCTOR:
Fractal Building Systems
MATERIALS:
Blobb (an inhouse constructive aluminium profile) for construction polycarbonate
AREA:
30 m²
PROJECT DURATION:
1 month (design), 2 weeks (construction), 3 days (on site)
OPENING:
27 september 2001

Color-changing walls of light were created to show one of the uses of the brand new Blobb profile.

241
ROTOR GROUP grand stand

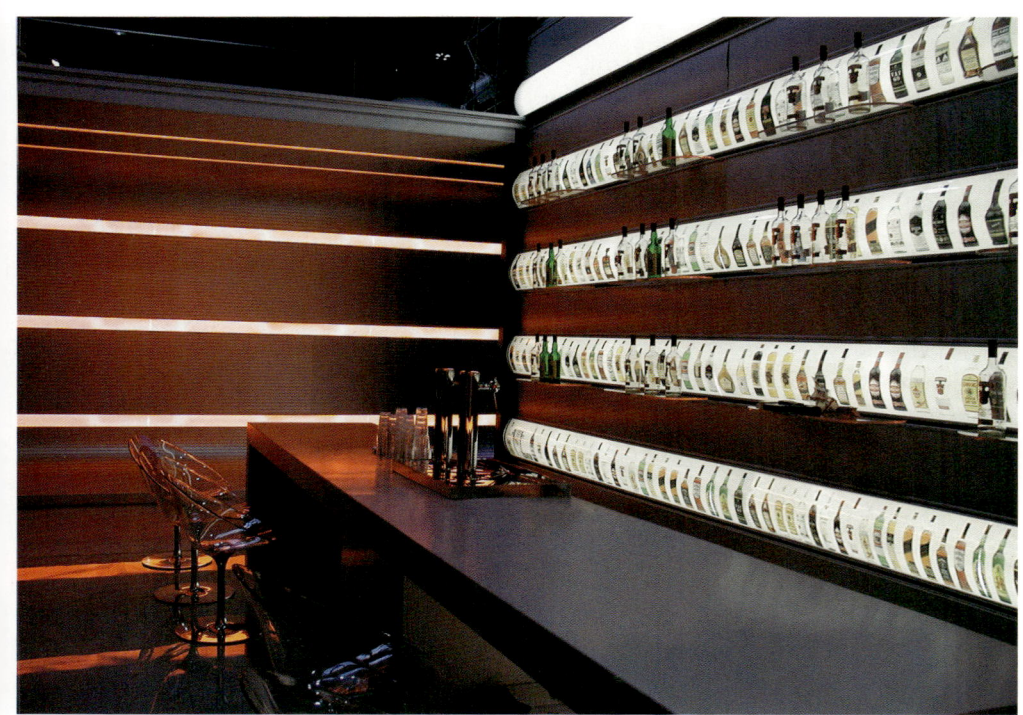

242
grand stand **ROTOR GROUP**

PROJECT:
MODULAR UNDERWATER-VESSEL
KORTRIJK, BELGIUM

The vessel's walls were made out of specially formed translucent 'bath-tubes', all lit from behind with TL-strips. All other walls and some of the floors were covered with neoprene – diving suit material – to intensify the underwater character of the stand. The decor was conceived using small and big aquariums. Stand visitors were able to inhale pure oxygen in order to prepare them for the next 'dive'.

243
ROTOR GROUP grand stand

PROJECT
MODULAR UNDERWATER-VESSEL
KORTRIJK, BELGIUM

WHERE:
Interieur 2000, Kortrijk, Belgium
WHEN:
13 - 22 October 2000
CLIENT:
Modular Lighting Instruments
MARKET SECTOR:
lighting fixtures
DESIGNER OF STAND:
Bernard Rommens
DESIGN TEAM:
Rotor
GENERAL CONSTRUCTOR:
Fractal Building Systems
MATERIALS:
thermal-formed acrylic sheets (green 'bath-thub' walls), neoprene (walls), water & fish (aquariums) steel (frameworks),
AREA:
192 m²
PROJECT DURATION:
3 months (design), 2 months (construction), 2 weeks (on site)
OPENING:
13 October 2000

244

grand stand **ROTOR GROUP**

PROJECT:
GINO VASELLI
BRUSSELS, BELGIUM

WHERE:
Batibouw 2003, Brussels, Belgium
WHEN:
20 February - 2 March 2003
CLIENT:
Modular Lighting Instruments
MARKET SECTOR:
lighting fixtures
DESIGN TEAM:
Rotor
Toon Stockman, Bram Couvreur
GENERAL CONSTRUCTOR:
Fractal Building Systems
MATERIALS:
cycling wheels, wood,
Kubus (an inhouse constructive aluminium profile)
AREA:
144 m²
PROJECT DURATION:
5 weeks (design), 2 weeks (construction), 1 week (on site)
OPENING:
20 February 2003

This stand is conceived as a indoor velodrome. At that time, Modular supported the well known cyclist, Gino Vaselli, and this stand was a tribute to him. (Of course, none of this was real, but spectators were convinced Modular really had their own cycling team.)

grand stand **ROTOR GROUP**

PROJECT:
FRACTAL 100% DESIGN STAND 2002
LONDON, UK

WHERE:
100% Design, London, UK

WHEN:
26 - 29 september 2002

CLIENT:
Fractal Building Systems

MARKET SECTOR:
aluminium profiles (shopfitting/standbuilding/interior architecture)

DESIGNER OF STAND:
Yannick Florin

DESIGN TEAM:
Fractal/Rotor

GENERAL CONSTRUCTOR:
Fractal Building Systems

MATERIALS:
Blobb (an inhouse constructive aluminium profile), acrylic plates (foamalux)

AREA:
30 m²

PROJECT DURATION:
1 month (design), 2 weeks (construction), 3 days (on site)

OPENING:
26 september 2002

A wobbly stand, made possible with the Blobb-profile and acrylic plates.

ROTOR GROUP grand stand

COMPANY NAME:
ROTOR GROUP

HEAD OFFICE:
Rumbeeksesteenweg 258 - 260
8800 Roeselare
Belgium

PHONE:
+32 (0)51 25 27 25

FAX:
+32 (0)51 25 27 88

E-MAIL:
rotor@supermodular.com

WEBSITE:
www.supermodular.com
www.fractal.be

MANAGEMENT:
Paul Rommens
Bernard Rommens

CONTACTS:
Peter Coussee
Toon Stockman

STAFF:
15

KEY DESIGNERS:
Paul Rommens
Bernard Rommens
Peter Coussee
Yannick Florin
Toon Stockman

FOUNDED:
1998

COMPANY PROFILE:
Rotor Group consists of Modular Lighting Instruments, Fractal Building Systems and Rotor. In-house agency Rotor® is the creative cel behind Modular Lighting Instruments® and sister company Fractal®. Rotor's® think-tank conceives mind-blowing exhibition stands for both companies at Interieur – Xpo Kortrijk or Euroluce – Milan, just to mention two. Obviously, this approach is similar in creations for third parties.

CLIENTS:
- Modular Lighting Instruments
- Fractal Building Systems
- BMW
- Addict
- Rolls Royce
- Mazda
- Nike
- Audi
- Vodafone
- Ericsson
- Citroen
- Loewe
- Bose
- Police Amsterdam

SERVICES:
- Exhibition and stand design
- Exhibition and stand build
- Retail design
- Shop design
- Displays
- Graphic design
- Event design

OPERATES:
Worldwide

SCHMIDHUBER + PARTNER

MUNICH, GERMANY

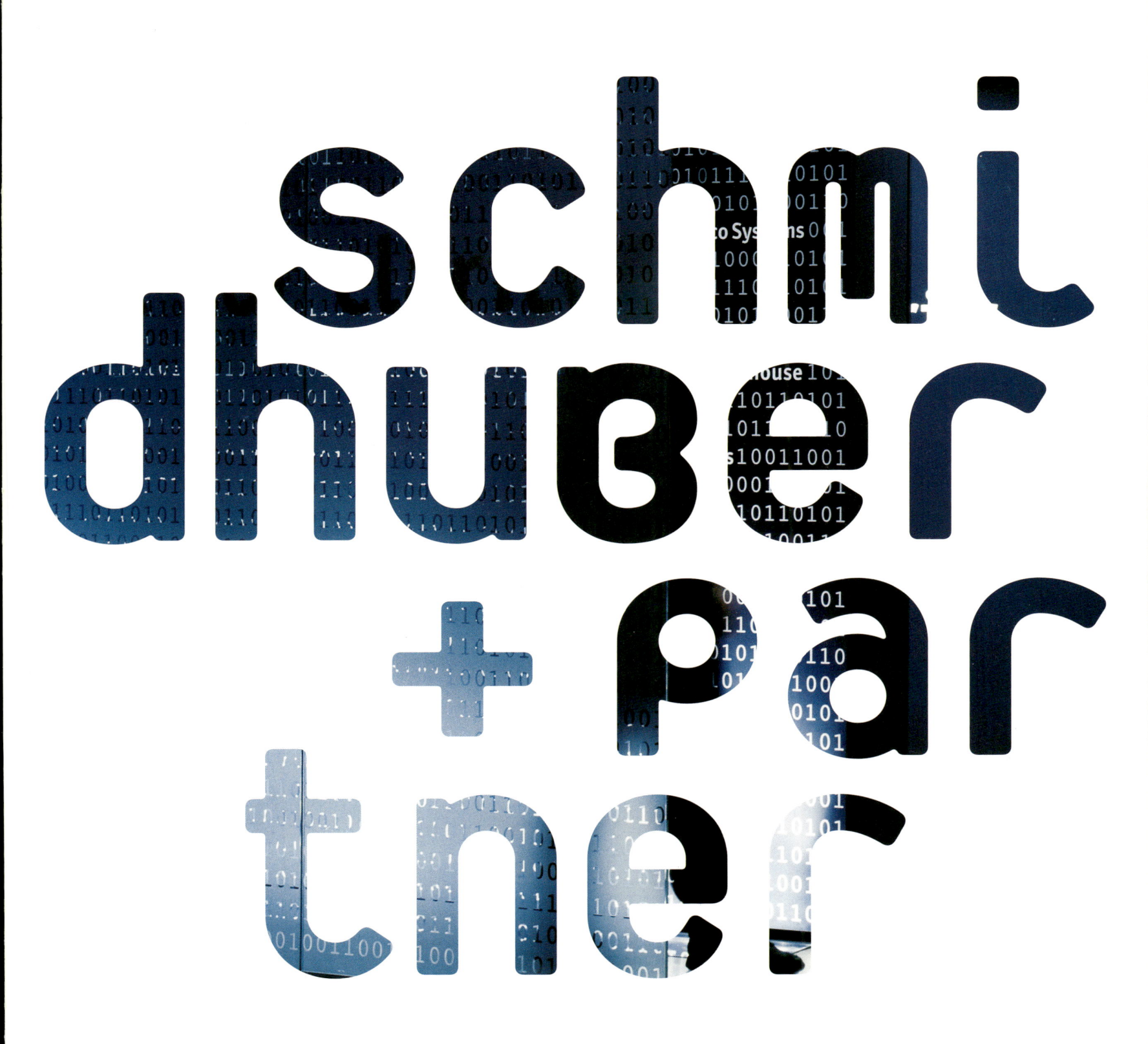

schmidhuber + partner

PROJECT:
KPMG
CEBIT 2000, HANNOVER, GERMANY

WHERE:
CeBIT 2000, Hannover, Germany
WHEN:
March 2000
CLIENT:
KPMG Consulting
MARKET SECTOR:
consulting, IT
CONCEPT, COMMUNICATION AND REALISATION:
KMS, Munich
ARCHITECTURE AND REALISATION:
Schmidhuber + Partner, Munich
LIGHTING PLANNING:
Four to One, Hürth
CONSTRUCTION:
Ambrosius Messebau, Frankfurt
MATERIALS:
floors: wood, bordered with stainless steel profile
walls: blue wall panels, translucent glass panes with binary code, glass breastwork
lighting: ground level: ceiling strip lighting (translucent flashed glass), lamps integrated in floor
upper level: floor lamps, floor washers
AREA:
floor space 75 m², upper level 28 m²
PHOTOGRAPHER:
Stefan Müller-Naumann, Munich

The appearance of the famed consulting and auditing firm KPMG achieved iconic status in the IT category at the 2000 CeBIT in Hannover. On the front pages of the Financial Times, the German TAZ and other newspapers, its design was lauded as exemplary. A concise yet powerful visual guiding principle: modulated transparency.
The installation's 'outer skin' of translucent glass makes a vital and complex visual impression. The numbers 0 and 1 in the order of the binary code serve as a figurative design element. Special lighting modulates the outer skin's translucency. The different layers of information are mixed to produce moiré effects which change depending one's angle of view.
The protagonists here are the visitors. As vague silhouettes, they blend in with the lines of binary information when they walk through the corridor between translucent glass and blue wall panels: an aesthetically effective symbol for the interactive cooperation between digital processes and real human actions. And it is because of the clarity and intensity of this manner of presentation that the KPMG motto 'time for clarity' made a lasting impression on the visitors.
The motto and the design not only represented the KPMG concept at the CeBit, but subsequently at a variety of locations and occasions. House trade fairs, info parks, tech days, and special events – the installation's modular construction was specially developed to enable flexible deployment in spaces ranging from 12 m² to 100 m².
At the CeBit, the design embodied the perfect sensual expression for the clarity of KPMG's business strategy. The 'transmitters' are active: 'it's time for clarity'. Whenever, as in this case, need and reality become one, the effect of the solution can be best measured in terms of the special attention paid to an installation by clients, the media and the general public.

253
grand stand

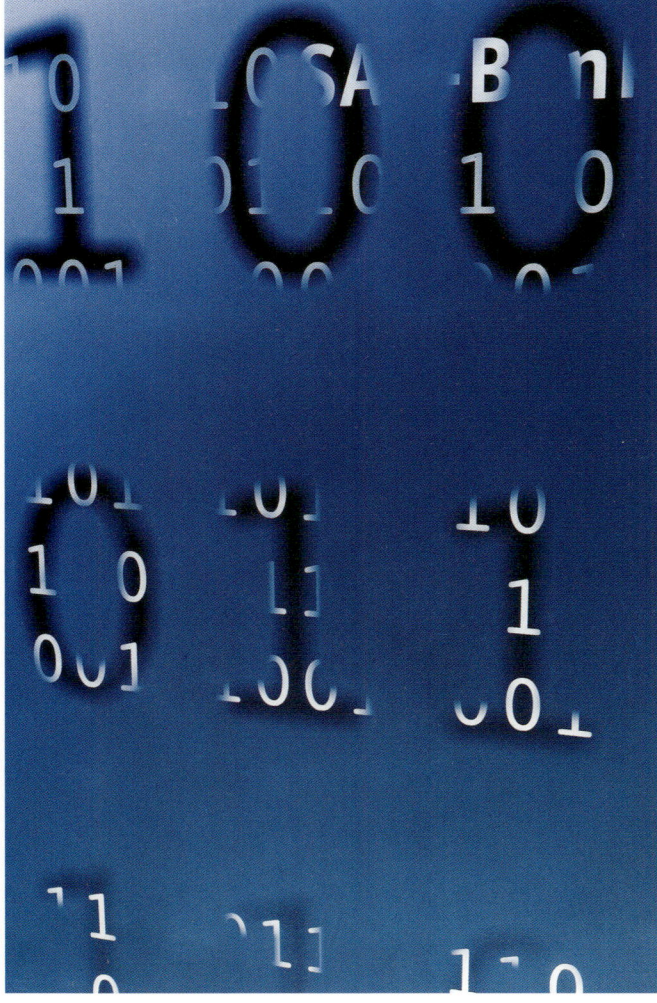

grand stand

PROJECT:
LAMBORGHINI
IAA 1999, FRANKFURT, GERMANY

WHERE:
IAA 1999, Frankfurt, Germany
WHEN:
September 1999
CLIENT:
Lamborghini
MARKET SECTOR:
automobiles
ARCHITECTURAL CONCEPT AND REALISATION:
Schmidhuber + Partner, Munich
COMMUNICATION CONCEPT AND REALISATION:
KMS, Munich
LIGHTING PLANNING:
Delux Lighting, Rolf Derrer, Zurich
CONSTRUCTION:
Ambrosius Messebau, Frankfurt
AREA:
floor space 370 m², upper level 90 m²
PROJECT DURATION:
June 2001 - September 2001
PHOTOGRAPHER:
Jens Weber, Munich

Combining the themes of monolithic form and a cult-like devotion to the brand ultimately leads to a new definition of the relationship between body and space. Schmidhuber's goal was to create an archetypal space: the temple, the cult space, the 'pure space' which the name Lamborghini conveys.

Here, as in the past, the starting point is the juxtaposition of the automobile's chiselled look with a massive, monolithic volume, whose high density and immense weight are visible and radiate strength. In Paris, the car presided from above, on a massive block. Now, going one step further, Schmidhuber wanted to make even stronger the association between the massive surroundings and the racy automobile by integrating the Lamborghini into the steel block. The team hollowed out the block to create a space for the car. In contrast with prior installations, the car had now truly dug its way into the 'primitive rock'.

By means of its revolving monolithic context, the cult object was given a mystical presentation space which was, formally speaking, reduced to an absolute minimum but at the same time laden with mystery and atmosphere.

SCHMIDHUBER + PARTNER grand stand

LEADING THE RIGHT

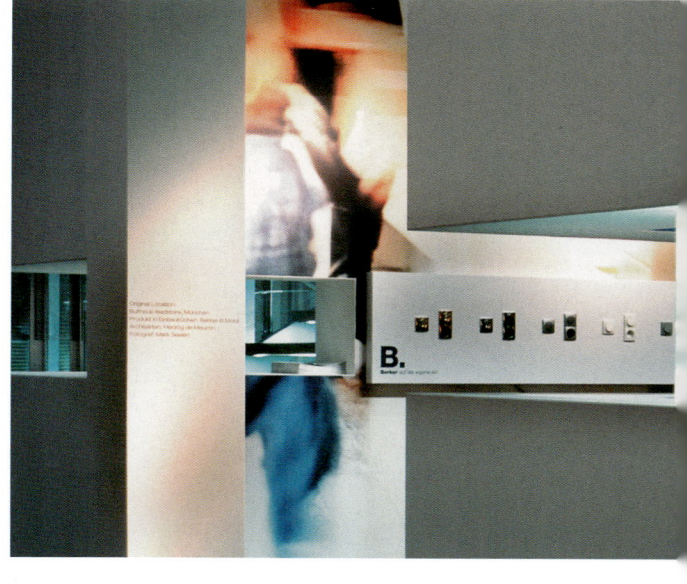

256
grand stand **SCHMIDHUBER + PARTNER**

WAY?

PROJECT:	
BERKER	
LIGHT & BUILDING 2002, FRANKFURT, GERMANY	

WHERE: Light & Building 2002, Frankfurt, Germany
WHEN: April 2002
CLIENT: Gebr. Berker & Co.
MARKET SECTOR: electrical technology
CONCEPT AND REALISATION: Schmidhuber + Partner, Munich
PLANNING PARTNER FOR COMMUNICATION: Thomas Biswanger, Ingolstadt
LIGHTING PLANNING: Lightnews, Munich
MEDIA PLANNING: merida2, Cologne
CONSTRUCTION: Ambrosius Messebau, Frankfurt
MATERIALS:
floors: cherry parquet (ground floor), carpeting (upper floor)
walls: wood with white-painted surface, partially covered with photo wallpaper
Staircase steel with solid cherry wood steps
presentation elements: Displays and all surfaces: white lacquer
furniture: uniform furniture scheme for all surfaces (aluminium, cherry wood, plastic, leather)
lighting: 3-phase rig system with reflector, built-in ceiling reflector, floor lamps, highlighting in the staircase steps and wall slits
AREA: floor space 476 m², upper level 200 m²
PHOTOGRAPHY: Studio Schroll, Hagen

'What's leading the right way?' This was Berker's motto at the 2002 Light + Building trade fair in Frankfurt, where it deployed, for the second time, its timeless and classic Berkerhaus. The motto on a giant strip creates a highly visible connection between the various areas represented in the installation. In six rooms, or lofts, real-life stories are told in pictures: stories about the lofts, their electrical switches and the people who use them. Real people who live in homes with Berker products present them to the visitor.

New products, innovative switch design and technology are placed in a future-oriented presentation about today's home: an 'open house' with scenes into which visitors themselves can step. Light, form and colour demonstrate a special quality of life. Design quality and technical innovation are presented convincingly.

The first thing one notices about the Berkerhaus is its white façade. The slit takes over the function of the window as design element: it is a signal, a stimulus for interaction. Its repetition in a spatial sequence ensures a high degree of recognition at the fair. In each of the lofts, a loft display, a mobile presenter and a pictorial presentation give potential purchasers a comprehensive view of Berker's product range. The product samples are within arm's reach on the display. The mobile presenter organises product variants according to colour, material and shape. Prospectuses and forms are readily visible and available. Wherever visitors go, there are always company representatives ready to answer their questions.

The intense collaboration between Berker and the architects is clearly reflected in the upper level's architectural exhibit, Today's Home. The exhibit's initiator, the magazine of the Süddeutsche Zeitung newspaper, here asks how today's home could look once it takes into account of the overlapping worlds typifying our time.

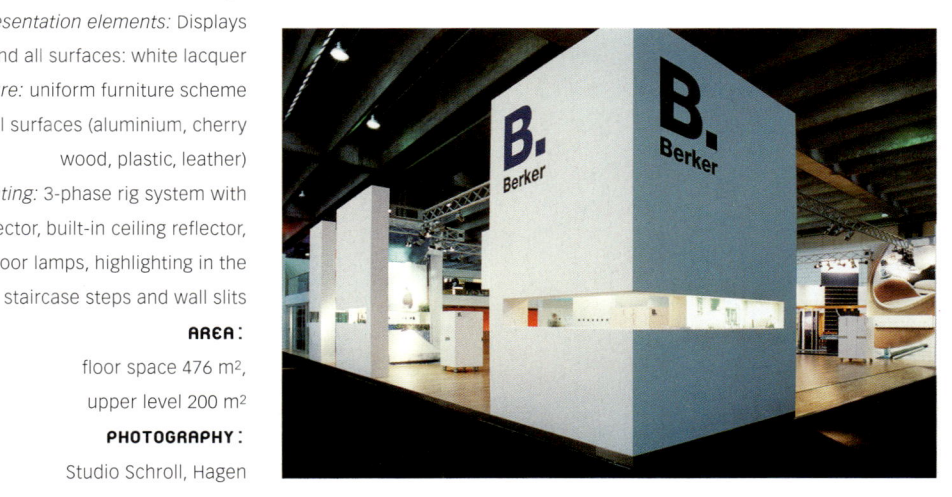

SCHMIDHUBER + PARTNER grand stand

PROJECT:
LEXUS
MONDIAL DE L'AUTOMOBILE, PARIS, FRANCE

WHERE:
Mondial de l'Automobile, Paris, France

WHEN:
October 2000

CLIENT:
Toyota Motor Europe

MARKET SECTOR:
automobiles

ARCHITECTURAL CONCEPT AND REALISATION:
Schmidhuber + Partner, Munich

COMMUNICATION:
Milla & Partner, Stuttgart

CONSTRUCTION:
Born & Strukamp, Düsseldorf

MATERIALS:
floors: ash veneer on white glazed MDF, partially slotted
walls: lacquered with Nextel, cream-white with gold glimmer,
stalks: Polycarbonate

AREA:
approx. 750 m²

PHOTOGRAPHY:
Uwe Spoering, Köln

The installation's basic idea is to be found in its styling as a landscape. In the middle of competing statements in a cluttered trade fair hall, the Lexus Motorshow is directly accessible, a prominent, independent, atmospheric space – promotion by emotion.
In the installation's foreground are the brand-new revolving automobiles, visible on all sides. In the middle ground, metre-high 'stalks' – resembling blades of grass or rush – are organised in rows: the location of Lexus' primary messages.
In the background, an image horizon: an approximately 18 x 2 metre wide screen; cinematic product communication in a specially-designed acoustic environment. The moving pictorial impressions run on three different transparent levels behind one another, and stimulate the viewer's individual associations utilising multiple image layers.
In this way, the primary dimensions of the Lexus brand image, namely motion, individuality and balance, as well the content of the Lexus brand, are reflected associatively. A perfect ensemble stimulates the viewer's fantasies and desires. A composition composed of light, colours and materials, displayed objects, details, information and visual associations unfolds its intensity without distractions or excess. Everything is directed toward the total effect, and an expressively powerful whole. The image horizon varies in tempo from calm to dynamic or pulsating. The notion of individuality is conveyed through the language of the changing images.

259
SCHMIDHUBER + PARTNER grand stand

260
grand stand

PROJECT:
DURAVIT/LAUFEN
ISH 2001, FRANKFURT, GERMANY

WHERE:
ISH 2001, Frankfurt, Germany

WHEN:
April 2001

CLIENT:
Duravit/Ambrosius Messebau

MARKET SECTOR:
sanitary products

CONCEPT AND REALISATION:
Schmidhuber + Partner, Munich

STRUCTURAL CALCULATION:
Ambrosius Messebau, Frankfurt

LIGHTING PLANNING:
Ambrosius Messebau, Frankfurt

CONSTRUCTION:
Ambrosius Messebau, Frankfurt

AREA:
800 m² floor space

PHOTOGRAPHY:
Vaclav Reischl, Reischl & Liptak, Stuttgart

The presentation centred around a functionality-based living domain showing the stylistic possibilities of the new bathing culture expressed in Duravit's products.

The individual sanitary products are unique objects, designed with the highest criteria in mind. Art and design were the inspiration for this class of sanitary ceramics. Individual sanitary components are removed from their normal context; employing the principle of formal reduction, a high degree of attention to the individual object is attained. By means of accentuated illumination and light-and-shadow effects, the pure form of the object is underscored to emphasise its sculptural quality.

The World of the Bath is shaped by bodily perceptions – hot and cold, wet and dry – as well as emotional associations, resulting in the world's most beautiful places for hygienic activities. This connection between product and experience stimulates new images in the visitor's mind, a process that should be encouraged.

The aim was to unify both conceptual aspects into one installation design uniquely communicating Duravit/Laufen, working with the opposition pairs of dynamic/static and movement/mass.

The 'slab' motif: The first, eye-catching element of the installation's design is the wall. Schmidhuber used an archaeological motif for the entire floorspace, creating a kind of 'Stonehenge' landscape. The monoliths function as the primary structure; they shape the direct surroundings of the sanitary objects, which are placed before or against these stones. As a secondary structure, the spaces between the slabs are given a free treatment using light textile surfaces which help define the product families.

The second defining feature of the design is the 'wave', which by means of textile strips, moves freely through the 'Stonehenge' landscape, functioning as a sort of ceiling. The element symbolises water, and serves to support the emotional perception of and direct association with Duravit's corporate identity. Bathing culture, the rediscovered joy derived from body consciousness and joie de vivre are all addressed.

The installation concept is designed both for the high-profile ISH appearance and smaller, regional ones. The individual presentation unit is comprised of two monolithic slabs and a secondary structure of guyed light textile strips. Associated aspects can be incorporated through the choice of materials and surface design for the monoliths.

PROJECT:
O₂ CAN DO
CEBIT 2003, HANNOVER, GERMANY

WHERE:
CeBIT 2003, Hannover, Germany

WHEN:
March 2003

CLIENT:
O₂ Germany

MARKET SECTOR:
telecommunications, IT

ARCHITECTURE CONCEPT AND REALISATION:
Schmidhuber + Partner, Munich

COMMUNICATION CONCEPT AND REALISATION:
KMS Team, Munich

LIGHTING PLANNING:
Delux, Rolf Derrer, Zurich

MEDIA PLANNING:
In Scena, Rudi Hennies, Berlin

CONSTRUCTION:
Messebau Tünnissen, Kranenburg

MATERIALS:
floors: basic surface, ash wood, painted white
platform and upper level, high nap carpeting
walls: melamine resin board, aluminium colour
bubble wall, acrylic glass basin filled with water
horizon: inflated membrane construction, revue foil
counters: painted white, acrylic glass top
displays: painted white or in silver colour
sitting cubes: white imitation leather

AREA:
floor space: 1,425 m²
upper level: 378 m²

PROJECT DURATION:
October 2002 - March 2003

PHOTOGRAPHER:
Frank Kleinbach, Stuttgart

Following the successful launch of the O₂ brand in 2002, the company's installation at the 2003 CeBIT trade fair reflects the concrete fulfilment of the brand's promise, O₂ can do. It presents O₂'s range of products and services all their facets from the standpoint of usefulness to the customer. The installation picks up on O₂'s successful 2002 presentation, but utilises a new communication concept. Primary elements, such as the all-embracing horizon, the lounges and the presentation counters have undergone further evolution in a manner consistent with the installation concept. The essential principle behind the design is an analogy to a shopping mall. Just as in a shopping centre, visitors are given a vivid impression of O₂'s multifaceted range of products and services. The communication takes up the brand's promise, but alters it by focussing on the verb 'do', in turn replacing its general sense with that of concrete activities: the lounge, with the theme 'multimedia messaging' is dubbed can communicate, the lounge with the theme games/music can entertain, and so forth. The installation's presentation area is raised almost a half metre above the hall floor. Illumination from below the platform contributes to the impression of suspense; the illuminated upper surfaces of the hand rails continue the contours of the presentation area whilst also reinforcing the suspension effect. The focal point of the generously-proportioned, open central area is an approximately 20-metre-long counter reminiscent of a modernly appointed shop. Each of its sections is dedicated to a different situation from daily work or leisure (e.g.: can enjoy, can travel, can eat & drink) demonstrating how O₂ can take care of all of one's needs via mobile radiotelephone. Above the counter are double 20-metre-long LED strips, on which films are displayed. The films traverse the entire length of the strips at high speed and are, through their aesthetic quality, a visual attraction in themselves.

Six lounges in the peripheral area serve as places for in-depth consultation, product demonstrations or simply relaxation. In relaxed surroundings, visitors can try out O₂'s wide spectrum of services at the custom equipped lounge tables. The upper level continues the lounge's theme in the can smoke Bar. The entire installation is framed by a horizon, a hanging construction consisting of an inflated membrane in the company's blue colour. Excellent distance recognition is ensured by the horizon's outer side, which features both the brand and its promise, whilst on the inner side the core message is communicated by means of changing typography, whose continuous upward movement supports the effect of lightness, as well as the impression that the horizon is floating in the air, taking up, in so doing, the brand-specific air and oxygen metaphors. This, in combination with the LED strips' horizontal movement, results in a vibrant and aesthetically attractive total effect.

O₂ can do

263
SCHMIDHUBER + PARTNER grand stand

COMPANY NAME:
SCHMIDHUBER + PARTNER

HEAD OFFICE:
Nederlinger Straße 21
80638 Munich
Germany

PHONE:
+49 (0)89 15 79 97 0

FAX:
+49 (0)89 15 79 97 99

E-MAIL:
shp@schmidhuber.de

WEBSITE:
www.schmidhuber.de

MANAGEMENT:
- Prof. Klaus Schmidhuber
- Susanne Schmidhuber
- Siegfried Kaindl
- Gerd Pilz
- Doris Eizenhammer
- Sonja Wright

CONTACTS:
Susanne Neumann

STAFF:
34

FOUNDED:
1983

COMPANY PROFILE:
Our field is the interface between landscape, architecture and interior design. Here, we work toward the creation of unique places, architecture, spatial contexts and narratives for the purpose of sensual communication. The individual – with his/her special design needs – and the impressions and messages to be communicated are at the heart of our deliberations. These result in the formulation of a new concept, in which functional, constructive, economic and ecological aspects are all given ample attention. Our aim: to achieve the best possible result in collaboration with the engineering specialists, constructors and ultimate users involved, while always ensuring punctual completion at the price agreed. We create added value through design.

CLIENTS:
- Analog Devices
- AUDI, Ingolstadt
- Automobili Lamborghini S.p.A
- Management of Hospital and Old Age Home, Die Barmherzigen Schwestern, Munich
- Biotronik & Co., Berlin
- BMW Group, Munich
- Daimler Chrysler, Stuttgart
- Deutsche Bundesbank (formerly: Landeszentralbank im Freistaat Bayern)
- Deutsches Museum, Munich
- Duravit, Hornberg,
- Dyckerhoff & Widmann/Walter Bau
- E.ON Energie, Munich
- E.ON Wasserkraft, Landshut
- GBW AG Bayrische Wohnungs-Aktiengesellschaft
- Gebrüder Berker, Schalksmühle
- Infineon Technologies, Munich
- KPMG Consulting, Frankfurt and Berlin
- Dritter Orden Hospital, Munich
- Münchener Hypothekenbank, Munich
- Münchener Rückversicherungsgesellschaft, Munich
- O$_2$ Germany, Munich (formerly: VIAG Interkom)
- Siemens
- Toyota Motor Europe, Brussels
- TRIA Software AG, Munich
- Volkswagen AG, Wolfsburg
- VW (China) Investment Company
- Zoological Society, Frankfurt a.M.

SERVICES:
Trade fairs and exhibitions:
- International and regional trade fair presentations
- Trade fair pool development
- Press events
- Information centres and exhibitions
- EXPO events
- Brand centres/experience centres

Company architecture/ representative offices:
- Building architecture and showroom design
- Product presentation and sales personnel workplaces
- Shop design and customer service facilities
- Workshop environment and general functional processes
- Internal workplace design
- Meeting and conference rooms
- Exterior spatial design
- Logos/CI's

Administration and Banks:
- Entrances
- Workplace design and organisation for offices
- Training and seminar rooms
- Conference rooms, including media facilities
- Casinos, gastronomic facilities
- Internal service facilities/waiting rooms
- Information CI's

Hospitals, child and adolescent psychiatry, doctors' surgeries
- Hospitals/obstetrics units
- Specialists' surgeries
- Youth centres

Other fields of activity
- Shopping centres
- Care facilities
- Hotels
- Cafés and restaurants
- Zoos

AWARDS:
iF Exhibition Design Award
- iF Exhibition Design Award, ISH 2001, Frankfurt, **Third Prize (Bronze)** for Duravit installation
- iF Exhibition Design Award, CeBIT 2001, Hannover, **First Prize (gold)** for Creating Business installation, VIAG Interkom
- **Second Prize (silver)** for It's time for clarity installation, KPMG Consulting
- iF Exhibition Design Award, CeBIT 2000, Hannover, **First Prize (gold)** for Creating Visions installation, VIAG Interkom

FAMAB ADAM Award
- 2002 FAMAB Adam Award, **Second Prize** for an installation of 500 - 1500 m²: Was heißt hier auf die eigene Art installation for Berker, Light + Building 2002, Frankfurt
- 2001 FAMAB Adam Award, **First Prize** for an installation of up to 150 m²: It's time for clarity installation, KPMG Consulting, CeBIT 2000, Hannover
- 2001 FAMAB Adam Award, **Second Prize** for an installation larger than 1,500 m²: Creating Visions installation, VIAG Interkom, CeBIT 2001, Hannover
- 2001 FAMAB Adam Award, **Third Prize** for an installation in a foreign country: installation for Lamborghini, 1999 Bologna Motorshow

2002 Prize of the Deutscher Designer Club (DDC)
- Audi installation concept for: IAA Frankfurt 2001/Tokyo Motorshow 2001/Detroit NAIAS 2002

Reddot Design Award
- 2002 Reddot Design Award: **Best of the Best** for 2001/2002 Audi installation concept
- 2002 Reddot Design Award: Product Design Award for High Design Quality for Lamborghini installation, IAA 2001

Most Significant Exhibit Design
- Audi, Detroit Motorshow 2002, Award sponsored by: the Detroit Institute of Ophthalmology.

AIT/Intelligent Architectural Innovation Prize
- AIT/Intelligent Architectural Innovation Prize (Architecture and Technology), Light+Building 2002: mobile RGB and yellow light-walls for Audi installation Special Recognition
- AIT/Intelligent Architectural Innovation Prize (Architecture and Presentation), EuroShop 2002: The Stalk, identifying feature for Lexus installations

OPERATES:
Worldwide

TOTEMS COMMUNICATION

HOOFDDORP, THE NETHERLANDS

totems communication

ABOUT

totems communication

Thanks to a Dutch-German partnership, Totems is able to fall back on a broad base of both conceptual work and project management. The agency approaches exhibit design as a total experience which should seduce and move visitors. To this end, video-installations and films form an important means of communication. Despite the recession, stands should remain attractive and light-hearted, so that visitors leave with a smile.

TOTEMS CONCENTRATES ON ANALYSIS, conception, design and management of three-dimensional communications projects. The agency mainly focusses on trade shows, exhibitions, events and commercial interiors for large and medium-sized clients such as Wella, Grohe, TUI, KPN Telecom, Elsevier, Mercedes (DaimlerChrysler) and Audi.

PROJECTS CAN VARY FROM THE DEVELOPMENT OF A TOTAL CONCEPT TO COMMUNICATION ONLY (through media such as graphic design, displays, film or music). For example, an entire hall was designed for Wella at Hairworld in Berlin, a trade show for hairdressers. Rather than expressing the quality, technology and innovation of the brand – aspects that had formerly determined the image of Wella – the concept referred to the more emotional value of vanity. To do so, the entire hall was transformed into a glittering jewelery-box, with enormous diamonds and pearls as separate elements, creating spaces for fashion shows and demonstrations to be held in between.

IN GERMANY HOWEVER, WITH LARGE AND COMPLEX PROJECTS it is common to contract out the architecture and communication to different firms. In that case, Totems is commissioned for the communication. When given the choice, Totems also prefers to focus on content, rather than being responsible only for design.

FILMS AND VIDEO INSTALLATIONS HAVE BECOME AN IMPORTANT CORNERSTONE IN THE WORK OF TOTEMS. They provide an excellent medium for storytelling within architecture. Through LED-screens and strips, images can be played simultaneously or independently. Usually, existing material is edited into loops, but sometimes new footage is made. This type of communication proves particularly suitable for the auto industry, since it exudes energy and dynamism – the same powerful terms by which cars are judged.

TOTEMS HAS MARKETED ITSELF AS A EUROPEAN AGENCY from the very beginning with one office in Hoofddorp (The Netherlands) and one in Stuttgart (Germany). The light and casual nature of Dutch culture combined with the German sense of quality and perfection offers the firm a broad foundation. To further expand the advantages of such cultural diversity, Totems has the

PROJECTS:
TOTEMS COMMUNICATION

PROJECT PAGE 268:
SPEED
PORTE DE VERSAILLES,
PARIS, FRANCE

PROJECT PAGE 272:
MYTHOS MERCEDES
DEICHTORHALLEN, HAMBURG,
GERMANY

PROJECT PAGE 274:
BE PART OF TUI
ITB BERLIN, GERMANY

ambition to launch a number of 'satellite offices' abroad. This would both offer a complement organisation and further enhance the existing organisation.

THIS FIRM IS VISUALLY ORIENTED and likes to come up with beautiful images that command attention. Totems often tries to convince the client of the quality of a design with only one powerful image. For example, TUI – Europe's largest travel organisation – was compared to a lady blowing soap bubbles. The underlying thought was that travelling was in fact a sort of time-loop: you leave home and come back to it after a while. The trip in between is a sort of dream, or a bubble you temporarily exist in. TUI was then portrayed as the person blowing bubbles and the attendees of the trade show were given the idea that a number of them were being blown into the hall. This was expressed in the form of large air-filled spheres with projections that offered various visualisations of dream worlds (water vacations snow vacations, etc.).

THE AGENCY'S STRATEGY IS TO SEDUCE VISITORS, but apart from the aesthetic sense, Totems always sees the need for content. A solid strategy typically does not surface in the first briefing from the client. The client usually needs to be advised on what the story might be. To reach a good proposal, three steps need to be taken. First, an analysis must take place to determine which core values are to be communicated. What is the identity or the profile of the company? Next, the dominant cultural trends need to be understood, in terms of which target groups there are, and how to address a new target group. From these two conditions, a clear and inspiring translation needs to be made in the form of a design. Clients need to keep selling lightness and to remain attractive at trade shows, or the backlash becomes too visible. It is important to be economical, but a client is better off going to fewer trade shows than cutting back on the design or the process. According to Totems, a certain cheerfulness should be found in every project, so that visitors leave with a smile.

> "BRAND COMMUNICATION WITH FOCUS AND SOUL. TOTEMS RELISHES THE CHALLENGE OF DISTILLING THE ESSENCE OF A BRAND AND COMMUNICATING IT WITH PASSION, ANYWHERE."

PROJECT PAGE 276:
WELCOME TO THE KIDS WORLD
INTERNATIONAL FAIR GROUND,
COLOGNE, GERMANY

PROJECT PAGE 278:
WOONBRON HOUSING SHOPS
ROTTERDAM, THE NETHERLANDS

PROJECT:
SPEED
PORTE DE VERSAILLES,
PARIS, FRANCE

Audi is a dynamic brand: up front, setting new standards, ever moving forward. It thrives on a passion for the automobile, a passion for beauty, technology and for driving fast, competing and challenging.
Following the present strategic brand positioning into sportiness, for the 2002 Paris exhibition Totems took the brand's passion for speed as the central theme, making visible what is at the core of the Audi brand. First, as a single word only. Then, as a breathtaking, sweeping image of flaming beauty: the 'Speed-motionblur'.
A number of films were developed, embedding product content into hyperdynamic motion blurs and image-splits. Pushing the borders of motion design, the moving images were then differentiated into a range of media, varying from large-scale LED surfaces to multi-sided monitor cubes and single small screens.
Parallel, a multiplicity of motionblur applications in other communication elements was developed – from 300 m² backwall graphics up to menu cards and giveaways.

268
grand stand **TOTEMS COMMUNICATION**

Cette f

Audi gagne pour la troisiè

1. Biela / Kristensen / Pirro
2. Capello / Herbert / Pesca
3. Krumm / Peter / Werner

Biela / Kristensen / Pirro a
Amélioration de 7 tours s

Tom Kristensen - 2:33.493
Amélioration de l'actuel

Nouvelle Audi A8

allroad quattro 4.2

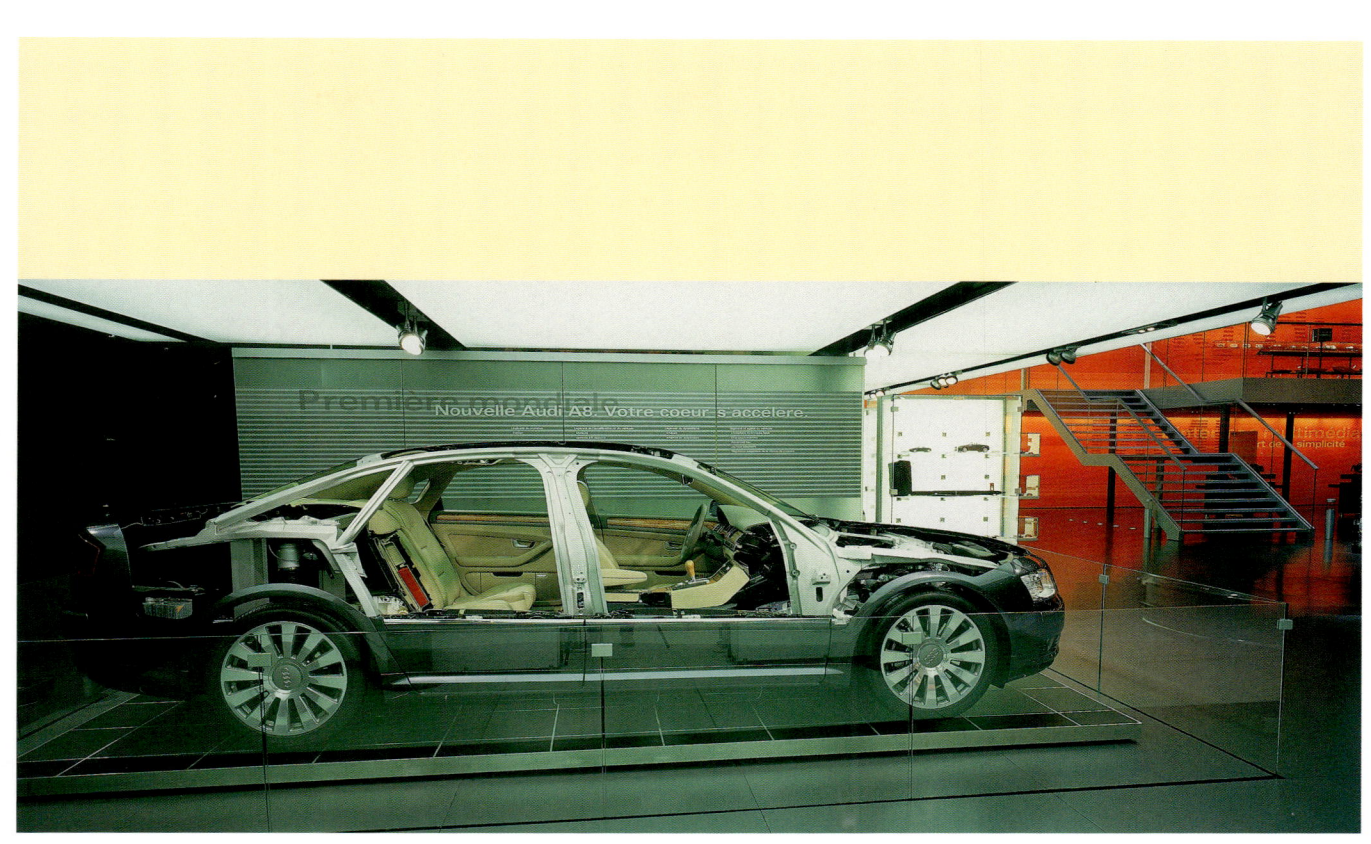

Nouvelle Audi A8. Votre cœur s'accélère.

Le sport automobile

Cette fois-ci, nous ne sommes pas uniquement venus au Mans pour gagner, mais pour entrer dans l'histoire.

Infineon Audi R8

PROJECT
SPEED
PORTE DE VERSAILLES,
PARIS, FRANCE

WHERE:
Porte de Versailles, Paris, France

WHEN:
22 September 2002 - 13 October 2002

CLIENT:
Audi

MARKET SECTOR:
automotive

COMMUNICATION:
Totems Communication

ARCHITECTURE:
Tools-Off Architecture

CONSULTANTS:
media technology:
Michael Nicht + Partner

GENERAL CONSTRUCTOR:
Ambrosius Messebau

MANUFACTURERS:
lighting: Four to one: scale design
film production: MetropolisFilm
graphics production: Schüttenberg

AREA:
1,050 m² (excluding elevations)

BUDGET:
€ 750,000 (communication only)

PROJECT DURATION:
6 months
(April 2002 - October 2002)

OPENING:
22 September 2002

270
grand stand **TOTEMS COMMUNICATION**

TOTEMS COMMUNICATION GRAND STAND

PROJECT:
MYTHOS MERCEDES
DEICHTORHALLEN, HAMBURG, GERMANY

WHERE: Deichtorhallen, Hamburg, Germany
WHEN: 4 August - 14 October 2001
CLIENT: DaimlerChrysler
MARKET SECTOR: automotive
ARCHITECTURE: Totems Communication
COMMUNICATION: Totems Communication
CONSULTANTS: *lighting:* Jerry Appelt, procon multiMedia
MANUFACTURERS: *graphics:* Stadelmayer Werbung
showcases: Buchbinderei Fröhlich
AREA: 1,650 m²
BUDGET: € 435,000
PROJECT DURATION: 7 months
OPENING: 3 August 2001

Myths are the sort of stories that cause strong emotions. Myths grow stronger, more surreal and more desirable as time goes by. During the Mythos SL exhibition, 15 classic cars were exhibited in 13 big spaces, each offering the experience of a different mythic SL story. Each story is a portrait of its age, presenting the spirit of the people involved in the process of creation, their surroundings, and their objects of desire. Various small exhibits were gathered and displayed in open showcases, drawing attention to a variety of interesting details.
The dominant and towering dimensions of these spaces with 12-metre-high ceilings are set against a strong horizontal direction of the design. Rectangular information panels display all design-related content and create a linear path of orientation, helping visitors find their way through the exhibition, playfully taking them past the different elements of soul-stirring car design. Every position shows an element that is both characteristic of its time and recognisable in its features.

273 TOTEMS COMMUNICATION GRAND STAND

PROJECT:
BE PART OF TUI
ITB BERLIN, GERMANY

WHERE:
ITB (Internationale Tourismusbörse), Berlin, Germany
WHEN:
7 - 11 March 2003
CLIENT:
TUI
MARKET SECTOR:
tourism
ARCHITECTURE:
Totems Communication
COMMUNICATION:
Totems Communication
GENERAL CONSTRUCTOR:
Gielissen Interiors & Exhibitions
MANUFACTURERS:
lighting constructions:
Classissimo Produktion
farbic strips and walls:
Langhammer + Vogt
AREA:
3,000 m²
BUDGET:
€ 1,200,000
PROJECT DURATION:
5 months

Browsing through a field of man-sized blades of artificial grass, large air-filled clouds attracting attention from afar, hostesses supplying refreshments in the hotel area and local sports instructors presenting first hand stories about favorite holiday activities. The TUI stand at the 2003 International Tourism Tradeshow (ITB) in Berlin offered visitors a completely different world. Furthermore, TUI's corporate presentation has been designed to clearly reflect the diversity of the integrated tourism group and the World of TUI as a master brand. 'With the participation of travel organisations, airlines and the hotel industry' creative director Erik Hoebergen explains, 'it was important for us to design a stand that all these different parties could identify with, binding them together in a clear, unmistakeble symbol representing the TUI company. Moreover, with both professionals and end consumers visiting, we wanted everybody to feel welcome.' Hence the motto 'Be part of TUI!', inviting all visitors to be part of the holiday excitement that unites everybody. With possibilities to meet, talk and exchange stories everywhere, the Totems concept suitably emphasises that people are the centre of attention in the new world of TUI.

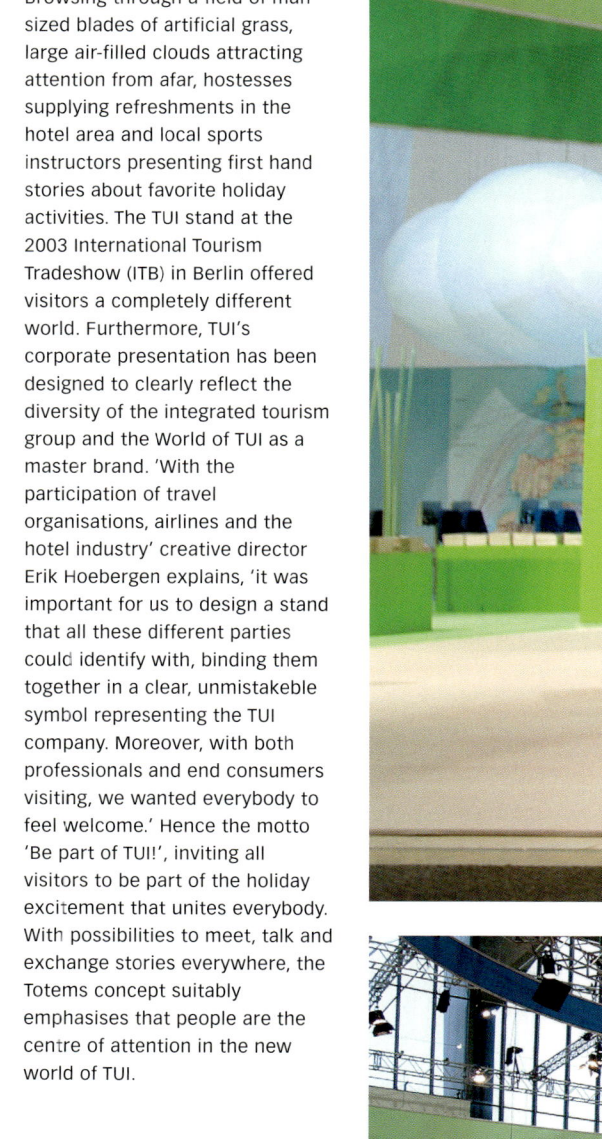

275

GRAND STAND

grand stand **TOTEMS COMMUNICATION**

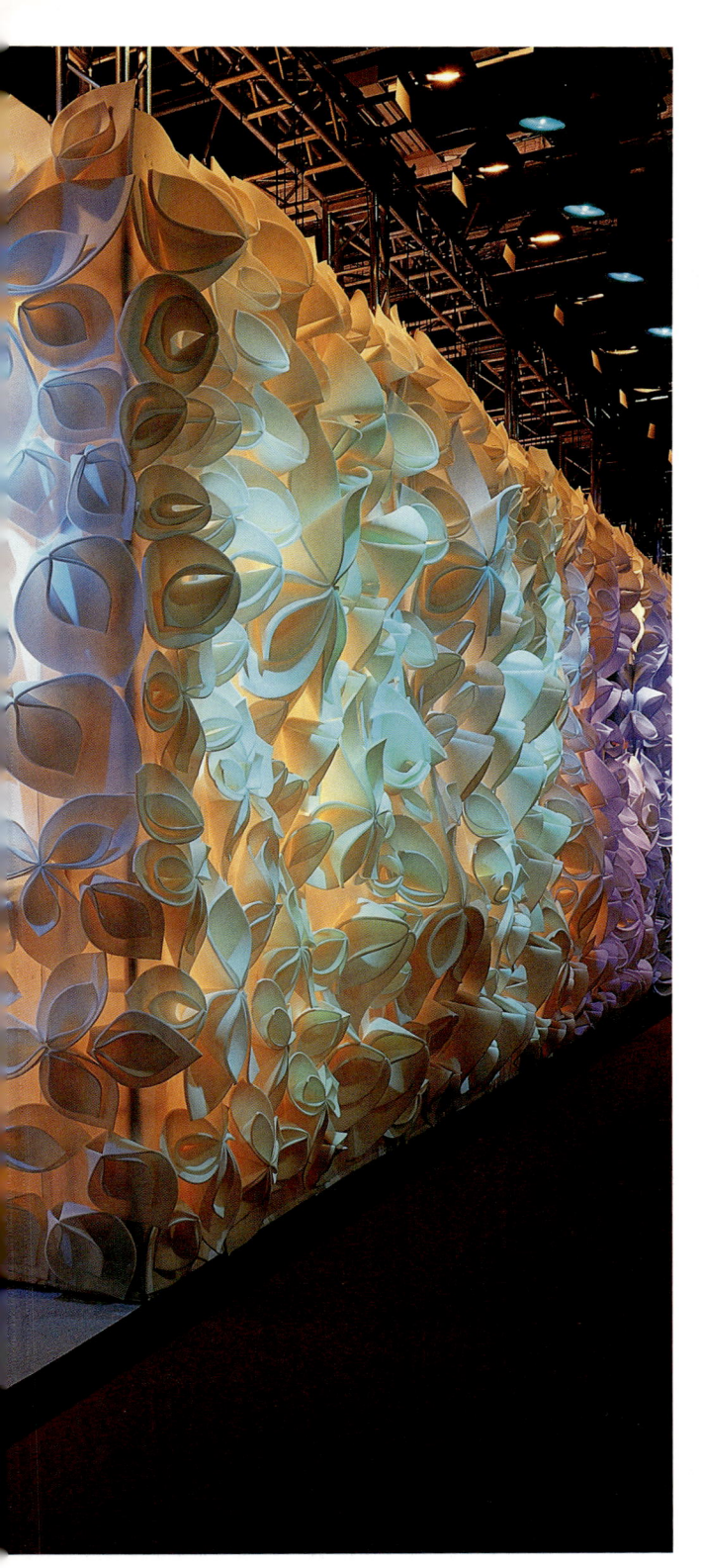

PROJECT:
WELCOME TO THE KIDS WORLD
INTERNATIONAL FAIR GROUND,
COLOGNE, GERMANY

WHERE: 'Kind + Jugend', Cologne, Germany
WHEN: 27 - 29 July 2001
CLIENT: Julius Zöllner
MARKET SECTOR: furniture, textile and accessories for kids
ARCHITECTURE: Totems Communication
COMMUNICATION: Totems Communication
MANUFACTURERS:
lighting: Procon multiMedia
graphic sculpture: Totems Communication
furniture and floors: Balloni deko
walls and lampshades: ARTec
AREA: 425 m²
BUDGET: € 160,000
PROJECT DURATION: 3 months

Julius Zöllner has built a strong reputation for style and hospitality. To stress this quality, a stand was conceived that invited visitors to come closer and enter. Light fabrics cover the façade on all sides, creating one opulent sculpture of warmth with 3000 reflective flowery forms. Smooth changes in both color and light intensify feelings of security and aesthetic pleasure. Conceived as a singular architectural construction, the outer skin poses a seductive invitation to enter the sheltered, harmonious spaces inside. Here, Zöllner products are presented in clearly-structured settings – yet with the playfulness of a child's room.
A linear ground plan directs visitors from the entrance to the lounge. In this light-hearted temporary environment another theatrical statement on hospitality is found.

TOTEMS COMMUNICATION GRAND STAND

PROJECT:
WOONBRON HOUSING SHOPS
ROTTERDAM, THE NETHERLANDS

WHERE:
Rotterdam, The Netherlands
WHEN:
early 2002
CLIENT:
Woonbron Maasoevers
MARKET SECTOR:
retail
INTERIOR ARCHITECTURE:
Totems Communication
COMMUNICATION:
Totems Communication
GENERAL CONSTRUCTOR:
Intrica Rotterdam
MANUFACTURERS:
varying per site
AREA:
150 - 300 m² (varying per site)
BUDGET:
> € 500,000
PROJECT DURATION:
approx. 3 years
OPENING:
2002 and 2003

The identity of Woonbron-Maasoevers as a reliable and trustworthy, but also new, fresh and friendly organisation is translated into a retail environment by creating an open and clear architecture with strong, clear forms and natural materials. The concept is defined by flexibility: it can be applied to a variety of sites without losing its appeal, uniformity and identity.
A clear set of architectural guidelines was defined, including floor and wall finishing, coatings, colours and lighting.
Independent customer orientation is available through interactive media offering information ranging from basic subject information to real-time availability of real-estate.
Other elements include a service-element (with children's play area, library and beverage area), a manned information point and open/closed meeting areas.

TOTEMS COMMUNICATION GRAND STAND

COMPANY NAME:
TOTEMS COMMUNICATION

HEAD OFFICE:
Polarisavenue 87
Postbus 2026
2130 GE Hoofddorp
The Netherlands

PHONE:
+31 (0)23 568 55 11

FAX:
+31 (0)23 568 55 12

E-MAIL:
amsterdam@totems.com

WEBSITE:
www.totems.com

OTHER LOCATIONS:
Stuttgart, Germany

MANAGEMENT:
Gerard de Gorter
Peter van Lier
Florian Gerlach

CONTACTS:
Erik Hoebergen

STAFF:
25

FOUNDED:
1997

MEMBER OF:
BNO, Association of Dutch Designers

COMPANY PROFILE:
Totems is an agency at the forefront of 3D communication and design. The staff consists of experienced concept developers, architects, 3D and graphic designers. Totems is dedicated to finding stories in its clients' most basic values. Based on fresh, inspired concepts, content is brought alive as multidimensional stories, communicating spaces, objects and images of astonishing aesthetic quality.

CLIENTS:
- Audi
- DaimlerChrysler
- Exact
- Elsevier
- Gasunie
- Lufthansa
- Ritter Sport
- TUI
- Wella

SERVICES:
- Concept development
- Exhibition & stand architecture
- Interior architecture
- Graphic design
- Event scenography
- Stage design
- Scenorio & scriptwriting
- Film development

OPERATES:
Worldwide

GRAND STAND
CONCEPT & DESIGN

INDEX: GRAND STAND CONCEPT & DESIGN

PROJECT NAME:	CLIENT:	PARTICIPANT:	PAGE:
Be part of Tui	Tui	Totems Communication	274
Berker	Gebr. Berker & Co	Schmidhuber + partner	256
Biennale/Danish Pavillion	Danish Ministry of Culture	Kvorning Design	126
Blue Bull	Blue Bull	Raumschiff	231
Bticino at Saie Due	Bticino	Migliore + Servetto	172
Cabletel Mobile	Cabletel	Land Design Studio	140
Chello	Chello	Exhibits International	103
City of Abstracts	Frankfurt Ballett	Atelier Markgraph	31
Constructing Atmospheres	Messe Frankfurt	Atelier Markgraph	36
Copenhagen, Denmark Helsinki, Finland Tallinn, Estonia	Danish Centre for Architecture/ Dominique Perrault	Kvorning Design	130
D'art Design Gruppe at Euroshop	D'art Design	D'art Design Gruppe	78
Danfoss Test Station	Danfoss	Raumschiff	228
Dinobirds	Natural History Museum	Land Design Studio	148
Discover the Lab.01	Daimler Chrysler	Atelier Markgraph	28
Drawing Dreams-Dante Ferretti	Cinicitta Holding	Migliore + Servetto	174
Duravit/Laufen	Duravit/Ambrosius Messebau	Schmidhuber + partner	260
Ellesse	Ellesse International	Arno Design	13
ENBW product presentation	Energie Baden-Württemberg	Raumschiff	220
Energis at Internetworking Event	Energis	Promhouse	214
Ericsson	Ericsson	The GC Group	116
First Class Connections	New Skies Satellites	Oil for 3D	194
Fractal at 100% Design	Fractal Building Systems	Rotor Group	246
Fractal at Euroshop	Fractal Building Systems	Rotor Group	240
Freep Deez	Modular Lighting Instruments	Rotor Group	238
Futureroom Installation	Futureroom	Raumschiff	223
Futures Gallery	Thinktank	Land Design Studio	146
Gauss European Presentations	Gauss Interprise	Raumschiff	227
Gino Vaselli	Modular Lighting Instruments	Rotor Group	245
Grundig at IFA	Grundig	Arno Design	14
Hans Bartelds Zaal	Amev (Div. of Fortis Group)	Promhouse	204
Haworth at Neocon	Haworth Inc.	Lorenc + Yoo Design	160
Hyatt European presentation	Hyatt Int. hotels & resorts	Raumschiff	226
'Ja, ik wil'/'Yes, I do'	Nieuwe Kerk Amsterdam	Exhibits International	92
Kickers	Kickers International	Arno Design	22
KPMG	KPMG Consulting	Schmidhuber + partner	252
Krizia Moving Shapes	Krizia	Migliore + Servetto	178
Lamborghini	Lamborghini	Schmidhuber + partner	254
Lee Jeans at Bread and Butter	Lee Jeans	Creneau International	60
Lee Jeans at Interjeans	Lee Jeans	Creneau International	62
Let's go	Basler Lacke and Wyssbrod	Oil for 3D	188
Let's go miles	Yellomiles	Atelier Markgraph	34
Levi Strauss at Interjeans	Levi Strauss Europe	Creneau International	64
Levi Strauss at Interjeans	Levi Strauss Europe	Creneau International	66
Lexus	Toyota Motor Europe	Schmidhuber + partner	258
Lifetime Movie Network	Lifetime Movie Network	Lorenc + Yoo Design	164
Light Weights	Danish Music Information Centre and Danish Centre for Accessibility	Kvorning Design	134

PROJECT NAME:	CLIENT:	PARTICIPANT:	PAGE:
Microsoft: Waar is Hans?	Microsoft	Exhibits Internatioanl	100
Midem 2002+2003	Danish Ministry of Culture and Danish Music Information Centre	Kvorning Design	132
Minimal Constructions	Craftman's Guild of Copenhagen	Kvorning Design	128
Modular Underwater Vessel	Modular Lighting Instruments	Rotor Group	242
Mono at Tendence	Mono Seibel	D' art Design Gruppe	84
Montana at HMW	Montana	Arno Design	23
Moving Objects	Royal College of Art	Land Design Studio	142
Mythos Mercedes	Daimler Chrysler	Totems Communication	272
Nasdaq Marketsite	Nasdaq	Exhibits International	102
National Maritime Museum	National Maritime Museum	Land Design Studio	150
New Horizons	New Skies Satellites	Oil for 3D	192
New Skies	New Skies Satellites	Oil for 3D	190
Nissan	Nissan Europe	Exhibits International	96
O$_2$ can do	O$_2$ Germany	Schmidhuber + partner	262
Open Systems	Open Systems	The GC Group	113
Orange Boat	Orange Communications	The GC Group	115
Orange Cube	Orange Communications	The GC Group	108
Orange Dome	Orange Communications/Nokia	The GC Group	110
Orange Modulare	Orange Communications	The GC Group	118

CONCEPT & DESIGN grand stand

INDEX GRAND STAND CONCEPT & DESIGN

PROJECT NAME:	CLIENT:	PARTICIPANT:	PAGE:
Philips AEG Licht	Philips AEG	D'art Design Gruppe	80
Picnic on top of the world	New Skies Satellites	Oil for 3D	196
Playzone at Millennium Dome	New Millennium Experience Company	Land Design Studio	144
Relaxsense	Pitti Uomo	Cibic & Partners	52
Risanamento	Risanamento	Cibic & Partners	55
Samsonite at Tendence	Samsonite	D'art Design Gruppe	76
Schill & Seilacher	Schill & Seilacher	Raumschiff	230
Schwarzkopf at Hairworld 2000	Schwarzkopf Professional	Raumschiff	224
Shaping the future of print media	Heidelberger Druckmaschinen	Atelier Markgraph	30
Sony at IBC 2001	Sony Business Europe	Promhouse	210
Sony at IBC 2002	Sony Business Europe	Promhouse	212
Sony-Ericsson at CTIA	Sony-Ericsson North America	Lorenc + Yoo Design	158
Speed	Audi	Totems Communication	268
Speedo at ISPO	Speedo International	Arno Design	12
Sto at Farbe Spring	Sto ag	Arno Design	18
Super Audio CD	Philips/Sony cooperation	Promhouse	207
Telecom Italia	Telecom Italia	Cibic & partners	44
The Danish Wave	Danish Cultural Institute and Danish Centre for Architecture	Kvorning Design	124
The Famous Grouse Experience	Highland Distillers	Land Design Studio	147
'The making of' Pirelli calendar	Armani, Pirelli	Migliore + Servetto	182

PROJECT NAME:	CLIENT:	DESIGNER:	PAGE:
The Orange Experience	Orange	Oil for 3D	198
The Story of Passion	Daimler Chrysler	Atelier Markgraph	39
Tod's Ferrari	Tod's Ferrari	Migliore + Servetto	176
Toys R Us	Toys R Us	Exhibits International	101
Under one roof	European Aeronautic Defence and Space Company	Atelier Markgraph	32
Unilever	Unilever	Exhibits International	98
VDP at Interpack	Verband Deutscher Papierfabriken	D'art Design Gruppe	82
Verkehrszentrum Deutsches Museum München	Deutsches Museum München	Atelier Markgraph	35
Vink at Euroshop 2002	Vink Holding	Promhouse	208
Welcome to the kids world	Julius Zöllner	Totems Communication	276
Whirlpool	Whirlpool/Bauknecht	Cibic & partners	48
Woonbron housing shops	Woonbron Maasoevers	Totems Communication	278
Wordspring Discovery Center	Wycliffe Bible Translators	Lorenc + Yoo Design	166
Wrangler at Interjeans	Wrangler	Creneau International	70
X-Novo	Webert	Cibic & partners	46
XX by Mexx	Mexx	Creneau International	68
Zamias	Zamias Services	Lorenc + Yoo Design	162
Zanders at Drupa	Zanders Feinpapiere	D' art Design Gruppe	86

285

CONCEPT & DESIGN grand stand

COLOPHON:
GRAND STAND
DESIGN FOR TRADE FAIR
STANDS AND EXHIBITIONS

PUBLISHERS:
Frame Publishers
www.framemag.com
avedition
www.avedition.com

GRAPHIC DESIGN AND TRAFFIC:
Lava – www.lava.nl

GRAPHIC PRODUCTION:
def. – www.def.nl

WRITERS:
Jörg Boner, Conway Lloyd Morgan,
Edwin van Onna, Simone Petsch
Lars Heger, Carly Butler

COPY EDITING:
Matt Stewart

TRANSLATION:
D'Lain Camp, Nick Lakides,
Daniela Mecozzi

COLOUR REPRODUCTION:
Plusworks – www.plusworks.nl

PRINTING:
Tien Wah Press, Singapore

DISTRIBUTION:
Germany, Austria and Switzerland
ISBN 3-89986-009-8
ISBN 3-89986-005-5 (Grand Stand:
    Concepts and Design)
ISBN 3-89986-006-3 (Grand Stand:
    Design and Construction)
avedition – Publishers for
architecture and design
Königsallee 57
D-71638 Ludwigsburg
Germany
www.avedition.com

All other countries
ISBN 90-77174-03-6
ISBN 90-77174-05-2 (Grand Stand:
    Concepts and Design)
ISBN 90-77174-06-0 (Grand Stand:
    Design and Construction)
Frame Publishers
Lijnbaansgracht 87
NL-1015 GZ Amsterdam
The Netherlands
www.framemag.com

© 2003 Frame Publishers
© 2003 avedition – Publishers for
    architecture and design

Bibliographic information published
by Die Deutsche Bibliothek
Die Deutsche Bibliothek lists this
publication in the Deutsche
Nationa bibliografie; detailed
bibliographic data are available in
the Internet at http://ddb.de.

Copyrights on the photographs,
illustrations, drawings and written
material in this publication are
owned by the respective
photographers, the graphic
designers, the manufacturers and
their clients, and the authors.

This work is subject to copyright.
All rights are reserved, whether the
whole or part of the material is
concerned, specifically the rights of
translation, reprinting, re-use of
illustrations, recitation,
broadcasting, reproduction on
microfilms or in other ways, and
storage in data bases. For any kind
of use, permission of the copyright
owner must be obtained.

Printed on acid-free paper produced
from chlorine-free pulp. TCF ∞
Printed in Singapore
987654321

FRAME

THE INTERNATIONAL MAGAZINE OF INTERIOR ARCHITECTURE AND DESIGN > JUL/AUG 2003

MILANORAMA

7 Literary Quotes for 7 Libraries
How Smart Materials Can Spark Sharp Ideas
The Far-East Guide to Shopping

www.framemag.com

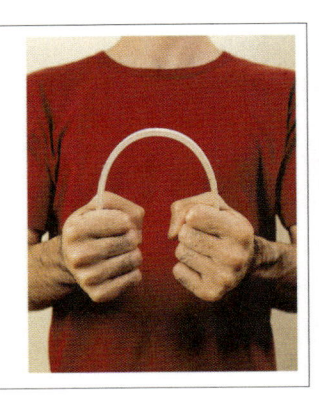

Material World: Innovative Structures and Finishes for Interiors

Boasting no less than 100 innovative materials for architects and designers, this book also offers clever ideas on how to use them. Discover materials smart enough to react to changes in their surroundings. Get acquainted with materials that create exciting optical effects. Learn about exceptionally strong yet lightweight composites, flexible building materials and great finishes for all types of architectonic projects.

Features
- A marvellous range of 100 materials grouped into eight sections: Smart Technology / No Waste / Optical Effects / Flexible Structures / Sound Control / Strong Building / Free Form / Finishing Touch
- Photographs and in-depth descriptions of all materials, including composition, properties and applications
- Detailed contact information for all manufacturers and designers mentioned in the book
- Extensive glossary

Publication details
- Written and edited by Edwin van Onna
- Introduction by Ed van Hinte
- 244 pages
- hardback
- 23 x 29.7 cm
- co-publication by *Frame* and Birkhäuser
- ISBN 90-806445-6-0

Price
Europe €65 / other countries €73 (postage included)

how to order

- Visit our online shop at www.framemag.com
- Complete this form and fax to +31 20 428 0653 or mail to Frame, Lijnbaansgracht 87, NL-1015 GZ Amsterdam, the Netherlands

Please send me:

___ book(s) *Material World: Innovative Structures and Finishes for Interiors*

Name
Company
Address
Postcode/Zip Code   City
Country
T   F   E
Payment (credit-card payment ensures prompt delivery)
☐ Bill me (Europe only)
☐ Charge my credit card: ☐ Visa ☐ MasterCard ☐ American Express
Number
Expiry date
Name on credit card
CVC2 code   CARD VERIFICATION CODE FOR PAYMENT BY VISA OR MASTERCARD. THIS IS THE LAST 3 DIGITS OF THE NUMBER ON THE WHITE STRIP ON THE BACK OF THE CARD
Signature